A SPIRITUALITY OF PERFECTION

Faith in Action in the Letter of James

Patrick J. Hartin

A Michael Glazier Book
THE LITURGICAL PRESS
Collegeville, Minnesota

Cover design by David Manahan, O.S.B.
Art: EL GRECO, *Portrait of Saint James the Less*, c. 1610–15, Oil on canvas, 24.75 x 19.75 inches, 1971.18, photo by Joseph Levy, The Hyde Collection Art Museum, Glens Falls, New York

A Michael Glazier Book published by The Liturgical Press

1   2   3   4   5   6   7

Library of Congress Cataloging-in-Publication Data

Hartin, P. J. (Patrick J.)
   A spirituality of perfection : faith in action in the Letter of
James / Patrick J. Hartin.
      p.   cm.
   "A Michael Glazier book."
   Includes bibliographical references and index.
   ISBN 0-8146-5895-4 (alk. paper)
   1. Bible. N.T. James—Criticism, interpretation, etc.
   2. Perfection—Biblical teaching. 3. Bible. N.T. James—Theology.
   I. Title.
   BS2785.6.P55H37   1999
   227'.9106—dc21   98-56223
                                                              CIP

To my parents,
whose faith in action
taught me to treasure
friendship with God

Contents

Preface

My special interest in the letter of James began over sixteen years ago while teaching a course to undergraduate students on the letter of James. In reading the text, these students raised intriguing questions concerning the relationship between James and the Sermon on the Mount. This sparked for me an inquiry that continues until today. I thank them for sending me on this journey.

The focus of this study is the letter of James. Attention is given to one particular theme, namely perfection, that has special importance for the letter's religious thought. At the outset of the investigation, two issues presented themselves: Why is perfection such an important concept for the letter of James, and what does James actually understand by this term? I have noticed a strange phenomenon among those with whom I shared this research interest. Whenever I mentioned that I was researching the notion of perfection in James, a polite eyebrow would be raised as if to say: "Why would you want to consider such a topic?" Hopefully, this study will provide the answer by showing that what James (and Matthew) intends by perfection is very different from our modern understanding and that the concept of perfection unlocks an important self-understanding of Christianity.

The letter of James continues to fascinate me with its witness to a very distinctive religious thought world and way of life. By taking James seriously, the reader has an opportunity to open up new vistas onto the developing religious matrix of Christianity. This study aims at allowing James to be read in its own right, instead of through the eyes of other traditions, such as Paul. This study also takes one spiritual value, namely perfection, as a way of entering into the spirituality of this letter to discover implications for today's reader. The theological character of this writing is exciting since its ethical teaching derives from an understanding of God that can be shared with people of other faiths. In a postmodern world where diversity is the hallmark, James resonates with its own distinctive vision. The letter of James witnesses to the diversity of the world of the first century as well as to that of the twenty-first century.

I should like to thank all those who have helped me in different ways in the production of this book. First of all, my students from the University of the Witwatersrand, the University of South Africa, and Gonzaga University who have continued to help me read this letter with new eyes. I should like to thank all my colleagues, particularly in the Religious Studies Department at Gonzaga University, who have shared their insights with me on this topic. From these discussions, new avenues have opened for me. In particular, I should like to thank Marc Lenneman for his tireless reading and editing of the initial manuscript and to Michael and Bob van Cleve for their assistance with research and computer technology. Finally, I should like to thank all the editors of The Liturgical Press for their assistance in bringing this project to fruition: Linda Maloney, Annette Kmitch, Colleen Stiller, and Mark Twomey.

I dedicate this book to my parents who were my first teachers in the community of faith and whose lives showed me faith in action.

Unless otherwise noted, all the English biblical quotations in this study are taken from the *New Revised Standard Version of the Bible: Catholic Edition* (Nashville: Thomas Nelson, Catholic Bible Press, 1989).

CHAPTER ONE

A Call to Perfection

Approaches to the Letter of James

Among New Testament writings, the letter of James must certainly be one of the most tantalizing. It consistently defies attempts by scholars to reach consensus on even the most basic of aspects. One of the most Jewish of all New Testament writings in thought,[1] this letter is also among the most Hellenistic in language and style.[2] Scholars assign the authorship and date of James to the two extremities of the time chart: from being one of the earliest of New Testament writings (prior to 62 C.E.), to being one of the latest (around 120 C.E.).[3] While

---

[1] There is little in the thought of James that does not reflect the world of Judaism. See, for example, James's concept of God, his treatment of the Law, as well as his idea of the gathering in of the twelve tribes in the Dispersion, to name but a few of the ideas in the letter that have a foundation in the religious thought world of Judaism. These concepts will be examined in detail in the course of this study.

[2] Joseph B. Mayor (*The Epistle of St. James: The Greek Text with Introduction, Notes, Comments and Further Studies in the Epistle of St. James* [Grand Rapids, Mich.: Zondervan (1913), 1954] ccxliv) evaluates the quality of the Greek in this way: "On the whole I should be inclined to rate the Greek of this Epistle as approaching more nearly to the standard of classical purity than that of any other book of the N.T. with the exception perhaps of the Epistle to the Hebrews."

[3] Peter H. Davids (*The Epistle of James: A Commentary on the Greek Text,* The New International Greek Testament Commentary [Grand Rapids, Mich.: Paternoster Press, 1982] 4) gives a very useful chart of the judgment of scholars on the dating of James. His overview of their positions is limited to references to works from this century until 1980. What is noteworthy in this chart is the vast divergence of viewpoints. However, the views are almost equally divided between attributing the letter in some way to James the Just, and those who judge it to be pseudonymous. More recent scholarship seems to tend toward an earlier dating of the letter. See, for example, Luke Timothy Johnson, *The Letter of James: A New Translation with Introduction and Commentary,* The Anchor Bible 37A (New York: Doubleday, 1995) 121.

James[4] mentions Jesus Christ directly only twice in the entire writing (1:1 and 2:1), and also makes no reference to Jesus' death and resurrection (beliefs that formed the heart and foundation of Paul's teaching), nevertheless James shows more connections with the sayings of Jesus than with any other New Testament writing.[5]

From the sixteenth century onward, New Testament scholarship's main concern has been with James's relationship to the thought and writings of Paul. James's teaching on faith and works (2:14-26) was the center of concern and was judged to be in conflict with Paul's teaching on justification by faith alone.[6] Largely because of Martin Luther's negative assessment,[7] James has been mainly confined to the margins of New Testament scholarship. Only in more recent times is James undergoing a rehabilitation because of a number of important aspects occurring within recent New Testament scholarship. I believe that the following aspects, all independent of each other, contribute toward a more favorable interest in the letter of James:

(1) The interest stimulated by Walter Bauer's book *Rechtgläubigkeit und Ketzerei im ältesten Christentum.*[8] Undoubtedly one of the more challenging books of the twentieth century,[9] this work prompted scholars to reimagine the origins and development of earliest Christianity. While this book was originally published in Germany in 1934, its views went largely ignored.[10] Only with its reprint in Germany in 1964,

---

[4] Throughout this study "James" will refer either to the letter of James or to the author without intending to accept a particular person as the author.

[5] See my work on the relation of James to the Jesus traditions in Patrick J. Hartin, *James and the Q Sayings of Jesus,* Journal for the Study of the New Testament 47 (Sheffield: Sheffield Academic Press, 1991); and "James and the Sermon on the Mount/Plain," *Society of Biblical Literature 1989 Seminar Papers,* ed. D. J. Lull (Atlanta: Scholars Press, 1989) 440–57.

[6] See Martin Luther, *Luther's Works: Word and Sacrament I,* vol. 35, ed. T. Backmann (Philadelphia: Fortress Press, 1960) 362.

[7] Ibid., 396.

[8] Walter Bauer, *Rechtgläubigkeit und Ketzerei im ältesten Christentum,* BHT 10 (Tübingen: Mohr-Siebeck, 1934).

[9] Helmut Koester calls it "one of the most brilliant monographs in the field of New Testament studies in this century" (Helmut Koester, "Epilogue: Current Issues in New Testament Scholarship," *The Future of Early Christianity: Essays in Honor of Helmut Koester,* ed. Birger A. Pearson [Minneapolis: Fortress Press, 1991] 470).

[10] There were two reasons Bauer's thesis was ignored. First, Tübingen had a reputation for a scholarship that mainline scholars viewed with great suspicion. At the same time, his view appeared just as Hitler was beginning his climb to power (1934). With the aftermath of the ensuing world war, the world was not receptive to any ideas (let alone new and unorthodox ones) coming out of Germany.

and a subsequent English translation in 1971, did the significance of these views begin to be recognized.[11] Instead of envisaging the growth of Christianity in a monolithic way following the traditional outline of the origins of the Christian movement in the Acts of the Apostles, Bauer proposed the development of numerous independent Christian communities each with its own theologies and understandings. The usual construct of a "primitive Christianity," according to Bauer, never existed, and the earliest "heresies" were simply varied understandings of the Christian message that arose in different geographical localities. Only much later, after the fourth century, did a uniform and orthodox understanding of Christianity begin to emerge. Prior to Bauer's work, the usual understanding had been to view Paul and his theology as representative of all areas of early Christianity. Now, following Bauer's perspective, Paul's thought and theology would be but one among numerous other understandings of the message of Jesus. Diversity was the hallmark of the early Christian movement.

Against that backdrop, the letter of James comes into its own right. Instead of being an embarrassment to the hegemony of Pauline Christianity, it becomes a marvelous representative of another branch of early Christianity, one that presents the Christian message in very different terms. James is a witness to the beauty and diversity of that early Christian movement. My hope will be to illustrate this further in this study. In our present postmodern world where diversity is treasured for the wealth that different cultures, perspectives, beliefs, etc., bring, the letter of James with its distinctiveness and difference resonates with this postmodern consciousness.

(2) Upholding the importance of James in its own right means that James can be read in terms of its own thought and teaching rather than in contrast to that of Paul. The usual way in which James has been read over the centuries has been to see it in opposition to Paul's thought.[12] This perspective has had a long entrenched history, and even today many support this position.[13] However, the model on which that type

---

[11] Walter Bauer, *Orthodoxy and Heresy in Earliest Christianity*, trans. R. A. Kraft and G. Krodel (Philadelphia: Fortress Press, 1971).

[12] Ferdinand C. Baur had advanced the view that in the early Church a theological conflict developed between Gentile Christianity (of whom Paul was the greatest proponent) and Jewish Christianity (of which James and Peter were the staunchest supporters). See Ferdinand C. Baur, *Paul, the Apostle of Jesus Christ, His Life and Work, His Epistles and His Doctrine: A Contribution to the Critical History of Primitive Christianity*, 2d ed. (London: Williams and Norgate, 1876).

[13] Among the more noteworthy proponents was Martin Hengel, who argued that the letter of James was a direct attack against Paul's views and practice. Martin

of construction is based, namely a model of conflict, does not do justice to the careful examination of the letter of James. Instead, the acknowledgment of the plurality and diversity of New Testament traditions helps to set the letter of James free to stand on its own as a significant New Testament writing. As Johnson notes: "The most important gain from breaking the Pauline fixation is that it liberates James to be read in terms of 108 verses rather than 12 verses, in terms of its own voice rather than in terms of its supposed muting of Paul's voice."[14]

(3) New methods for the study of the New Testament have emerged over the past few decades, which give new insights into the wealth of the New Testament. Until the 1970s, studies in the New Testament tended to be largely literary, textual, and theological. Since then, interest in other approaches has developed, especially in methods that give more attention to the social context of the writings themselves. Using models gleaned from sociology and anthropology, scholars have endeavored to shed new light on the New Testament writings and the world out of which they emerged.[15] These approaches have also had an influence upon the letter of James. The work by Pedrito U. Maynard-Reid[16] is a case in point.[17] Using a sociological perspective, Maynard-Reid analyzed one theme in the letter of James, namely that of rich and poor. He attempted to shed new understanding on this topic through an examination of the social context of the

---

Hengel, *Acts and the History of Earliest Christianity*, trans. J. Bowden (Philadelphia: Fortress Press, 1979) 112–26; and "Jakobusbrief als antipaulinische Polemik," *Tradition and Interpretation in the New Testament*, ed. G. F. Hawthorne and O. Betz (Grand Rapids, Mich.: Eerdmans, 1987) 248–78.

[14] Johnson, *The Letter of James*, 114.

[15] See, for example, Bruce J. Malina, *Christian Origins and Cultural Anthropology: Practical Models for Biblical Interpretation* (Atlanta: John Knox Press, 1986); Gerd Theissen, "Die soziologische Auswertung religiöser Überlieferungen: Ihre methodologischen Probleme am Beispiel des Urchristentums," *Kairos* 17 (1975) 284–99; Gerd Theissen, "Theoretische Probleme religionssoziologischer Forschung und die Analyse des Urchristentums," *Neue Zeitschrift für systematische Theologie und Religionsphilosophie* 16 (1974) 35–56; Norman Gottwald, ed., *The Bible and Liberation: Political and Social Hermeneutics* (Maryknoll, N.Y.: Orbis Books, 1983) 337–457.

[16] Pedrito U. Maynard-Reid, *Poverty and Wealth in James* (Maryknoll, N.Y.: Orbis Books, 1987).

[17] See also A. M. Charue, "Quelques Avis aux Riches et aux Pauvres dans l'Epître de St. Jacques," *Collationes Namurences* 30 (1936) 177–87; Albert S. Geyser, "The Letter of James and the Social Condition of His Addressees," *Neotestamentica* 9 (1975) 25–33.

community and world of James. Such an approach does not content it-self with an archaeological investigation of times past; instead, it also wishes to explore how such a theme applies to our present time. This sociological examination of the theme of rich and poor uncovers in James's context the evil structures that enable the rich to become richer and the poor poorer. James's condemnations are seen to speak not just to his own time, but to every generation where unjust situations of so-cial discrimination abound. As such, the letter of James emerges with a message that challenges our present and calls attention to the bibli-cal theme of God's option for the poor, an option that must be incar-nated in our present. As Maynard-Reid says: "That James takes up their cause as an apostle of Jesus Christ demonstrates his option for the poor. Like James, we, as modern representatives of Jesus Christ, are called to take that option and to take up the cause of the oppressed."[18]

Studies such as that of Maynard-Reid show the importance of the letter of James for situations of exploitation and oppression. James gives voice to the marginalized and the oppressed. "Is it not the rich who oppress you? Is it not they who drag you into court? Is it not they who blaspheme the excellent name that was invoked over you?" (2:6-7). In recent times, some scholars have critiqued the Bible for express-ing only the voice of the powerful,[19] however, James is a unique writing in that it gives expression to the voice of the oppressed. It en-courages the reader to see the world through the eyes of those who are discriminated against and dispossessed.[20]

(4) The community dimension of the letter of James has become more evident. This letter has generally been read with an eye to the ad-vice (paraenesis) being directed toward individuals. However, a closer analysis of the letter reveals that all the advice given is community ori-ented.[21] For example, the usual way in which James marks off his sec-tions of instruction is with the simple phrase: "My brothers and sisters" (ἀδελφοί [μου]) at 1:2, 16, 19; 2:1, 14; 3:1; 4:11; 5:7, 12, 19). The morality that James espouses is no individualistic ethic, but one that embraces believers together in their concern for one another. This community re-

---

[18] Maynard-Reid, *Poverty and Wealth in James*, 98.

[19] See, for example, Itumeleng J. Mosala, *Biblical Hermeneutics and Black Theology in South Africa* (Grand Rapids, Mich.: Eerdmans, 1989).

[20] Another work that gives expression to a reading of James within the context of the oppressed and the poor is that of Elsa Tamez, *The Scandalous Message of James: Faith without Works Is Dead* (New York: Crossroad, 1992).

[21] See Luke Timothy Johnson, "Friendship with the World/Friendship with God: A Study of Discipleship in James," *Discipleship in the New Testament*, ed. Fernando Segovia (Philadelphia: Fortress Press, 1985) 166–83.

sponsibility clearly emerges in the final pericope of the writing (5:13-20) where the members of the community are challenged to show concern for bringing a wandering brother or sister back to the community. Awareness of this dimension generates a reading of the letter with new eyes.

(5) Engagement with the text is another important insight.[22] In line with an openness to new approaches toward the interpretation of texts is the understanding that interpretation is not a detached, dispassionate process. Rather, interpretation serves a purpose. The text speaks to the interpreter. As a reader of the text, I interact with the text. I am called to encounter the text. When readers approach a text, they do more than ask the question, "What is said?" Readers also question, "Why is this said?" or "What effect does this have?" and so forth. Further, in a writing such as the letter of James where advice dominates, the readers are addressed directly with an invitation to put into practice the advice that is presented. This calls forth a response from the readers to react by either accepting or rejecting the advice. In other words, readers are called to test the validity of the ethical stance embraced by the document. For example, in the opening of chapter 2 the writer says, "My brothers and sisters, do you with your acts of favoritism really believe in our glorious Lord Jesus Christ?" (2:1). Here the readers are asked to endorse the validity of the statement that true faith cannot coexist with an ethical lifestyle that discriminates against others. Thus, the letter not only offers advice, but shows how this advice is intimately connected with the very foundational understanding of one's faith. In this way the letter calls for faith in action. It calls for the engagement of its message on both the individual and societal level. This study will endeavor to embrace this engagement with the text.[23]

(6) A unique aspect of the letter of James that separates it from other New Testament writings is its theological rather than christological approach.[24] James has been criticized for its lack of interest in and reference to the death and resurrection of Jesus.[25] However, this omis-

---

[22] See Johnson, *The Letter of James*, 162.

[23] See especially chapter seven.

[24] I am indebted for this insight to Johnson, *The Letter of James*, 164.

[25] This was behind the conclusions of scholars such as L. Massebieau, "L'Epître de Jacques est-elle l'Oeuvre d'un Chrétien?" *Revue de l'Histoire des Religions* 32 (1895) 249–83; and F. Spitta, "Der Brief des Jakobus," *Zur Geschichte und Literatur des Urchristentums*, vol. 2 (Göttingen: Vandenhoeck & Ruprecht, 1896) 1–239. They argued that because of the lack of obvious Christian references (only two allusions to Jesus Christ) this was originally a Jewish writing that had been baptized.

sion also produces a very positive result. James undoubtedly shows its roots in Jewish thought. There is nothing in the thought and teaching of James that does not find resonance in the world of Judaism. In fact, the theological stance of James is consistent with the basic theological perspectives of Judaism. James's concept of God (namely, that God is Creator, the Father of Lights, the source of all wisdom, the one who bestows gifts on all who ask, the one lawgiver) is such that religions such as Judaism and Islam could embrace this view. This New Testament writing provides a link to other monotheistic faiths and gives expression to aspects of faith that they share in common. James celebrates an understanding of God that has consequences for one's life, a celebration of life that Judaism and Islam also cherish. Rather than stress our divisions, the letter of James helps us to see aspects of our respective faiths that we share in common. A reminder to Christians of their Jewish roots, James is also a reminder to other believers of the eternal truths we celebrate together. As a writing that reflects on the practical nature of one's actions, its proposed ethic is one that all humans can embrace. The concern for the elimination of discrimination, injustice in the treatment of the poor, the avoidance of violence, and many other themes are all values that today's world can embrace regardless of religious belief or nonbelief. Again, the letter of James provides a pathway to dialogue with the wider community in matters of values and ethical principles. In our multicultural and multireligious world, the letter of James is a valuable document providing us with a means for fostering dialogue. It offers impetus for social action in a way no other New Testament writing does.

(7) Finally, the letter of James has a contribution to make in the realm of the quest for the historical Jesus. While the letter of James seldom mentions Jesus,[26] it does show a closeness to Jesus' sayings.[27] In this area of Jesus' teaching, James has the possibility of making an important contribution. In recent times there has been a renewed interest in the search for the historical Jesus. In fact, a proliferation of books on the historical Jesus has presently emerged.[28] In addition to this influx

---

[26] Only twice directly at 1:1; 2:1.

[27] See Hartin, *James and the Q Sayings of Jesus*, 139–72.

[28] See the following works, to name but a few: John D. Crossan, *The Historical Jesus: The Life of a Mediterranean Jewish Peasant* (San Francisco: HarperSanFrancisco, 1991); John P. Meier, *A Marginal Jew: Rethinking the Historical Jesus*, vols. 1 and 2 (New York: Doubleday, 1991 and 1994); Luke Timothy Johnson, *The Real Jesus: The Misguided Quest for the Historical Jesus and the Truth of the Traditional Gospels* (San Francisco: HarperSanFrancisco, 1996); Marcus J. Borg, ed., *Jesus at 2000* (Boulder,

of literature, scholarly groups, such as the Jesus Seminar and the International Q Project, examine the traditions behind the Gospels in an attempt to get closer to the historical Jesus. An analysis of the letter of James reveals no direct references to Jesus and his teaching and no sayings of Jesus quoted as such. Nevertheless, similarities with the teaching of Jesus in the Gospels have been demonstrated.[29] Drawing from a source that is independent of the other New Testament traditions, the letter of James offers insight into the sayings of Jesus that also made their way into the Gospels, particularly the Gospels of Matthew and Luke. One of the principles that research concerning the historical Jesus advances for the establishment of the authenticity of a tradition is whether multiple independent attestation can be demonstrated for the saying or tradition.[30] The letter of James is such an independent tradition. In this way, it could provide another witness to the traditions dealing with the sayings of Jesus.

Aim of This Study

In the light of the above indications of renewed interest in the letter of James this study approaches this writing with the purpose of giving attention to the following four aspects:

The Discovery of a Unifying Theme for the Letter

Many different approaches have been adopted to define the structure of this letter. Dibelius, for example, argued that James was made up of a disjointed set of "paraenetical" material brought together with no unifying thought running through it.[31] According to Dibelius this is

---

Colo.: Westview Press, 1997); and Graham Stanton, *Gospel Truth? New Light on Jesus and the Gospels* (Valley Forge, Pa.: Trinity Press International, 1995).

[29] See, for example, the lists of correspondences that have been noted by different scholars, such as: Gerhard Kittel, "Der geschichtliche Ort des Jakobusbriefes," *Zeitschrift für die neutestamentliche Wissenschaft und die Kunde der älteren Kirche* 41 (1942) 84; Mayor, *The Epistle of St. James,* lxxxv–lxxxviii; W. D. Davies, *The Setting of the Sermon on the Mount* (Cambridge: Cambridge University Press, 1964) 402–3; Franz Mussner, *Der Jakobusbrief: Auslegung,* 4th ed. (Freiburg: Herder, 1981) 48–50; Davids, *The Epistle of James,* 47–8; Peter H. Davids, "James and Jesus," *Gospel Perspectives: The Jesus Tradition outside the Gospels,* vol. 5, ed. David Wenham (Sheffield: JSOT Press, 1985) 66–7; Hartin, *James and the Q Sayings of Jesus,* 139–43.

[30] See Crossan, *The Historical Jesus,* xxxi–xxxii; Meier, *A Marginal Jew,* vol. 1, 174–5.

[31] Martin Dibelius made this approach famous in his commentary on the Letter of James (*James: A Commentary on the Epistle of James,* trans. Michael A. Williams

the very nature of paraenesis,[32] and James illustrates this approach well. What connects the various pericopes in James together are catch-words, not continuity of thought.[33]

Elsewhere, I have adopted an opposite approach, arguing for a certain unifying structure that can be discovered from the way in which the opening chapter operates with regard to the rest of the letter.[34] This opening chapter functions much in the way that a symphony's overture does: the major themes of the letter are first introduced, then developed in a more elaborate way in the body of the letter.[35] For example:

- the theme of rich and poor (1:9-11; 2:1-13; and 5:1-6).
- the theme of faith and works (1:22-25; 2:14-26; and 4:13-17)
- the theme of speech and the tongue (1:26-27; 3:1-12; and 4:11-12)
- the theme of enduring testing (1:2-4, 12-18; and 5:7-11).
- the theme of wisdom (1:5-8; 3:13-18; and 4:1-10).

Certain convictions operate as unifying principles and help give coherence to these major themes that James develops in the body of the letter. Johnson[36] argues that one of the fundamental principles evident behind James's teaching is the opposition between the world and God. James 4:4 gives expression to this idea very succinctly: "Do you not know that friendship with the world is enmity with God?"[37]

[Philadelphia: Fortress Press, 1975]). The influence that this commentary has had, particularly in setting forth the view of James as paraenesis, cannot be over-emphasized.

[32] Dibelius (*James*, 5) defines paraenesis in this way: "By paraenesis we mean a text which strings together admonitions of general ethical content. Paraenetic sayings ordinarily address themselves to a specific (though perhaps fictional) audience, or at least appear in the form of a command or summons."

[33] Ibid., 6.

[34] Hartin, *James and the Q Sayings of Jesus*, 23–34.

[35] For a detailed discussion of the structure of the letter of James see Hartin, *James and the Q Sayings of Jesus*, 23–34 and 245. James's opening chapter contains two introductory formulae of joy and blessedness which replace the traditional Pauline thanksgiving at the beginning of a letter. Within these formulae of joy and blessedness occur a number of themes that become the major themes for the letter. James returns to these themes at least twice in the body of the letter.

[36] Johnson, *The Letter of James*, 14.

[37] From another perspective Timothy B. Cargal (*Restoring the Diaspora: Discursive Structure and Purpose in the Epistle of James*, SBL Dissertation Series 144 [Atlanta: Scholars Press, 1993]) sees the letter as operating with a number of oppositions. These oppositions carry the thought forward (pp. 229–32) and operate as the unifying principles for the thought of the letter.

I believe that James's frequent use of the adjective "perfect" provides another such overarching principle. This study will show how James's concept of perfection operates as a unifying theme by giving meaning to the other themes developed throughout the letter. An examination of the meaning of perfection will show how this concept permeates the paraenetical advice of the letter and comes close to the present day understanding of integrity. While James himself does not use this word, it will be my argument that the understanding of perfection that so dominates the thought of this letter can be captured by this term "integrity." In order to illustrate this, my starting point will be to examine the use of the adjective "perfect" in James, as well as in his Jewish-Christian environment.

The Spirituality of the Letter of James

The reflection on James's understanding of perfection helps give expression to the main spiritual impulses of the letter, and this study will culminate in an attempt to define this spirituality. Two aspects are important to any spirituality: the aspect of faith, what one believes, and the aspect of action, how that belief system influences the way in which one acts. The letter of James is the New Testament writing par excellence that takes seriously the call to put faith into action. Faith is the guiding force behind all the actions one performs, be it in the avoidance of discrimination, in the correct use of the tongue, etc. All this gives expression to the perfect law of liberty, the law of love (1:25; 2:8). Again, the aspect of perfection will emerge as the pulsating heart of the spirituality of the letter. James's belief system gives expression to the way in which believers are called to lead their lives. The letter's basic understanding of God is that of a God who is transcendent and gives all gifts to those who ask. In particular, God is the source of all wisdom (1:5). This study examines James's spirituality by illustrating how its understanding of perfection plays a key role in the definition of God, as well as the way one is called "to be in the world." Every perfect gift comes from God, and the perfect law of love becomes the guiding principle for every action.

The Eschatological Dimension of the Letter

As a paraenetical writing, James offers advice on how to lead one's life in the midst of changing situations. These situations (to which the letter refers in graphic illustration) occur as different contexts of testing. Within these situations of testing one is called to embrace a life of patient endurance that will lead to perfection (1:4). The opening (1:2-

8) and the closing (5:7-11) provide the framework within which James's paraenetical advice is situated. The opening states the goal, namely the attainment of a life in which one lacks nothing, a life in which one is perfect. The conclusion provides the call to be patient because the coming of the Lord is near. James sees the community to whom he writes living at the end of history. "The Judge is standing at the doors!" (5:9). The call in the letter is for perseverance so that they will be found perfect at the coming of the Lord.

Another aspect of this study will be to show how eschatology provides the horizon for the letter's paraenetical wisdom advice. Much scholarship has been devoted to the examination of the categories of eschatology, apocalypticism, and wisdom. This study endeavors to make a contribution to this discussion by providing some indications of the relationship among these traditions within the letter of James.

Engagement with the Text

Finally, this monograph will attempt to interact with the text in the sense of seeing how the text speaks to our present time. This study is not simply an archaeological investigation of a writing from the first century that has interest in reflecting the thought and views of the first generation Christians as they struggled to hand on their interpretation of Jesus' teaching in their new surroundings. As part of the Christian canon, James is a writing that is judged to have universal relevance. From this standpoint, part of this investigation will be to see how the themes and perspectives of this letter speak to a world very different from the one in which it was written. Every generation of believers struggles to put their faith into action. The letter of James, more than any other, is the writing of the New Testament that devotes its full energies to illustrate faith in action. What directions does the letter of James give to Christians today who are striving to put their faith into action?

A Spirituality of Perfection?

Perfectionism today is "out of fashion."[38] I am not sure if it ever was in fashion. For most people, perfectionists are those individuals who are very demanding, both of themselves as well as of others. They are hard to get along with for they are often very impatient with those unable to live up to the high standards they set for themselves. They make one uncomfortable because one feels unable to measure up to them. For this reason, no one really loves a perfectionist. They appear

---

[38] See Bonnie Bowman Thurston, "Matthew 5:43-48," *Interpretation* 41 (1987) 170.

psychologically abnormal, living beyond the abilities of most of us who are only too aware of our own human frailties and weaknesses.

Therefore, when we turn to the New Testament and hear Jesus' statement in the Sermon on the Mount, "Be perfect, therefore, as your heavenly Father is perfect" (Matt 5:48), we feel very uncomfortable. Our sensitivities to the idea of perfectionism are immediately alerted. The same is true when we turn to the letter of James. Here the notion of perfection occurs more than in all the Gospels combined. Consequently, focusing on the concept of perfection in the letter of James also causes much disquiet.

In the history of interpretation, the understanding of perfection and who is able to attain it has embraced very divergent attitudes. Among these we can illustrate the following approaches:

A Moral Understanding

Different nuances emerge by way of offering a moral understanding for the concept of perfection.

Some argue that only a select few are able to attain the demands for perfection. According to this view, perfection is equated with the evangelical counsels *(consilia evangelica)* of poverty, chastity, and obedience which formed the basis of the vows taken by monks and, later, by priests and nuns.

Others argue that the demands for perfection are attainable by all. This is the basic premise in the teaching of John Wesley who understood perfection as sanctification. Christian perfection implies being renewed in the image of God. The Christian responds to God's activity by faith which illustrates itself through loving God with one's whole being.[39]

---

[39] John Wesley writes in his work "A Plain Account of Christian Perfection" *(John and Charles Wesley: Selected Writings and Hymns,* ed. Frank Whaling [New York: Paulist Press, 1981] 319): "On Monday, June 25, 1744, our first conference began, six clergymen and all our preachers being present. The next morning we seriously considered the doctrine of sanctification, or perfection. The questions asked concerning it and the substance of the answers given were as follows:

Q. What is it to be *sanctified?*
A. To be renewed in the image of God, *in righteousness and true holiness.*
Q. What is implied in being *a perfect Christian?*
A. The loving God with all our heart, and mind, and soul (Deut. 6:5).
Q. Does this imply that *all inward sin* is taken away?
A. Undoubtedly: or how can we be said to be *saved from all our uncleanness?* (Ezek. 36:29)."

The same approach to perfection is adopted by Pope John Paul II in his encyclical The Splendor of Truth *(Veritatis splendor)*.[40] He sees the call to perfection as addressed to everyone, not just to a select few. This perfection is capable of being achieved through adherence to the person of Jesus and the imitation of his example of love.[41]

This examination of the letter of James wishes to discover James's specific understanding of perfection and to see where the concept fits against the perspectives indicated above.

An Eschatological Understanding

This understanding of perfection begins with an emphasis on the eschatological end which is seen to lie behind the concept of perfection. All morality is judged to be driven by an eschatological dimension. The eschatological kingdom of God gives direction to every action.[42] There is a certain truth in this argument, for there is without doubt an eschatological dimension that gives direction to one's actions. However, a problem arises when this is made the exclusive approach with which to interpret everything. As a consequence, every ethical decision is forced to operate under this umbrella—no room is left for other

---

[40] Encyclical letter The Splendor of Truth *(Veritatis splendor)*, addressed by the Supreme Pontiff Pope John Paul II to All the Bishops of the Catholic Church Regarding Certain Fundamental Questions of the Church's Moral Teaching (Boston: St. Paul Books and Media, 1993).

[41] For example, Pope John Paul II reflects upon the dialogue between Jesus and the rich young man in Matt 19:16-30, and in particular Jesus' response to him: "If you wish to be perfect, go, sell your possessions, and give the money to the poor, and you will have treasure in heaven; then come, follow me" (Matt 19:21). The Pope writes: "This vocation to perfect love is not restricted to a small group of individuals. *The invitation,* 'go, sell your possessions and give the money to the poor,' and the promise 'you will have treasure in heaven,' *are meant for everyone,* because they bring out the full meaning of the commandment of love for neighbor, just as the invitation which follows, 'Come, follow me,' is the new, specific form of the commandment of love of God. Both the commandments and Jesus' invitation to the rich young man stand at the service of a single and indivisible charity, which spontaneously tends towards that perfection whose measure is God alone; 'You, therefore, must be perfect, as your heavenly Father is perfect' (Mt 5:48). In the Gospel of Luke, Jesus makes even clearer the meaning of this perfection: 'Be merciful, even as your Father is merciful' (Lk 6:36)." (Pope John Paul II, The Splendor of Truth 18, 31–2).

[42] Herbert Preisker, *Das Ethos des Urchristentums* (Gütersloh: Bertelsmann, 1949) 130–4.

motives, such as the desire to conform to the will of God in the present for the way in which one should act.

A State of Perfection

There are those who take cognizance of the human situation of frailty and weakness, and transpose the notion of perfection onto the future. They see perfection in terms of a state that one is to attain after death. People speak of the state of perfection as occurring when one has attained one's destiny in union with Christ after death.

The Gnostic Approach[43]

Gnosticism as a religious movement became exceedingly more and more influential in the centuries after the New Testament era. The Gnostics used this term to refer to themselves as "the perfect," just as they referred to Jesus in this way. In the Gnostic sermon *The Gospel of Truth,* those who are considered to be the elect are referred to as "the perfect": "It is to the perfect that this, the proclamation of the one they search for, has made itself known, through the mercies of the father."[44] In the Gnostic myth of creation, the first man, Adam, is described as "the perfect man": "Then—[deriving] from *prior acquaintance and* perfect intellect through [disclosure] of the desire of the invisible spirit and the desire of the self-originate—the perfect human being, the first manifestation and true [person] was named 'the Geradamas' [Ger-Adamas]."[45]

The Way Forward

The issue here is one that occurs frequently in studies on the New Testament. It is a question of language. The problem is essentially that modern understandings and preconceptions with regard to perfection are transposed uncritically upon documents from twenty centuries ago. Presuppositions and misunderstandings of meaning are forced

---

[43] The perennial question related to the Gnostic writings is: "To what extent were these Gnostic ideas prevalent at the time of the New Testament?" This is a much debated point among scholars. Without entering into a discussion of this vexing question, I limit myself here to drawing attention to the importance that this notion of "the perfect" or "perfection" had in Gnostic circles.

[44] "The Gospel of Truth," *The Gnostic Scriptures,* ed. Bentley Layton (New York: Doubleday, 1987) 254.

[45] "The Secret Book according to John," *The Gnostic Scriptures,* ed. Layton, 34.

upon the text. In fact, the challenge is to discover first of all the biblical understanding of perfection before disregarding the notion as unacceptable. Perfection according to the biblical mind is neither a state of perfection after death, nor is it a state of perfectionism here on earth.

This study will examine the concept of perfection in the biblical writings as a background for understanding its usage in the letter of James. Our aim will be not just to examine the usage of this notion, but more especially to see how this concept functions within the thought world of the letter of James, and how ultimately a spirituality of perfection emerges.

James owes his distinctive understanding of perfection to his Jewish and Greek heritage. Once the concept of perfection in James has been examined against this Greek and Jewish background, I will argue that, in fact, the concept of integrity captures James's meaning more fully. The call to perfection that James makes is essentially a call to integrity.

CHAPTER TWO

An Overview of the Concept of Perfection in the Ancient World as a Background to the Letter of James

The Concept of Perfection in the Classical Greek World

Before examining the concept of perfection in the letter of James and the spiritual understanding that it generates, it is necessary to investigate the notion of perfection within the wider world to which James was heir. This examination will show how the concept of perfection in the letter of James is indebted to its context and can only be fully understood against that background.

Terminology for perfection was used widely in ancient writings. The Greek adjective τέλειος *(teleios)* is the word that was most widely associated with the notion of perfection. By examining its usage in its distinctive contexts, we can give more precision to its meaning. Such an exercise is important because to appreciate the biblical understanding of perfection one must first view it in relation to the Greek concept of perfection.

In the cultic usage of the Greek world, τέλειος referred to animals or things that were declared suitable for sacrifice because they were considered ritually without blemish.[1] The phrase "perfect holy offerings" (ἱερά τέλεια) was used to embrace sacrifices that met all the ritual requirements.[2] On the other hand, the term τέλειος was also used

---

[1] For example, Homer, *The Iliad*, I.65–66: "in hope that perchance he may accept the savour of lambs and unblemished goats [ἀρνῶν κνίσης αἰγῶν τε τελείων] and be minded to ward off from us the pestilence" (A. T. Murray, *Homer: The Iliad* [New York: G. P. Putnam's Sons, 1928] 6–7).

[2] As Paul J. Du Plessis (*ΤΕΛΕΙΟΣ: The Idea of Perfection in the New Testament* [Kampen: J. H. Kok, 1959] 75) says: "Offerings are called ἱερὰ τέλεια when executed in complete or full accordance with rubrical prescriptions and lacking in none

in a biological sense to refer to an animal or person that was fully grown or mature. An adult was described as being a "mature person" (τέλειος ἀνήρ). For example, Xenophon gives a fourfold classification of human development: childhood, youth, mature years (οἱ τέλειοι ἄνδρες), and elders.[3] Finally, the adjective "perfect" (τέλειος) was also used in a religious sense to describe the gods. For example, Zeus was addressed as "O perfect Zeus" (Ζεῦ Ζεῦ τέλειε).[4] As a description, it was connected with the nouns "end" or "goal" (τέλος) indicating that these gods had accomplished everything that they set out to do. It was a further way of indicating the almighty power that Zeus and the other gods possess.[5]

In Greek philosophy, the notion of perfection also developed a precise meaning. A brief overview of three of the more influential Greek philosophers reveals an idea of perfection that is future oriented and one that was very difficult to acquire.

Parmenides (born in the latter part of the sixth century B.C.E.) is generally regarded as the one who inaugurated Western metaphysics. His philosophy was expressed by means of a poem[6] that was in essence a reaction against the views of the philosopher Heraclitus who had taught that all things are in a state of flux or change. In contrast, Parmenides developed a perspective on the world that argued that change was an illusion. Parmenides's thought rested upon the statement that reality, or being, exists. There is one reality that is complete and perfect. Nothing can be added to it, nor taken away from it. Change is therefore impossible. The plurality of individual things was, therefore, not real. For

---

of the constituent rites." Du Plessis's doctoral dissertation was one of the first comprehensive studies on the notion of perfection in the New Testament. I acknowledge my debt to him for many of his valuable insights.

[3] Xenophon (*Cyropaedia*, 1.2.4) writes: "This square, enclosing the government buildings, is divided into four parts: one of these belongs to the boys, one to the youths, another to the men of mature years [τελείοις ἀνδράσιν], and another to those who are past the age for military service. And the laws require them to come daily to their several quarters—the boys and the full-grown men [οἱ τέλειοι ἄνδρες] at daybreak . . . ." (Walter Miller, trans., *Xenophon's Cyropaedia*, vol. 1, The Loeb Classical Library [New York: The Macmillan Co., 1954] 12–3).

[4] See Aeschylus, *Agamemnon*, 973.

[5] Du Plessis, *The Idea of Perfection*, 77.

[6] As Frederick Copleston observers: "Parmenides wrote in verse, most of the faragments we possess being preserved by Simplicius in his commentary" (*A History of Philosophy*, vol. 1, *Greece and Rome*, An Image Book [New York: Doubleday, 1985] 48).

Parmenides and those who followed him, the notion of perfection embraced that of totality and unity: all things are one.[7]

Plato (428/7–348/7 B.C.E.), one of the world's most significant thinkers, brought the philosophical inquiry forward by trying to harmonize the views of Heraclitus and Parmenides with his concept of the "Ideas."[8] Things are imperfect because they are multiple. However, every individual thing exists insofar as it participates in a corresponding Idea that exists as separate, unchangeable, and perfect. Taken together, these Ideas contain all perfection. Material objects share in that perfection to the extent to which they are related to these Ideas. Perfection lies in the ideal order and is withdrawn from the present order of existence. For example, to describe justice or beauty or goodness one starts with various forms of justice or beauty or goodness in the world around us and slowly one arrives at the true Idea, the perfection, of justice or beauty or goodness.[9]

In his writing the *Phaedrus,* Plato demonstrates how perfection is attained: the philosopher strives to remember what had once been seen in the world of Ideas.[10] By liberating oneself from the shadows of this world and ultimately attaining the world of Ideas, one reaches the world of true being. In other words, one remembers when one's soul

---

[7] Ibid., 47–53.

[8] As Copleston (*A History of Philosophy,* 52) says: "Plato attempted a synthesis of the two, a combination of what is true in each. He adopts Parmenides' distinction between thought and sense, and declares that sense-objects, the objects of sense-perception, are not the objects of true knowledge, for they do not possess the necessary stability, being subject to the Heraclitean flux. The objects of true knowledge are stable and eternal, like the Being of Parmenides; but they are not material, like the Being of Parmenides. They are, on the contrary, ideal, subsistent and immaterial forms, hierarchically arranged and culminating in the Form of the Good."

[9] Plato, *Phaedo,* 65–6. For example, Plato (*Phaedo,* 66) writes: "Would not that man do this most perfectly who approaches each thing, so far as possible, with the reason alone, not introducing sight into his reasoning nor dragging in any of the other senses along with his thinking, but who employs pure, absolute reason in his attempt to search out the pure, absolute essence of things, and who removes himself, so far as possible, from eyes and ears and in a word, from his whole body, because he feels that its companionship disturbs the soul and hinders it from attaining truth and wisdom? Is not this the man, Simmias, if anyone, to attain to the knowledge of reality?" (Harold N. Fowler, trans., *Plato in Twelve Volumes,* vol. 1, *Euthyphro, Apology, Crito, Phaedo, Phaedrus,* The Loeb Classical Library [Cambridge, Mass.: Harvard University Press, 1977] 229).

[10] For Plato, "God" (θεός) stands for that transcendent world of Ideas (Cornelia J. de Vogel, *Greek Philosophy: A Collection of Texts, with Notes and Explanations,* vol. 3, 2d ed. [Leiden: Brill, 1964] 135).

was "perfect" before it was united to the body. A person who rekindles such memories and attains the world of Ideas is "perfect" (τέλειος).[11] Platonic perfection consists in the contemplation of the world of Ideas through "the eye of the soul."[12] They become like "mystic(s) initiated into that state of perfection."[13] Plato saw the world of Ideas as hierarchically ordered with the Idea of the good at the apex. The aim of philosophers is to contemplate the nature of the good. In this way they perfect themselves by conforming themselves morally to the nature of the good.[14]

Aristotle (384/3–322/1 B.C.E.) was another influential Greek philosopher who had an enduring legacy. Originally a student of Plato's Academy, Aristotle found in Plato a mentor who had a lasting influence. Copleston expresses the influence in this way: "Though in later years his [Aristotle's] own scientific interests tended to come much more to the fore, the metaphysical and religious teaching of Plato had a lasting influence upon him."[15] After Plato's death in 348/7 B.C.E., Aristotle developed his own empirical philosophy more fully.

[11] As Plato says in the *Phaedrus* (249C, D): "And therefore it is just that the mind of the philosopher only has wings, for he is always, so far as he is able, in communion through memory with those things the communion with which causes God to be divine. Now a man who employs such memories rightly is always being initiated into perfect mysteries and he alone becomes truly perfect; but since he separates himself from human interests and turns his attention toward the divine, he is rebuked by the vulgar, who consider him mad and do not know that he is inspired" (Fowler, *Plato in Twelve Volumes,* vol. 1, *Phaedrus,* 480–3).

[12] Plato, *Republic* VII, 533d: "the eye of the soul" (τὸ τῆς ψυχῆς ὄμμα) (Paul Shorey, trans., *Plato in Twelve Volumes,* vol. 6, *The Republic,* The Loeb Classical Library [Cambridge, Mass.: Harvard University Press, 1980] 202–3).

[13] Du Plessis, *The Idea of Perfection,* 81. Plato writes in the *Phaedrus* (250B, C): "But at that former time they saw beauty shining in brightness, when, with a blessed company—we following in the train of Zeus, and others in that of some other god—they saw the blessed sight and vision and were initiated into that which is rightly called the most blessed of mysteries, which we celebrated in a state of perfection, when we were without experience of the evils which awaited us in the time to come, being permitted as initiates to the sight of perfect and simple and calm and happy apparitions, which we saw in the pure light, being ourselves pure and not entombed in this which we carry about with us and call the body, in which we are imprisoned like an oyster in its shell" (Fowler, *Plato in Twelve Volumes,* vol. 1, *Phaedrus,* 484–5).

[14] As Hans K. La Rondelle (*Perfection and Perfectionism* [Berrien Springs, Mich.: Andrews University Press, 1971] 13) says: "According to Plato, man's obligation is to strive after virtue or inner harmony of the soul, the perfection of his nature, and thus to perfect himself here and now by making himself morally alike to 'God' as much as possible: *homoiosis theoi kata to dunaton.*"

[15] Copleston, *A History of Philosophy,* 266.

Aristotle rejected the Ideas of Plato as metaphors existing only in the mind and explained perfection from his concept of potency and act. Imperfection is potency, the capacity for being; while perfection is act, the being itself. Every thing is able to attain its maximum perfection when all its potentialities are realized.[16] For Aristotle, perfection means that no further development or change is possible in the quality of something—it lacks nothing, but is excellent in all aspects.[17]

In reflecting on human nature, Aristotle argued that human nature contained within itself the principle that drove the human being forward toward the goal of perfection.[18] Here he shows the connection between "end or goal" (τέλος) and "perfect" (τέλειος): something is perfect in that it has achieved its goal or arrived at its end.[19] Aristotle identified a teleological principle working within human nature that constantly drove the person ever onward in the quest for the attainment of the goal of perfection.[20]

While the thoughts of these great Greek philosophers did vary, they all shared a certain common perspective. Perfection was something one strived for in the future—one is on the way to perfection. Thus perfection, especially in the thought of Plato and Aristotle, approached more

[16] Ibid., 52.

[17] Aristotle gave a very detailed description of the term τέλειος in this way: "'Perfect' or 'complete' [τέλειος] means: (a) That outside which it is impossible to find even a single one of its parts; e.g., the complete time of each thing is that outside which it is impossible to find any time which is a part of it. (b) That which, in respect of goodness or excellence, cannot be surpassed in its kind; e.g., a doctor and a musician are 'perfect' when they have no deficiency in respect of the form of their peculiar excellence. And thus by an extension of the meaning we use the term in a bad connexion, and speak of a 'perfect' humbug and a 'perfect' thief; since indeed we call them 'good'—e.g. a 'good' thief and a 'good' humbug. (c) And goodness is a kind of perfection. For each thing, and every substance, is perfect when, and only when, in respect of the form of its peculiar excellence, it lacks no particle of its natural magnitude. (d) Things which have attained their end, if their end is good, are called 'perfect'; for they are perfect in virtue of having attained the end" (Aristotle, *Metaphysica, V*, XVI, 1021b. 12–25. This translation is from Hugh Tredennick, trans., *Aristotle in Twenty-Three Volumes*, vol. 17, *The Metaphysics, Books I–IX*, The Loeb Classical Library [Cambridge, Mass.: Harvard University Press, 1989] 266–7).

[18] Aristotle argues that the good is that at which all things aim (*Ethica Nicomachea* I, 1, 1094a).

[19] Du Plessis (*The Idea of Perfection*, 73) also argues that "the distinct qualities of *telos* are to be kept in mind when considering the circle of meanings characteristic of *teleios*."

[20] As La Rondelle (*Perfection and Perfectionism*, 14) says: "This is a teleological principle, which by nature propels man to his goal of perfection, the fulfillment of the natural destination of man."

closely the meaning of attaining completeness in the sense that one has attained the goal (τέλος) for which one was striving.[21]

The Distinctive Idea of Perfection in the Hebrew Scriptures and the Septuagint

From this wider context of the ancient Greek world, attention now turns to examine a more immediate context, namely the Greek translation of the Hebrew Scriptures, the Septuagint. In looking at the Septuagint as a possible source of influence for the New Testament writers, two groups of terms must be considered when trying to gain an understanding of the concept of τέλειος: (1) those Hebrew terms translated by the word τέλειος, and (2) other related terms (even though not translated by τέλειος). The related terms are important because they give the theological background for the use of the term. A word is never used in a vacuum, but operates within a particular theological framework. Michel[22] argued that when examining the meaning of τέλειος, it was not just a matter of searching for the usage of the word itself, but it was also a question of examining the conceptual range of meanings that the word embraced. He observed one such range of meanings in the conceptual understanding of righteousness.[23] Attention will be given to this connection with righteousness in what follows.

Hebrew Terms Translated by the Greek Word τέλειος

In the Septuagint, the Greek word τέλειος is used on occasions to translate the Hebrew words *"tamim"* and *"shalem"* (שלם, תמים) that carry the meaning of "unblemished, undivided, complete, and whole."[24]

---

[21] As F.M.J. Waanders (*The History of TELOS and TELEO in Ancient Greek* [Amsterdam: Grüner, 1983] 237) says: "All available evidence leads me to believe that the most frequent meaning of τέλειος ('having τέλος') is 'complete.' It is to be found as an attribute of animals (which may be specified as victims by the context), meaning 'full-grown' (from Homer onwards), as a special case of 'complete'; further as an attribute of persons who are 'accomplished' in some respect (Plato, Isocrates, Aristotle, etc.: #203); as an attribute of συλλογισμός, 'complete' (which does not need conversion of terms, or *reductio ad impossibile,* to become evident)—*not* 'perfect,' in some profoundly philosophical way; etc. These applications are based on τέλος in the sense 'realization, completeness.'"

[22] Otto Michel, *Der Brief an die Hebräer* (Göttingen: Vandenhoeck und Ruprecht, 1936) 8.

[23] Ibid.

[24] Gerhard Delling, "τέλειος," *Theological Dictionary of the New Testament*, vol. 8, ed. Gerhard Friedrich, trans. Geoffrey W. Bromiley (Grand Rapids, Mich.: Eerdmans, 1972) 72.

The Hebrew adjective *"tamim"* (תמים) is translated by the Greek word τέλειος in the following passages: Gen 6:9; Exod 12:5; Deut 18:13; 2 Kgs 22:26 (LXX).[25] To understand these passages it is necessary to see them in the context of the wider background of the usage of the term *"tamim"* throughout the Hebrew Scriptures.

Schnackenburg[26] argues rightly, I think, that the origin for the notion of *tamim* is found in the realm of the sacrificial worship of Israel. There it took on the meaning of "unblemished," referring especially to an animal that was without defects. For example, the sacrificial laws of Leviticus prescribed on numerous occasions that only animals that were "unblemished" *(tamim)* were to be sacrificed.[27] This means that only what was whole, complete, and without defects could be offered to God. In this context, one can see the notion of perfection arising. If a

[25] The Hebrew *"tamim"* (תמים) is translated by the Greek τέλειος in the following instances:
- Gen 6:9: "Noah was a righteous man, *blameless* [*tamim*] in his generation";
- Exod 12:5: "Your lamb shall be *without blemish* [*tamim*], a year-old male";
- Deut 18:13: "You must remain completely loyal [*tamim*] to the Lord your God";
- 2 Kgs 22:26 (LXX): "With the loyal you show yourself loyal; with the blameless [*tamim*] you show yourself blameless."

Otherwise, *"tamim"* is translated by the Greek adjective ἄμωμος, "unblemished, blameless" (Delling, "τέλειος," 72, n. 20). Nevertheless, in order to understand what is meant by τέλειος it is necessary to examine the full range of meanings that the Hebrew term *"tamim"* generates.

[26] Schnackenburg, "Christian Perfection according to Matthew," *Christian Existence in the New Testament,* vol. 1 (Notre Dame, Ind.: University of Notre Dame Press, 1968) 160–1.

[27] For example:
- Lev 1:3: "If the offering is a burnt offering from the herd, you shall offer a male *without blemish* [*tamim*]."
- Lev 1:10: "If your gift for a burnt offering is from the flock, from the sheep or goats, your offering shall be a male *without blemish* [*tamim*]."
- Lev 3:1: "If the offering is a sacrifice of well-being, if you offer an animal of the herd, whether male or female, you shall offer one *without blemish* [*tamim*] before the Lord."
- Lev 3:6: "If your offering for a sacrifice of well-being to the Lord is from the flock, male or female, you shall offer one *without blemish* [*tamim*]."
- Lev 4:3: "If it is the anointed priest who sins, thus bringing guilt on the people, he shall offer for the sin that he has committed a bull of the herd *without blemish* [*tamim*] as a sin offering to the Lord."

In all the above instances, the word used in the Septuagint to translate the Hebrew *"tamim"* is ἄμωμος ("unblemished"). However, in Exod 12:5 the word τέλειος is used: "Your lamb shall be without blemish [πρόβατον τέλειον], a year-old male."

being remained true to its original constitution, then it was considered perfect. In other words, Hebrew thought conceived perfection in an intimate relationship to the original state of a being, to its wholeness as originally constituted. This is radically different from the Greek concept where perfection was an ideal toward which one strived.

The word *"tamim"* was not only used to refer to the cultic condition of animals. It was also applied to human action or conduct whereby one walks blamelessly before the Lord. For example, "You must remain *completely loyal* [*tamim*] to the LORD your God" (Deut 18:13). As Schnackenburg says: "To be 'blameless' before the Lord (Deut 18:13) means to belong to him wholeheartedly, without practicing idolatry, sorcery and other abominations (cf. 18:9-12)."[28] The concept expresses the unconditional giving of one's heart to God; above all it rejects idolatry or the worship of other gods.

Terms such as "walking before the Lord" and the "way" are the most usual images for human conduct in the Hebrew Scriptures. The adjective *"tamim"* is often connected with these images. For example: "I am God Almighty; walk before me and be blameless [*tamim*]" (Gen 17:1). Here the concept of *tamim* is not presented as an ideal. Rather, Abraham, to whom the above passage is directed, is able to actualize it in his moral conduct. The same is true of Noah: he was presented as a model of the perfect person: "Noah was a righteous man, blameless [*tamim*] in his generation" (Gen 6:9). The Septuagint translates the term *"tamim"* by τέλειος here at Gen 6:9 as well as at Deut 18:13 and 2 Kgs 22:26. One can say that these Old Testament individuals are *tamim* because they are "complete, sound, free from defect, and, in this sense, *perfect.*"[29]

The Hebrew expression *"shalem leb"* (שׁלם לב, "a heart that is whole or perfect") is another phrase with which the Greek word τέλειος is connected. The Septuagint uses the Greek word τέλειος to translate the Hebrew *"shalem"* in the following examples:

- "Therefore, *devote yourselves completely* [αἱ καρδίαι ἡμῶν τέλειαι] to the Lord our God, walking in his statutes and keeping his commandments, as at this day" (3 Kgs 8:61 [LXX]).

- "For when Solomon was old, his wives turned away his heart after other gods; and *his heart was not true* [καὶ οὐκ ἦν ἡ καρδία αὐτου τελεία] to the Lord his God" (3 Kgs 11:4 [LXX]).

---

[28] Schnackenburg, "Christian Perfection according to Matthew," 162.

[29] See Samuel R. Driver and George B. Gray, *A Critical and Exegetical Commentary on the Book of Job,* International Critical Commentary (New York: Charles Scribner's Sons, 1921) 3.

• "He committed all the sins that his father did before him; *his heart was not true* [καὶ οὐκ ἦν ἡ καρδία αὐτου τελεία] to the Lord his God, like the heart of his father David" (3 Kgs 15:3 [LXX]).

• "Nevertheless *the heart of Asa was true* [ἡ καρδία Ασα ἦν τελεία] to the Lord all his days" (3 Kgs 15:14 [LXX]).

• "And you, my son Solomon, know the God of your father, and serve him *with single mind* [ἐν καρδίᾳ τελείᾳ] and willing heart" (1 Chr 28:9 [LXX]).

From these examples emerges the understanding of τέλειος as wholehearted devotion to the Lord. One is completely and perfectly dedicated to being faithful to the Lord in carrying out the Lord's commands.

Other Related Terms

Other adjectives are also used to describe this "completeness" of the Israelite in relation to God. For example:

• *"yasar"* (ישׁר, upright): "Mark the blameless, and behold the *upright*, / for there is posterity for the peaceable" (Ps 37:37).

• *"saddiq"* (צדק, righteous): "O let the evil of the wicked come to an end, / but establish *the righteous*, / you who test the minds and hearts, / O righteous God" (Ps 7:9).

• *"amen"* (אמן, fidelity): "Now therefore, if you acted in good *faith* and honor . . ." (Judg 9:16).

In particular, the word *"saddiq"* appears to be almost synonymous with the word *"tamim."* As Du Plessis says: "Something is *saddiq* if it answers to its purpose, if it is as it should be, or is what can be expected of it."[30] More importantly, the notion of *saddiq* embraces a dimension of relationships. A person is in a relationship with God as well as with a community. God has intended and has initiated this righteous relationship. Here the notion of *tamim* intersects: if one is part of this relationship with God and the community, and if one strives to maintain this relationship in all one's actions, then one is *tamim*, perfect.

Wholehearted dedication to the Lord is demonstrated in a life of obedience to the Torah, to the laws of the Lord. "Those who walk blamelessly [*tamim*], and do what is right, / and speak the truth from their heart; / who do not slander with their tongue, / and do no evil to their friends, / nor take up a reproach against their neighbors . . . . Those who do these things shall never be moved" (Ps 15:2-5). Since the

[30] See Du Plessis, *The Idea of Perfection*, 96.

Torah is the expression of the will of the Lord, "blamelessness" is identified with a life of obedience to the Torah, to the Law. "Crooked minds are an abomination to the LORD, / but those of blameless ways [*tamim*] are his delight" (Prov 11:20).

Summary

These examples show that the conceptual meaning of τέλειος emerges from a wide range of contexts that embrace the notions of completeness, wholeness, and living in a divine relationship. It implies that faith and action, "faith and works," are joined together in an unbreakable bond. The letter of James demonstrates a close connection to this perspective. For James, faith must express itself in a particular way of life through actions that conform to that belief.

While it is true that the notion of τέλειος represents a wide range of conceptual meanings, three essential aspects emerge from the above consideration that give expression to the biblical notion of perfection that τέλειος endeavors to capture:

(1) The idea of wholeness, or completeness, whereby a being remains true to its original constitution.

(2) The giving of oneself to God wholeheartedly and unconditionally which includes a relationship between God and God's people. Above all it rejects idolatry or the worship of other gods. It is akin to the adjective *"saddiq."* If the person was grounded in this relationship, she or he would be seen as whole, perfect. Perfection includes a community relationship, not just an individual dimension.

(3) The wholehearted dedication to the Lord that is demonstrated above all in obedience to God's will. This in turn includes a life led in obedience to the Torah, to the laws of the Lord. The Hebrew phrase "walking with God" (Gen 5:22, 24; 6:9; Mic 6:8; Mal 2:6) calls for moral obedience in which faith and works are intrinsically united.

The Concept of Perfection in the Wider World of Second Temple Judaism

The concept of perfection, as conveyed by the Hebrew word *"tamim,"* continued to exercise an importance in the life of the Jewish people. This was evident in the way the Greek translation of the Hebrew Scriptures gave attention to the concept of τέλειος. But, one observes its importance as well in two very different worlds of second temple Judaism: the world of Qumran and the world of Philo.

The World of Qumran

Whereas in the Old Testament the basic notion of *tamim* had a cultic meaning, in the Dead Sea Scrolls coming from the community of Qumran the perspective changed focus.[31] A life that is true to the Torah forms the essence for the way this term is used in the writings of this community. In fact, in Qumran the word *"tamim"* appears quite frequently.[32] Above all, it embraces the path one follows in order to abide by the Torah. Common expressions occur such as "those who walk in perfection"[33] and "in perfection of the path."[34] Such phrases implied that the community of Qumran would carry out the fullness of the stipulations of the Torah and the laws of the community. This language applied only to members of the Qumran community itself where they referred to themselves as "the perfect ones."[35] When they used such a designation for themselves, it was not to stress their own achievements, but rather to acknowledge what God had accomplished

---

[31] The translation of the Dead Sea Scrolls used here (unless otherwise noted) is from Florentino García Martínez, ed., *The Dead Sea Scrolls Translated: The Qumran Texts in English*, trans. Wilfred G. E. Watson (Leiden: Brill, 1994).

[32] As Delling ("τέλειος," 73) says: "The contexts in which תמים appears in the Qumran writings show clearly that the reference is to total fulfillment of God's will, keeping all the rules of the community."

[33] For example:
- 1QS 1:8: ". . . and walk in perfection in his sight . . . ."
- 1QS 2:2: ". . . the men of God's lot who walk unblemished in all his paths . . . ."
- 1QS 3:9: "May he, then, steady his steps in order to walk with perfection."
- 1QS 8:18: ". . . walking on the perfect path."
- 1QS 8:21: "All who enter the council of holiness of those walking along the path of perfection . . . ."
- 1QS 9:6: ". . . and (like) a house of the Community for Israel, (for) those who walk in perfection."
- 1QS 9:8: ". . . and the goods of the men of holiness who walk in perfection."
- 1QS 9:9: ". . . and walking on a perfect path."
- 1QS 9:19: ". . . the men of the Community, so that they walk perfectly . . . ."

See also Beda Rigaux, "Révélation des Mystères et Perfection à Qumran et dans le Nouveau Testament," *New Testament Studies* 4 (1957–58) 237–62.

[34] For example:
- 1QS 5:24: ". . . in order to upgrade each one to the extent of his insight and the perfection of his path . . . ."
- 1QS 8:21: "All who enter the council of holiness of those walking along the path of perfection . . . ."
- 1QS 9:9: ". . . have not cleansed their path, withdrawing from evil and walking on a perfect path."

[35] For example:

through them.[36] This was the specific emphasis that Qumran gave to the concept of perfection: incapability for humanity to walk in perfection by themselves. Humanity needs God's help to achieve perfection. For example: "As for me, in God is my judgment; in his hand is the perfection of my path with the uprightness of my heart" (1QS 11:2); "From his hand is the perfection of the path" (1QS 11:11).[37]

Everyone who joined this community was considered to be *tamim*. The new member of the community belongs to "the men of God's lot who walk unblemished [*tamim*] in all his paths" (1QS 2:2).[38] While everyone who joins the community is considered to be *tamim*, there appear to be different levels within the community itself. These levels depend upon how the individuals carry out their fidelity to the adherence to the Torah and the laws of the community.[39]

The opening of *The Rule of the Community* expresses concisely the way of life of a member of the Qumran community:

- 1QS 3:3: "In the source of the perfect he shall not be counted."
- 1QS 8:1: "In the Community council (there shall be) twelve men and three priests, perfect in everything . . . ."

Other terms used to designate themselves were "the men of perfect holiness" (1QS 8:20); "the council of holiness of those walking along the path of perfection" (1QS 8:21); "the men of holiness" (1QS 5:13; 8:17, 23; 9:8); "the assembly of holiness" (1QS 5:20).

[36] As J.P.M. van der Ploeg (*The Excavations at Qumran: A Survey of the Judaean Brotherhood and Its Ideas,* trans. Kevin Smyth [London/New York: Longmans, Green and Co., 1958] 119) says: "Thus the consciousness of their own sinfulness suppressed the thought of their own perfection."

[37] Rigaux ("Révélation des Mystères et Perfection à Qumran et dans le Nouveau Testament," 240–1) argues that there are three aspects in Qumran's notion of perfection: (1) a moral element illustrated through obedience and following the way; (2) a mystical element that comes from purification and the gift of the Spirit; (3) a "gnostic" element that shows a knowledge of the divine plan.

[38] Rigaux ("Révélation des Mystères et Perfection à Qumran et dans le Nouveau Testament," 238) expresses it in this way: "Or chez eux, cette voix parfaite est une désignation de la voie de l'Alliance nouvelle, de la forme de vie que procure la retraite au désert" ("Moreover, among them this perfect path is a reference to the path of the New Covenant, the type of life which withdrawal into the desert obtained").

[39] "And they shall be recorded in the Rule, each one before his fellow, according to his insight and his deeds, in such a way that each one obeys his fellow, junior under senior. And their spirit and their deeds must be tested, year after year, in order to upgrade each one to the extent of his insight and the perfection of his path, or to demote him according to his failings" (1QS 5:23-24).

For [the Instructor . . .] [book of the Rul]e of the Community: In order to seek God [with all (one's) heart and with all (one's) soul; in order] to do what is good and just in his presence, as commanded by means of the hand of Moses and his servants the Prophets; in order to love everything which he selects and to hate everything that he rejects; in order to keep oneself at a distance from all evil . . . in order to welcome into the covenant of kindness all those who freely volunteer to carry out God's decrees, so as to be united in the counsel of God and walk in perfection in his sight . . . (1QS 1:1-8).

This, then, is the life of those who are *tamim* in their relationship to God.

Standing within the tradition of the Hebrew Scriptures and remaining faithful to the theme of perfection, the members of the Qumran community focused attention upon one aspect, namely the way in which they as a community were to lead their lives. Their wholehearted dedication to the Lord was demonstrated by their fidelity to the Torah and to the laws of their own community. Perfection in the sense of obedience to the path outlined by the Torah and their community laws was a necessary ingredient for the preservation of the bonds of their society. In this sense perfection had an important worldly task that was essential to the preservation of the society itself.

Philo of Alexandria

A very different approach to the understanding of perfection is observed in the prolific writings of Philo of Alexandria (from about 20 B.C.E. to about 50 C.E.). He was undoubtedly the greatest Jewish philosopher of the Second Temple period of Judaism who lived outside Palestine in Alexandria, Egypt. With him the worlds of Judaism and Hellenism intersect, for his thought owes much to both traditions. In the philosophical realm his greatest debt is to the Platonic understanding of the world of Ideas with its contrast between the heavenly pattern and the worldly copy.[40]

The concept of perfection occupies an important place in Philo's writings. The adjective τέλειος occurs more than four hundred times, while the verb τελειόω occurs some fifty-three times.[41] Philo considers human perfection on two levels: that of virtue and that of wisdom.

On the level of virtue, the striving for perfection is the highest virtue and consists ultimately in the absence of all emotion. Here the

---

[40] See Charles Carlston, "The Vocabulary of Perfection in Philo and Hebrews," *Unity and Diversity in New Testament Theology: Essays in Honor of George E. Ladd,* ed. Robert A. Guelich (Grand Rapids, Mich.: Eerdmans, 1978) 145 and 159, n. 492.

[41] See Gunther Mayer, *Index Philoneus* (Berlin/New York: De Gruyter, 1974).

influence of Stoic thought is evident with the search for *apatheia* (ἀπάθεια, freedom from pain) dominating the direction of life. This explains why Philo defines the perfect person in this way: "The perfect person always endeavors to attain to a complete emancipation from the powers of the passions."[42] Philo describes Abraham as "the perfect man" who did not let his emotions hinder him when faced with the trial of sacrificing his son.[43]

On the level of knowledge or wisdom, true perfection consists in the vision of God, which is identified as the most perfect virtue.[44] In the vision of God, virtue and wisdom are brought harmoniously together. Moses, of all humans, is the one who experienced the closest vision of God. There, in the vision of God, Moses was made perfect so that he might in turn lead humanity from this world to an experience of the vision of God.[45]

Humanity is not able to attain perfection by its own efforts. It is only through a gift from God that this occurs. This understanding of perfection clearly shows Philo's Jewish roots. Wisdom (σοφία) which comes from God is the perfect path (τελεία ὁδός) to God.[46] God alone

---

[42] Philo, *Legum Allegoriae*, III, 131: "You see, then, how the perfect man is always endeavoring to attain to a complete emancipation from the power of the passions. But he who eradicates them being next to him, that is Aaron, labours to arrive at a state in which the passions have only a moderate power, as I have said before" (the translation of Philo's works used here are from Charles D. Yonge, trans., *The Works of Philo* [Peabody, Mass.: Hendrickson, 1993]).

[43] Philo, *Legum Allegoriae*, III, 203: "Accordingly he speaks with reference to the perfect man Abraham in the following manner: 'By myself have I sworn, saith the Lord, that because thou hast done this thing and hast not withheld thy son, thy beloved son from me, that in blessing I will bless them, and in multiplying I will multiply thy seed as the stars of heaven, and as the sand which is on the shore of the sea'" (See also Philo, *Quod Deus Immutabilis Sit*, 4).

[44] Philo, *De Ebrietate*, 83: ". . . and what can be more perfect among all the virtues than the sight of the only living God."

[45] As Erwin R. Goodenough (*An Introduction to Philo Judaeus*, 2d ed. [Oxford: Basil Blackwell, 1962] 147) expresses it: "In other words, the career of Moses is not so much the career of one who, like Abraham and Jacob, had the experience of development which we may reproduce, but was the career of the saviour of men who, given to them as a special loan from God, can lead them out of the world to the apprehension of God. For the mystic experience of men consists in 'going up to the aethereal heights with their reasonings, setting before them Moses, the type of existence beloved by God, to lead them on their way' (*De Cofusione Linguarum*, 95)."

[46] Philo, *Quod Deus Immutabilis Sit*, 142–3.

is truly perfect,[47] and it is only through God's grace that one can become perfect.[48] The person who endeavors to lead life according to the ordinances of the Torah is the perfect person.[49] God is the one who plants virtues in the soul and in this way leads the soul to perfect happiness.[50] By experiencing the vision of God, one experiences perfect happiness.[51] God is ultimately the climax of true and perfect happiness. It is here that the blending of Philo's Judaism and Hellenism come together. While expressing his thought in terms of Stoic and Platonic philosophy, Philo's emphasis on God shows that despite the importance he gives to the human ability to strive toward perfection, ultimately perfection remains something that is granted only by God.[52]

This brief examination shows that Philo (like the community of Qumran) had presented an ethical understanding of perfection.[53] For both, in union with their Jewish roots, the perfect person was seen to

[47] Philo, *Quis Rerum Divinarum Heres,* 121: ". . . that all excellence and perfection belong to one Being alone."

[48] Philo, *De Plantatione,* 93: "The portion of the subject which follows next, is the demonstration that perfection is found in no created thing, but that it does appear in them at times owing to the grace of the great Cause of all things."

[49] Philo, *De Specialibus Legibus,* IV, 140.

[50] Philo, *De Plantatione,* 37: "Therefore, we must suppose that the bounteous God plants in the soul, as it were, a paradise of virtues and of the actions in accordance with them, which lead it to perfect happiness."

[51] Philo, *Quod Deus Immutabilis Sit,* 92: "For when God bestows on any one the treasures of his own wisdom without any toil or labour, then we, without having expected such things, suddenly perceive that we have found a treasure of perfect happiness."

[52] Carlston ("The Vocabulary of Perfection in Philo and Hebrews," 145) summarizes his examination of Philo's use of the language of perfection by stating: "His main emphasis, however, lies elsewhere, in the soul's ascent, (*Legum Allegoriae,* III, 71; *Quod Deterius Potiori Insidiari Soleat,* 114; *Quis Rerum Divinarum Heres,* 69–70, 85; *De Fuga et Inventione,* 62; *De Somniis,* I, 225–6; *De Speicalibus Legibus,* I, 37–8; *Questiones et Solutiones in Genesin,* I, 86–7) in the 'mystic vision of God,' (*De Opificio Mundi,* 55; *Legum Allegoriae,* III, 100; *De Migratione Abrahami,* 34–5; *De Somniis,* I, 148–51; *De Abrahamo,* 122; *De Specialibus Legibus,* I, 165; *De Vita Contemplativa,* 11–12; *De Legatione Ad Gaium,* 5–6; *Questiones et Solutiones in Genesin,* IV, 20; *Questiones et Solutiones in Exodum,* I, 29, 40) in escape from the world of sense-perception, (*Legum Allegoriae,* II, 42, 44; *Quod Deterius Potiori Insidiari Soleat,* 158–60; *De Gigantibus,* 61; *De Migratione Abrahami,* 2, 184–95, 214–21; *Quis Rerum Divinarum Heres,* 69–71, 275–80; *De Specialibus Legibus,* I, 17), in contemplation of the heavenly Ideas, etc. Saint and Sage are indistinguishable in Philo."

[53] As Carlson ("The Vocabulary of Perfection in Philo and Hebrews," 145) says: "Perfection in Philo, then, includes elements of the religious, the philosophical, the pedagogical, and above all the ethical."

lead a life according to the ordinances of the Torah. Philo brought the reflection on perfection further by expressing his thought in Platonic and
Stoic terms. Since the heavenly world of Ideas is the perfect world, life's
aim is for the soul to escape from this present world of sense experiences
and to reach the contemplation of the heavenly realm of Ideas. This is
achieved only through the power of God leading the soul ever upward.

An Overview of the Concept of Perfection in the New Testament

Having examined the distinctive usage of the adjective "perfect"
(τέλειος) in the wider Graeco-Roman world, as well as in the Hebrew
Scriptures, the Septuagint, and Second Temple Judaism, there remains
one final area to investigate to make this examination complete, namely
the distinctive traditions that go to make up the New Testament. This
must of necessity be brief, for the focus of this study is not with the
New Testament as such, but with the letter of James. In providing such
an overview of this concept in the New Testament traditions, it is obviously not possible to treat every instance of its usage in great detail.
My intention here is to provide only a bird's-eye view that can ultimately act as a foil whereby James's thought can emerge more clearly
when viewed against this wider context.

The Synoptic Gospel Traditions

The use of the adjective τέλειος is very rare in the Synoptic Gospels,
occurring only three times. All of these occurrences are found in the
Gospel of Matthew (twice at 5:48 and once at 19:21) where it is used
attributively.[54] The verb τελειοῦν is more frequent in the Gospels,
appearing especially in Luke (and John) where it is used almost indis-
criminately together with the other verb τελεῖν. I am limiting myself,
however, to the attributive use of τέλειος.

In the Gospel of Matthew, the adjective τέλειος occurs in two
episodes: the Sermon on the Mount (5:48) and Jesus' encounter with
the rich young man (19:16-30). It is not my intention to give a detailed
exegesis of these verses here, but to draw attention to the fact that the
way τέλειος is used here conforms to the threefold meaning that was
identified for the biblical notion of perfection that τέλειος attempted to
capture. For example:

[54] More attention will be given in chapter six to Matthew's usage of this term
where the closeness of thought between Matthew and James will be illustrated.
Here, I simply wish to illustrate very briefly how Matthew's understanding of perfection reflects closely the world of Judaism.

(1) The idea of wholeness or completeness is evident here. In a sense Jesus' call "to be perfect" in Matt 5:48 is a call to wholeness, to attain God's original intention or will. This is apparent in the series of the antitheses preceding this saying (5:21-47), especially in the third antithesis related to divorce (5:31-32). In distinction to Moses, who permitted divorce, Jesus returns to the concept of creation in Gen 1:27 and 2:24. He calls for a return to the will of God whereby the original union of man and woman must be upheld. In Matt 19:16-30, the idea of completeness or totality is also the dominant motif. The young man's question to Jesus, "What do I still lack?" (19:20), and Jesus' answer show that the young man is still missing something in his life. This prevents him from attaining completeness in his allegiance to God.

(2) The giving of one's heart to God unconditionally. The context of Matt 5:48 emphasizes the love that should be the hallmark for every action. God's ways of acting become the motivation for the behavior of all believers. The case of the rich young man (19:21) shows that he is not wholly dedicated to God. His riches are an obstacle preventing him from giving total and unconditional service to God.

(3) The wholehearted dedication to the Lord is demonstrated above all in obedience to the will of God expressed in the Torah. Obedience is carried out through a life of observance to the Torah, to the laws of the Lord. In Matt 5:48, the one who is perfect is the one who has been obedient to God's will and has carried out God's commands to the fullest possible extent.[55] In carrying out those commands, one goes beyond the letter of the law to the intention behind the law. For example, beyond the command not to murder, the disciples are called to control their anger; beyond the law of adultery, they are called to avoid lust; in place of divorce, they are called to fidelity to their spouse; in place of oaths, they are called to embrace the truth; in place of hatred for enemies, Jesus calls for a love for enemies. In this way, the follower of Jesus exceeds the right behavior of the scribes and Pharisees.[56] Essentially the difference between the righteousness of the Pharisees and the followers of Jesus[57] is that the latter have an inner attitude that

---

[55] The Didache has the same notion of perfection: "For if thou canst bear the whole yoke of the Lord, thou wilt be perfect" (6:2) (Kirsopp Lake, trans., *The Apostolic Fathers*, vol. 1, *The Didache*, The Loeb Classical Library [Cambridge, Mass.: Harvard University Press, 1965] 319).

[56] See Ulrich Luz (*Matthew 1–7: A Commentary* [Minneapolis: Augsburg, 1989] 346): "'Perfect' is the one who keeps God's commandments without any reduction."

[57] Schnackenburg ("Christian Perfection according to Matthew," 178) says: "Matthew described this inner attitude in conscious contrast to the legal-minded

attempts to transform their whole being as they carry out God's will as expressed in the Law. For the disciples of Jesus, perfection is the characteristic mark, something that distinguishes them by a behavior of obedience to the law of God. This obedience demonstrates a total commitment to God's will,[58] and witnesses to "the higher righteousness" of the believers.

The rich young man has also led a life carrying out the stipulations of the Torah. After Jesus itemizes the commandments that should be observed, the young man responds: "I have kept all these; what do I still lack?" (Matt 19:20). He understands what the scribes and Pharisees had failed to understand, namely that one is called to do more than simply legalistically embrace and carry out the Ten Commandments. The "more" for him is a transformation of his inner attitude toward wealth and possessions. He is called to transcend possessions by giving away what he has. He is called to a "higher righteousness" than the scribes and Pharisees. Unfortunately, he is unable to embrace this: "He went away grieving, for he had many possessions" (Matt 19:22).

Matthew's use of the adjective τέλειος shows that his understanding of perfection reflects very closely the thought of the Hebrew Scriptures and the Septuagint regarding perfection. In particular, the threefold nuances are recaptured here extremely well. To be perfect indicates for Matthew, as it did for the Hebrew traditions, to be whole and complete. This brings about a wholehearted devotion to the Lord that is expressed in a life of obedience to the ways of the Lord as indicated through the Torah.

The Johannine Traditions

In his first letter, John gives one of the most graphic descriptions of perfection in the New Testament. "There is no fear in love, but perfect love casts out fear; for fear has to do with punishment, and whoever fears has not reached perfection in love" (1 John 4:18).[59] The context of this verse is the love of God ("God is love," 4:16), and fellowship with God means that one remains in the love that comes from God. For John, perfection consists in a love that is total, that lacks nothing. Such

---

piety of Pharisees and scribes which fails to realize the will of God, and closes rather than opens the kingdom of God to mankind (cf. Mt 23:13)."

[58] Leopold Sabourin, "Why Is God Called 'Perfect' in Mt 5:48?" *Biblische Zeitschrift, Neue Folge* 24 (1980) 266–8.

[59] ". . . but perfect love casts out fear [ἀλλ᾽ ἡ τελεία ἀγάπη ἔξω βάλλει τὸν φόβον] . . . has not reached perfection in love [οὐ τετελείωται ἐν τῇ ἀγάπῃ]" (1 John 4:18).

love enables one to remain in communion with God. This leads to a way of life that fulfills the commandments: "The commandment we have from him is this: those who love God must love their brothers and sisters also" (1 John 4:21). Again we notice the three distinctive characteristics of the Old Testament notion of perfection exemplified in this simple declaration of perfect love: (1) the aspect of wholeness and totality from which nothing is lacking. (2) Love establishes the bond of communion with God. God is the one who initiates this relationship and the believer is called to remain in this fellowship of love. (3) Finally, perfect love demands that one express this in a life that abides by God's commandments. The commandment of love in particular must inform every relationship.

Once again, the writings of John continue the biblical understanding of perfection. However, the Johannine writings give to the concept of perfection a distinctiveness of their own by bringing perfection into the heart of Jesus' message with its focus on the law of love. For John, perfection consists in sharing in the very nature of God who is love and in striving through every action to remain in this relationship of love.

The Pauline Traditions

Paul's usage of τέλειος is very distinctive in comparison to that of the rest of the New Testament writings. He uses the term frequently and widely (Rom 12:2; 1 Cor 2:6; 13:10; 14:20; Eph 4:13; Phil 3:15; Col 1:28; 4:12). Paul does not give expression to the threefold aspect of perfection that we have noted running like a thread from the Hebrew Scriptures and the Septuagint through Matthew and John. Instead, Paul focuses upon one aspect of perfection, namely, completeness or totality. This understanding of perfection takes on varying nuances depending upon the different contexts of its use.

For Paul, the idea of completeness or totality finds its most basic expression in the situation of Christians who experience the salvation wrought by Christ. "It is he whom we proclaim, warning everyone and teaching everyone in all wisdom, so that we may present everyone mature in Christ [τέλειον ἐν Χριστῷ]" (Col 1:28). What is given in Christ lacks nothing and in the order of salvation is perfect. Paul's goal was to bring everyone to experience this transforming presence of Jesus.

However, Paul envisages that a growth toward maturity needs to occur in the context of salvation. "Brothers and sisters, do not be children in your thinking; rather, be infants in evil, but in thinking be

adults" (1 Cor 14:20).[60] Here a contrast is presented between "children" (παιδία) on the one hand and "adults" (τέλειοι) on the other. In the world of Paul only an adult was considered a mature or fully human person. Consequently, to be a full Christian in Paul's eyes means that one must be mature. It is an implicit acknowledgment that believers need to grow in their allegiance to Christ in order to attain the fullness of life in Christ. The same idea continues in 1 Cor 2:6 where Paul again speaks of the mature: "Yet among *the mature* we do speak wisdom, though it is not a wisdom of this age or of the rulers of this age, who are doomed to perish." Again the contrast between the mature and the infants takes place.[61] The mature are able to understand the message that Paul proclaims, a message that he identifies as "wisdom." This wisdom embraces the message of the cross, the death and resurrection of Jesus, a message that the world itself is unable to accept.[62]

Finally, in the context of the body of Christ the notion of maturity also takes on a community dimension: ". . . to equip the saints for the work of ministry, for building up the body of Christ, until all of us come to the unity of the faith and of the knowledge of the Son of God, to maturity [εἰς ἄνδρα τέλειον], to the measure of the full stature of Christ" (Eph 4:12-13). Here, the writer envisages that the Church, as the body of Christ, should grow to maturity as "the perfect person." No longer is the call to work toward maturity addressed solely to the individual. Now the community, as a group, is called to work together to achieve this unity so that all the members may grow together toward maturity. Ultimately, the mature person lives under the power of the death and resurrection of Jesus and works together with others to constitute the body of Christ, the Church. Paul labors for this goal in order to present the members of this community to God and to Christ as "the mature" and to build up the body of Christ.[63]

While Paul did not embrace an understanding of perfection that expressed all the nuances of the term found in the Hebrew Scriptures and the Septuagint, nevertheless he remained faithful to the essence of its meaning. The concept of maturity or wholeness captured Paul's understanding of perfection very well. Those who have experienced the transforming presence of Jesus in their lives are the "mature" (τέλειοι) in Christ.

---

[60]   ". . . but in thinking be adults [ταῖς δὲ φρεσὶν τέλειοι γίνεσθε]" (1 Cor 14:20).

[61]   The reference to infants occurs at 1 Cor 3:1: "as infants in Christ" (ὡς νηπίοις ἐν Χριστῷ).

[62]   Delling, "τέλειος," 76.

[63]   Ibid.

The Epistle to the Hebrews

While the adjective τέλειος occurs only twice in the epistle to the Hebrews (5:14 and 9:11), the verb τέλειοῦν is the term the epistle uses most. As with the thought of Philo, the Platonized Hellenistic philosophical thought has decidedly influenced the outlook of this writing. It is particularly evident in the set of contrasts that the author builds up where the philosophical underpinnings of Platonic philosophy are clearly recognizable.

As noted, τέλειος is used only on two occasions. In Heb 5:14, the term means "fully grown, mature," and is contrasted with "the infant." "But solid food is for the mature [τελείων], for those whose faculties have been trained by practice to distinguish good from evil." The context of this passage deals with the contrasts that emerge in teaching the Christian message: "the basic teaching about Christ" (6:1) is given to the "infants," while deeper instruction in righteousness is given to the "mature," who are able to receive it.

In Heb 9:11, reference is made to the heavenly sanctuary as "the more perfect tabernacle"[64] (τελειοτέρας σκηνῆς) in its contrast to the earthly tabernacle. This heavenly tabernacle is more perfect because it is associated with the salvific work of Jesus as High Priest who is able to take away humanity's sins in a way any previous dispensation was unable to do. Here the epistle to the Hebrews is thinking within the framework of Platonic thought that makes a distinction between the two worlds, the earthly and the heavenly. For the writer of this epistle, all the Jewish institutions are seen to be good, but imperfect. They are reflections of the more perfect heavenly realm where Christ is. Christ offered the perfect sacrifice, which once and for all and in this way replaced all the many sacrifices that had previously been offered in the context of the Jewish institutions. As Carlston observes: "The heavenly sacrifice, the heavenly tabernacle, the heavenly high priesthood are all understood in Christianized Platonic terms as Christ, in his death, is seen as having offered a once-for-all sacrifice in the heavenly temple."[65] The epistle to the Hebrews and the writings of Philo share a common Jewish heritage together with a Platonic philosophical worldview that endeavors to reinterpret that tradition. However, it is the Christian kerygma that separates them sharply. For the author of the epistle to the Hebrews, the work and person of Christ brings perfection to the world and traditions of Judaism. These traditions and institutions

---

[64] This is the literal translation. The New Revised Standard Version translates it loosely as "perfect tent."

[65] Carlston, "The Vocabulary of Perfection in Philo and Hebrews," 148.

were but a shadow of the reality that was to come. So, while Philo and the author of the epistle to the Hebrews share much in common, the horizon of the Christian message separates them radically. For the author of the epistle to the Hebrews perfection is found in the work of Christ, in particular in his eternal sacrifice on the cross. As Carlson observes: "It would be hard to imagine anything more foreign to Philo's mode of thought."[66]

What is interesting is that with the epistle to the Hebrews one has come full circle. The origin of the use of the term τέλειος was seen to be in the Jewish cult where an unblemished offering is made to God in the temple. Now, in the epistle to the Hebrews, the cultic context returns, but this time the reference is to the heavenly worship where Christ offers an eternal sacrifice in the perfect temple. The concept of completeness, wholeness, remains the central thought, particularly in reference to those who are mature (Heb 5:14).

Conclusion

This chapter has examined the meaning and usage of the term τέλειος in the world to which James was heir and has provided a backdrop against which James's understanding of this term can be examined. The concept and terminology for perfection were indeed widespread throughout the Graeco-Roman world, and were also evident throughout the Hebrew Scriptures and the Septuagint. The distinctiveness of the concept of perfection in the Hebrew Scriptures and the Septuagint emerged in comparison to the wider Greek philosophical world. Despite the varied contexts and backgrounds, the notion of τέλειος in the world of the Septuagint gave expression to the biblical idea of wholeness and completeness that included an unconditional relationship between God and God's people. That relationship was demonstrated above all in a life led in obedience to the Torah. While not every instance of the use of the term contains all the above elements, nevertheless different nuances or stresses arise from the given context.

The brief overview of the New Testament usage of the concept of perfection has shown that there was no simple uniform understanding of this term in the New Testament writings. The biblical roots of the Old Testament and the Septuagint are clearly evident, but each New

[66] Ibid.

Testament writing used these traditions in its own specific way. The Gospel of Matthew's understanding of perfection continues to stress the threefold meaning that the Hebrew Scriptures gave to the understanding of perfection. The writings of John saw perfection as referring to a wholehearted relationship between God and the believer which is demonstrated by a life that is led according to the commandment of love. For the Pauline writings, the focus lies on the aspect of completeness and maturity experienced through the salvation brought by Christ. Only the epistle to the Hebrews showed itself at home in the wider philosophical world of Plato and his heir, Philo.

In examining the concept of perfection in the letter of James, attention will be given to the characteristic nature of James's thought on perfection as well as how this understanding of perfection relates to the rest of the letter of James. In fact, the examination will demonstrate how this concept gives meaning to the entire letter. However, before investigating James's understanding of perfection, it is necessary to discuss the nature or genre of this writing. Clarity on its genre will enable the meaning of perfection in James to emerge more fully. This issue is examined in the next chapter.

CHAPTER THREE

The Nature and Purpose of the Letter of James

The Importance of Genre

Before examining the concept of perfection in the letter of James, attention must be given to the nature or genre of this writing. James's understanding of perfection and its function within his writing can only be appreciated from a clear awareness of the genre of this work.

The literary genre of James has long been a source of discussion and debate among scholars.[1] The examination of a genre is not an end in itself, nor is it simply a question of providing a systematic classification into which James would suitably fit.[2] The identification of the genre of a work helps to determine its message because its structure is deliberately chosen for the purpose of its communication. As Johnson says: "function follows form."[3] In fact the definition of genre as provided by John J. Collins unites form, content, and function as determinative for any genre.[4]

---

[1] Luke Timothy Johnson (*The Letter of James: A New Translation with Introduction and Commentary*, The Anchor Bible 37A [New York: Doubleday, 1995] 16–26) provides a very good overview of the approaches adopted by scholars to the literary genre of James. He notes that the different understandings of what constitute a genre are largely responsible for the diverging perspectives that are adopted to the letter of James.

[2] See John G. Gammie, "Paraenetic Literature: Toward the Morphology of a Secondary Genre," *Semeia* 50 (1990) 42.

[3] Johnson, *The Letter of James*, 16.

[4] See John J. Collins, "Introduction: Towards the Morphology of a Genre," *Semeia* 14 (1979) 1–20; see also Adela Yarbro Collins, "Introduction: Early Christian Apocalypticism," *Semeia* 36 (1986) 1–11.

Elsewhere I have argued that James, while conforming to the outward form of a letter,[5] belongs within the literary genre of Wisdom literature[6] that was characterized as exhortatory literature popular throughout the Middle East and in particular Israel. Two aspects dominate Hebrew Wisdom literature, namely the presentation of the ethical way of life that is characterized by one living according to the path of wisdom and a deeper reflection on the nature of wisdom itself. Both characteristics of wisdom can be identified in the letter of James.[7]

Practical Wisdom Advice

A study of the structures through which James gives expression to his teaching shows that the letter adheres to many forms that are characteristic of Hebrew Wisdom literature.[8] Here attention will be given to a few of the forms that occur in the letter of James and are quite characteristic of the Hebrew wisdom tradition.

Wisdom Sayings and Admonitions

A notable feature of all Wisdom literature is the large number of sayings and admonitions. Arising from experience, they draw conclusions and offer advice on how to conduct one's life. For example: "For judgment will be without mercy to anyone who has shown no mercy; mercy triumphs over judgment" (Jas 2:13). The opening of the letter contains a host of admonitions that give expression to the wisdom advice: "My brothers and sisters, whenever you face trials of any kind, consider it nothing but joy" (1:2). While Dibelius's perspective was that these were isolated sayings,[9] a closer study of the letter reveals

---

[5] I have illustrated the way in which James conforms to the epistolary standards of the time in *James and the "Q" Sayings of Jesus,* JSNTS 47 (Sheffield: Sheffield Academic Press, 1991) 23–34.

[6] Patrick J. Hartin, "'Who Is Wise and Understanding among You?' (James 3:13): An Analysis of Wisdom, Eschatology and Apocalypticism in the Epistle of James," *Society of Biblical Literature Seminar Papers* (Atlanta: Scholars Press, 1996) 483–503; and Hartin, *James and the "Q" Sayings of Jesus,* 52–9.

[7] This chapter examines the exhortatory nature of wisdom as reflected in the letter of James. In the following chapter, the deeper reflection on the nature of wisdom will be examined as it emerges in the letter of James (see chapter 4, p. 65, the section entitled "Wisdom as the Horizon for Attaining Perfection").

[8] I have examined these wisdom forms in more detail in "Who Is Wise and Understanding among You?" 484–8.

[9] Martin Dibelius, *James: A Commentary on the Epistle of James,* trans. Michael A. Williams (Philadelphia: Fortress Press, 1975) 3. With regard to Jas 2:13, Dibelius argues that this is an "isolated saying" with no links to the preceding themes (see p. 147).

that these sayings are woven intimately into the argument of the pericope in which they are found.

Wisdom Forms of Comparison

A further characteristic of all Wisdom literature is the range of comparisons that are employed in order to explain and emphasize the urgency of the moral advice. Among the many forms evident in the letter of James the most noticeable are similes and metaphors ("The tongue is a fire," 3:6) and parables. Outside the Gospels, the letter of James is the only other New Testament writing that uses parables—the wisdom style of instruction so characteristic of Jesus. Illustration by means of a story involves the reader actively in deciphering the meaning. "For if any are hearers of the word and not doers, they are like those who look at themselves in a mirror . . ." (1:23) and "For if a person with gold rings and in fine clothes comes into your assembly, and if a poor person in dirty clothes also comes in . . ." (2:2-4) are two examples of parables in James.

Beatitudes

The beatitude is a characteristic feature of wisdom writings. The major distinguishing feature of the use of the beatitude in the Old and New Testaments is the promise that is attached to the blessing. In the Old Testament the fulfillment of the promise is seen to occur in the present, while in the New Testament the promise is reserved for the future in the eschatological age.[10] For example, "Happy the man who lives with a sensible wife / . . . . Happy is the one who does not sin with the tongue, / and the one who has not served an inferior" (Sir 25:8). In contrast, Luke 6:20 envisages the blessing as occurring in the future: "Blessed are you who are poor, / for yours is the kingdom of God."

The form of the beatitude occurs on two occasions in the letter of James:

(1) "Blessed is anyone who endures temptation. Such a one has stood the test and will receive the crown of life that the Lord has promised to those who love him" (Jas 1:12). The promise for those who endure occurs in the future where they will receive "the crown of life."

---

[10] See Friedrich Hauck, "μακάριος," *Theological Dictionary of the New Testament*, vol. 4, ed. Gerhard Kittel, trans. Geoffrey W. Bromiley (Grand Rapids, Mich.: Eerdmans, 1969) 367.

The promise for the future stands in direct and opposite correlation to what occurs here and now.

(2) "But those who look into the perfect law, the law of liberty, and persevere, being not hearers who forget but doers who act—they will be blessed in their doing" (Jas 1:25). Once again the blessing is given in the form of a correlation between the present and the future.[11]

In both instances the wisdom advice is taken up within an eschatological perspective that frames both the urgency and the motivation for one's life.

Woes

This form is found in both the prophets and the Wisdom literature. James uses this form with the intention of communicating wisdom exhortation to the readers. Two noteworthy examples occur in the letter:

(1) "Come now ["Αγε νῦν] you who say . . ." (Jas 4:13-17). The Greek phrase used here is a form of address associated with the prophetic mode of address.[12] James addresses his own community in the manner of the prophets of the Old Testament warning them against the dangers in the world around them. The rich that he refers to are not members of the community, but are used as a foil whereby the members within the community can be exhorted to change their ways.[13]

(2) "Come now ["Αγε νῦν], you rich people . . ." (Jas 5:1-6). In language that is similar to that of the prophets, James warns the rich against the punishments that are to befall them in the future: the last days are described as "a day of slaughter" (5:5). Once again, his concern is not that the rich change their ways of acting. Rather, this eschatological description offers encouragement and consolation to the community that has suffered at the hands of the rich.

James's use of the above two forms, namely the beatitude and the woe, is clearly distinctive. For him, wisdom is a vehicle through which he communicates his exhortation to the readers on how to lead their lives. To reinforce this appeal he incorporates material that is found in

[11] Ibid., 369.

[12] This is a phrase found again in the New Testament only at Jas 5:1. It occurs in Greek literature, particularly in the diatribe. It is also very common in prophetic speech patterns. The likelihood is that James is indebted chiefly to the Old Testament heritage for its usage, especially because the way of speaking here is identical to the prophetic way of address.

[13] As Dibelius (*James,* 231) says: "4:13-16 is delivered in the style of a prophetic address. The prophet cries out his words among the masses, unconcerned about whether his accusations reach the ears of those whom he accuses."

other literary genres. In this instance he uses the eschatological perspective to provide the urgency and the motivation for why they should act in a particular way: "You have lived on the earth in luxury and in pleasure; you have fattened your hearts in a day of slaughter" (5:5).

Besides the use of these characteristic wisdom forms, the content of the letter of James bears similarities to that of traditional Hebrew wisdom, particularly in many of the themes that are developed, such as the testing of one's faith (Jas 1:2; Prov 27:21; and Job 1 and 2); the control of one's tongue (Jas 1:26 and Sir 5:13); and the concern for the poor in society (Jas 1:27 and Prov 19:17; 31:9).

The Paraenetic or Protreptic Nature of This Wisdom Advice

In both form and content, then, the letter of James clearly shows that it is at home in the tradition of Wisdom literature.[14] One further aspect that needs attention in attempting to define its genre is the function or purpose to which this material is put.[15] Dibelius was the first to categorize this wisdom advice of James as "paraenesis."[16] By this, Dibelius understood the bringing together of much traditional moral material consisting mainly of isolated sayings that were loosely connected by means of catchphrases.[17] Paraenesis was designed to offer instruction and exhortation on how to lead one's life. Among the

[14] B. R. Halson has undertaken a detailed investigation of the connections of the letter of James to the Wisdom literature of the Old Testament ("The Epistle of James: 'Christian Wisdom?'" *Studia Evangelica,* vol. 4, Papers Presented to the Third International Congress on New Testament Studies Held at Christ Church, Oxford, 1965. Part 1: The New Testament Scriptures, ed. F. L. Cross [Berlin: Akademie-Verlag, 1968] 308–14). In particular, his examination of the vocabulary of the letter of James (especially the sixty-seven "hapax legomena" that no other New Testament writers use) has shown a marked similarity with that of the Wisdom literature of the Septuagint: "In his distinctive vocabulary then, we can say that the author of the Epistle of James has a marked predeliction for words from the Septuagintal Wisdom literature" (p. 309).

[15] Without doubt, the question of the purpose of a writing is most significant. Halson opened his article ("The Epistle of James," 308) by referring to Professor Henry Chadwick's insight that "the most important question we can ask about any book of the New Testament is, What is its purpose?"

[16] Dibelius, *James,* 21.

[17] As Dibelius (*James,* 3) says: "Besides Jas, one may point especially to Heb 13, to parts of the *Epistle of Barnabas* and of the *Didache;* in all these instances, what one finds is *paraenesis* in the form of unconnected sayings which have no real relationship to one another. The sayings of Jesus also belong in this category. For the 'speeches' of Jesus in Matthew and Luke consist of sayings loosely joined together, and these collections are extraordinarily similar in form to the first and final sections of Jas."

characteristics of paraenesis to which Dibelius gave importance was its distance from a specific context. He argued that it was very difficult to infer anything related to the background of the author or the situation of the readers from the traditional material that James had used.[18]

While Dibelius's identification of James in the role of paraenesis is generally acknowledged by most scholars,[19] further studies have shown the need to clarify and correct some of his views. An article by John Gammie ("Paraenetic Literature: Toward the Morphology of a Secondary Genre") is especially relevant here.[20] His starting point is most significant. He adopts the views of Luis Alonso Schökel who stressed that a distinction should be drawn between a primary literary genre and secondary literary genres and all their subgenres.[21] In applying this distinction to the letter of James, one would note that James belongs to the primary literary genre of Wisdom literature, while the secondary literary genre would be that of paraenetic literature with paraenesis itself as a further subgenre.[22] In this sense, paraenetic literature is a type of writing that embodies moral encouragement. Its main aim is to encourage a group to continue in the life they have begun or to further direct them on another course of action that the writer sets forth.[23] Paraenetic literature expresses this moral encouragement by means of a number of subgenres, two of which are significant for the study of the letter of James, namely paraenesis (or moral exhortation) and protreptic discourse (or moral demonstration).[24] Gammie defines paraenesis (moral exhortation) in this way as

[18]   Ibid., 21.

[19]   See Robert W. Wall, *Community of the Wise: The Letter of James,* The New Testament in Context (Valley Forge, Pa.: Trinity Press International, 1997) 18.

[20]   See Gammie, "Paraenetic Literature," 41–77.

[21]   Ibid., 45. See Luis Alonso Schökel, "Literary Genres, Biblical," *New Catholic Encyclopedia,* vol. 8, ed. William J. McDonald (New York: McGraw-Hill, 1967) 803–9.

[22]   As Gammie ("Paraenetic Literature," 45) says: "So it is being suggested here that one may most properly speak of: Wisdom Literature (a major literary genre), Paraenetic Literature (a secondary literary genre), and paraenesis (a sub-genre)." Gammie (p. 47) provides an excellent chart illustrating the breakdown of the secondary genres of Wisdom literature.

[23]   Ibid., 48.

[24]   I use the term "protreptic" in the way in which Gammie identifies it: "In modern, as in classical, usage the term protreptic, rather than *protrepsis* or *protrepseis,* is used whether applied to smaller units or to an entire work. . . . Thus retention of the term protreptic rather than the introduction of the term *protrepsis* (or an alternative) would seem to be the soundest decision in view of the classical precedent. Modern usage should, in our judgment, seek to show both some correspondence with, as well as awareness of, classical usage" (Gammie, "Paraenetic Literature," 57).

"a form of address which not only commends, but actually enumerates precepts or maxims which pertain to moral aspiration and the regulation of human conduct."[25] On the other hand, protreptic discourse (moral demonstration) refers to a more developed illustration or demonstration which is stylistically expressed in a clear, logical, and syllogistic manner.

Stowers[26] and Perdue[27] have developed this distinction between paraenesis and protreptic discourse by focusing on the audience as the dividing line. According to their view, protreptic discourse focuses on the unconverted, those who could potentially join the group, while paraenesis is directed toward instructing believers further in the way of life to which they have committed themselves.[28] While this distinction seems attractive, a more detailed examination shows that such a narrowly defined distinction is difficult to sustain. Using the book of Wisdom and the Letter of Aristeas[29] as examples, I feel Gammie has argued correctly that this distinction on the basis of audience alone is too restrictive and does not really capture the essence of the distinction between the two subgenres.[30] Rather than using the audience as the separating line, the best way to distinguish between paraenesis and

[25] Ibid., 51.

[26] Stanley K. Stowers, *Letter Writing in Greco-Roman Antiquity,* Library of Early Christianity (Philadelphia: Westminster Press, 1986).

[27] In a number of articles Leo G. Perdue has considered the character of paraenesis. "Liminality as the Social Setting of Wisdom Instructions," *Zeitschrift für die alttestamentliche Wissenschaft* 93 (1981) 114–26; "Paraenesis and the Epistle of James," *Zeitschrift für die neutestamentliche Wissenschaft und die Kunde der älteren Kirche* 72 (1981) 241–56; and "The Social Character of Paraenesis and Paraenetic Literature," *Semeia* 50 (1990) 5–39.

[28] See Stowers, *Letter Writing in Greco-Roman Antiquity,* 91–6; and Perdue, "The Social Character of Paraenesis and Paraenetic Literature," 23–5.

[29] The Letter of Aristeas is a writing that describes how the Jewish Law was translated from Hebrew into Greek in Alexandria. The dating of the letter is difficult to pinpoint. The dates lie between the third century B.C.E. and the first century C.E. (see R.J.H. Shutt, "Letter of Aristeas," *The Old Testament Pseudepigrapha,* vol. 2, ed. James H. Charlesworth [London: Darton, Longman and Todd, 1985] 7–34).

[30] See Gammie, "Paraenetic Literature," 54. Gammie correctly argues that the book of Wisdom is predominantly a writing that instructs the readers deeper in their religious life and traditions. The category of "protreptic" suits this writing best because of its nature of conducting a sustained argument. Using a further example, Gammie refers to the letter of Aristeas which aimed at converting those who already had a sympathetic attitude to the Jewish religion. Because the letter of Aristeas does not present a sustained argument but rather a series of sayings, it is more in conformity with the nature of paraenetic material.

protreptic discourse is through three other criteria to which Gammie draws attention: (1) the role of precepts; (2) the role of argumentation; (3) the role of vision or focus.[31] I shall apply these three criteria to the letter of James to show that the category of protreptic discourse, rather than that of paraenesis, applies to this writing

The Role of Precepts

For paraenesis, precepts are an essential ingredient, while for protreptic discourse they are optional. While some precepts do occur in the letter of James, the manner of expressing the teaching does not focus on the precept—instead the precepts serve the manner of the argument. For example, "Do not speak evil against one another, brothers and sisters" (Jas 4:11). This precept immediately serves the function of introducing a demonstration of not judging another, for God alone is the "one lawgiver and judge" (4:12).

The Role of Argumentation

Protreptic discourse aims at presenting a sustained argument by means of a developed demonstration. It is this stylistically crafted argument that distinguishes it from paraenesis. The whole purpose behind protreptic discourse is to persuade the audience. This feature distinguishes the letter of James from a writing such as the book of Proverbs. The latter generally consists in a collection of loosely connected exhortations or precepts, as for example:

> Do not withhold good from those to whom it is due,
>   when it is in your power to do it.
> Do not say to your neighbor, "Go, and come again,
>   tomorrow I will give it"—when you have it with you.
> Do not plan harm against your neighbor
>   who lives trustingly beside you.
> Do not quarrel with anyone without cause,
>   when no harm has been done to you.
> Do not envy the violent
>   and do not choose any of their ways (Prov 3:27-31).

---

[31] Gammie ("Paraenetic Literature," 54–5) lists three criteria for distinguishing between protreptic and paraenesis: "(1) presence or absence of precepts and the purpose for which they are adduced; (2) extent of sustained demonstration and organization with a view to persuade; and (3) breadth of topics covered and/or sharpness of focus."

On the other hand the letter of James consists of a series of peri-copes that contain sustained arguments. For example, the discussion on discrimination between rich and poor (2:1-7); the relationship between faith and works (2:14-26); the discussion on the tongue (3:1-12) or on merchants (4:13-17) are just a few such arguments.

The Role of Vision or Focus

Paraenesis has a very wide vision and scope, encompassing everything within its orbit, whereas protreptic discourse has a sharper and more refined focus. Benjamin Fiore indicates the distinction in this way: paraenesis is a very inclusive concept that covers almost every aspect of life, such as "culture, friends, enemies, good fortune."[32] A protreptic work, on the other hand, is much more focused.[33] The letter of James again demonstrates this distinction by concerning itself with maintaining "friendship with God" while avoiding "friendship with the world" (4:4). Other aspects that fall outside that focus are avoided (such as culture, good fortune, discipline of the young, fidelity to a spouse—themes characteristic of the book of Proverbs).

These three criteria support the designation of James as a protreptic discourse. The letter of James shows that it is much more than a simple collection of moral sayings and advice. It presents a vision that it wishes its readers to embrace. For this reason it offers arguments that demonstrate the lifestyle the readers should embrace. This is a lifestyle that sets the group apart from the wider society.

Instructions for a New Social Order

Part of the function of protreptic discourse and paraenesis is that of "social formation."[34] Berger and Luckmann called this "socialization which may be defined as the comprehensive and consistent induction of an individual into the objective world of a society or a sector of it."[35] This is precisely what James aims to achieve: to remind his readers of what it means to be part of the "twelve tribes in the Dispersion." In doing so, he points out the many values that separate these people

---

[32] Benjamin Fiore, *The Function of Personal Example in the Socratic and Pastoral Epistles*, AB 105 (Rome: Biblical Institute Press, 1986) 41.

[33] Ibid.

[34] See Perdue, "The Social Character of Paraenesis," 23–7.

[35] Peter L. Berger and Thomas Luckmann, *The Social Construction of Reality: A Treatise in the Sociology of Knowledge* (Garden City, N.Y.: Doubleday, 1966) 120.

from the wider society. The value of egalitarianism in particular should be the hallmark of this community. This is demonstrated in two ways. First, in the openness of the community in welcoming whoever comes into their midst. James sets before them the ideal: the community must be willing to embrace whoever enters: there is to be no distinction made between rich or poor (2:1-13). Faith in Jesus demands that one not discriminate against anyone: "My brothers and sisters, do you with your acts of favoritism really believe in our glorious Lord Jesus Christ?" (2:1). Second, egalitarianism shines forth in the very make up of the community. The only "officers" within the community are the teachers (3:1) and the elders (5:14). The teachers should view their role with tremendous seriousness for they are held accountable for all they say and teach. Their ministry is for the service of the community to lead them to an understanding of the "implanted word." The author sees himself in this group of teachers ("for you know that we who teach . . ." [3:1]). He is also one who values wisdom highly: "Who is wise among you" (3:13). Effectively, the teacher and the wise person are identical. As a teacher, James shares his wisdom with his hearers.

The elders too are at the service of the community. They are the ones called in to assist the sick. However, the responsibility for the community members is not something left up to these "officers." Rather, the whole community shares this responsibility, as the ending to the letter reveals: "My brothers and sisters, if anyone among you wanders from the truth and is brought back by another, you should know that whoever brings back a sinner from wandering will save the sinner's soul from death and will cover a multitude of sins" (5:19-20).

James's community is different from the wider society in which it is situated. In fact, the wider society appears as a threat. Part of the socialization process of the letter of James is to instruct and train the community to meet this threat from the world. They are to keep themselves "unstained by the world" (1:27). While the community is willing to welcome whoever comes into their midst, its openness does not mean that boundaries do not exist. The community clearly distinguishes itself from the world. The moral exhortations enable the community to see that its values are distinct from the values of the wider world. However, this does not mean that James's community is a group which retreats from the world similar to the way that the Qumran community withdrew itself. James never imagines that his community should set up institutions that would separate them from the wider society.[36] While living in the world, the community is to be con-

---

[36] See Luke Timothy Johnson, "Friendship with the World/Friendship with God: A Study of Discipleship in James," *Discipleship in the New Testament*, ed.

scious that what drives and motivates them are not the values of the world, but the values that come from their faith.

The Function of the Eschatological in the Letter

The final consideration to which attention will be given in discussing the nature of the letter of James is the place that eschatology plays within the context of this wisdom writing. Peter Davids describes the role of the eschatological in the letter of James in this way: "Yet eschatology is not the burden of the book; it is the context of the book."[37] This insight has importance because eschatology does not function in this writing as an end in itself. The letter of James is not directed toward providing a detailed explanation and teaching on eschatology. Rather, the eschatological provides the framework within which the wisdom instruction functions.

The letter is framed within an eschatological orbit. It opens with the address: "To the twelve tribes in the Dispersion" (1:1), who are identified as "the first fruits of God's creatures" (1:18). The community to whom James writes is painted in eschatological language. Situated outside Palestine, in the Diaspora,[38] James's community[39] embodies

---

Fernando F. Segovia (Philadelphia: Fortress Press, 1985) 172. However, Perdue sees things differently. He does consider James as constituting a "withdrawal group": "By withdrawal within this *Gemeinschaft*, a different social reality is constructed and efforts are undertaken to protect it from the threat of outside worlds. A good example of this sectarian position is the Epistle of James" (Perdue, "The Social Character of Paraenesis," 26). See also Perdue, "Paraenesis and the Epistle of James," 241–56.

[37] Peter H. Davids, *The Epistle of James: A Commentary on the Greek Text*, The New International Greek Testament Commentary (Grand Rapids, Mich.: Paternoster Press, 1982) 39.

[38] I understand the reference to the Diaspora (διασπορά) used here in the ordinary sense that refers to those areas outside the land of Palestine. This differs from many scholars such as Dibelius (*James*, 66), who views it in a metaphorical sense whereby it refers to Christians whose real home is not here on earth, but in heaven. Consequently, Christians living on earth are in fact living outside their true homeland and in this sense are in the Diaspora. This is certainly the meaning that 1 Peter gives to the term in 1:1, but it is not the meaning that I think is intended by James as can be seen from the rest of the letter. Davids (*The Epistle of James*, 64) also attributes the ordinary meaning to this phrase: "the true Israel [i.e., Jewish Christians] outside of Palestine [i.e., probably in Syria and Asia Minor]."

[39] When using the phrase "James's community," I have in mind the readers to whom James is writing. As noted consistently throughout this study, James's message is community oriented. James is addressing, not the individual as such, but rather the group, the community.

those eschatological hopes of the Jewish people in the reconstitution of its nation as "the twelve tribes."[40] The letter of James culminates with two pericopes that again provide a focus on the end of time (5:1-6 "the day of slaughter" is about to break upon the world; and 5:7-11 where the day of "the coming of the Lord is near"). Within this framework James presents his instructions and exhortations.

This eschatological framework provides the motivation for the way the believer is to lead his or her life. This motivation comes from both the present and the future eschatological perspectives. In the present, the readers are already "the first fruits of God's creatures" (1:18). As the eschatological age has already begun, they are to lead their lives according to this new rebirth. Their present existence gives direction and impulse to the way they are to live. In these last days, James is telling them what they should do if they are to stand before the judgment of God.

The future judgment of God acts as a warning. The teacher is singled out as the one with the greater responsibility: "for you know that we who teach will be judged with greater strictness" (3:1). The readers are further warned against acting as judges against their neighbors:

> Do not speak evil against one another, brothers and sisters. Whoever speaks evil against another or judges another, speaks evil against the law and judges the law. . . . There is one lawgiver and judge who is able to save and to destroy. So who, then, are you to judge your neighbor? (4:11-12).

The future judgment also acts as an encouragement for perseverance. Those who endure the test are promised "the crown of life" (1:12). Further, the poor are the ones who will be "heirs of the kingdom that he has promised to those who love him" (2:5).

In looking forward to the future, James is not advocating passivity, but rather is calling the readers to activity and involvement. They have received "the implanted word" which now they must bring to fruition in all their actions.[41] This has important implications for this study on perfection. When James calls on his readers to be perfect in 1:4, he is not calling on them to await a gift that is to be bestowed in the future

---

[40] Detailed attention will be given to the meaning and understanding of these terms, "the twelve tribes in the Dispersion" (1:1) and "the first fruits of his creation" (1:18) in the next chapter. (See the section entitled "Every Perfect Gift Is from Above [1:17]," p. 69). Here, James sees his readers, Jewish Christians, as the beginning of the reconstituted Israel. The Jewish people expected this to take place in the eschatological age.

[41] See Franz Mussner, *Der Jakobusbrief: Auslegung,* 4th ed. (Freiburg: Herder, 1981) 210.

at the end of time.[42] Rather, it is a gift received through the implanting of the word when they became believers. They must become "doers of the word" (1:22) leading lives that are mature, lives of authentic perfection. The aim is not to acquire perfection in the future, for perfection is a gift for the present. The call is to be found perfect and mature at the coming of the Lord.[43]

The community to whom James writes is a community that considers itself "the eschatological community of God."[44] James sees his community as living at the end of history. For him there is no problem about a delay in the coming of the Lord, for this coming is imminent ("The Judge is standing at the doors!" [5:9]).[45] Hence, the call in the letter is for perseverance and endurance so that they will be found perfect at the coming of the Lord. As Penner succinctly expresses it: "Hence, the eschatological focus of the framework pushes the community instruction in a particular direction: the community instruction is for the people living in the 'last days,' awaiting the imminent return of the Judge, and desiring to be found perfect and complete at the time of judgment."[46]

This explains the joy so characteristic of the letter's tone. Even in the midst of trials and testing (1:2 and 12) joy occurs. The reference to trials and testing is a further indication that James sees the community as living at the end of the ages. James 1:27 refers to "the distress" of the widows and orphans. The Greek term that James uses for "distress" (θλῖψις) is a technical word that is used particularly in apocalyptic literature for the sufferings experienced in the eschatological times. Heinrich Schlier, in his study of the use of this word in the Septuagint, argues that in the world of Israel it took on a special "theological significance from the fact that it predominantly denotes the oppression and affliction of the people of Israel or of the righteous who represent Israel."[47] When the New Testament writers took over this term, they did so by applying it to the sufferings that they were enduring particularly on the eve of the parousia.[48]

---

[42] As Wall (*Community of the Wise*, 49–50) argues.

[43] The next chapter will examine in detail the meaning and significance of James's concept of perfection as a present reality.

[44] Todd C. Penner, *The Epistle of James and Eschatology: Re-reading an Ancient Christian Letter*, JSNTS 121 (Sheffield: Sheffield Academic Press, 1996) 212.

[45] See Davids, *The Epistle of James*, 39.

[46] See Penner, *The Epistle of James and Eschatology*, 212.

[47] Heinrich Schlier, "θλίβω, θλῖψις," *Theological Dictionary of the New Testament*, vol. 3, ed. Gerhard Kittel, trans. Geoffrey W. Bromiley (Grand Rapids, Mich.: Eerdmans, 1972) 142.

[48] As Schlier says: "Similarly in Mt. 24 (Mk. 13) Jesus speaks of the sufferings before the *parousia*, of their first beginnings (ἀρχὴ ὠδίνων) in the form of a shaking

James uses this term, which elsewhere in the New Testament has become the technical term for the sufferings immediately preceding the parousia, to refer to the sufferings of the "widows and orphans." As I have argued elsewhere,[49] James has made this shift deliberately. He believes that the parousia is indeed imminent, but the usual signs accorded this arrival by apocalyptic literature are conspicuously absent. Consequently, James reinterprets the sufferings to refer to every suffering as an indication that the parousia is about to break in.[50]

This is also an indication of the way in which James has used the apocalyptic imagination. The focus of interest in James is not with the eschatological or the apocalyptic, but with community instruction for the present. This leads James to be very reserved in his use of apocalyptic symbolism.[51] He is undoubtedly aware of the apocalyptic imagination, after all it is part of the very world that he inhabits. However, James's interest is not with a description of this future apocalyptic cataclysmic in-breaking. This event provides the framework, not the purpose of his message. His purpose is to encourage his community to joy and expectation as they await the parousia: "Consider it nothing but joy" (1:2). This means that those who embrace the community instruction should be full of joy, eager with expectation as they strive to be found perfect at the Lord's coming. The future age is not to be approached with fear and trepidation, but with joy, peace, and happiness. Apocalyptic descriptions of the destruction of evil are outside the scope of James's writing. Instead, he wants his community to approach the future with joy, for the "glorious Lord" (2:1) will give "the crown of life" (1:12) to those who are found perfect.

---

of the historical and natural cosmos (24:4-8), of their continuation in the form of θλίψεις, or persecutions of the disciples (24:9-14), and of their consummation at the end of the age (24:15-28)" ("θλίβω, θλῖψις," 145).

[49] Hartin, "Who Is Wise and Understanding among You?" 494.

[50] Sophie Laws (*A Commentary on the Epistle of James*, Black's New Testament Commentaries [London: Black, 1980] 90) also argues for James's conscious reworking of the traditional understanding of θλῖψις: "It could be that he is trying to dispense with the old eschatological ideas, finding them no longer appropriate. . . . Alternatively James may be trying to keep the expectation alive and real in a situation where the traditional 'signs' are conspicuously lacking, and in that attempt he carries out a deliberate re-interpretation of the nature of the signs."

[51] James does share some of the thought patterns that are found in an apocalyptic worldview: he knows of the world of devils (2:19); that the world of the future brings about a judgment that necessitates a separation between good and evil (5:1-11); the future day of judgment is described as a "day of slaughter" (5:5); "the Judge is standing at the doors" (5:9); there is a "crown of life" (1:12) in store for

Conclusion

The letter of James presupposes a community of Jewish-Christians living outside Palestine whom the author sees as heirs to the heritage and promises of Israel. These promises have even now reached fulfillment in that the twelve tribe kingdom is being reconstituted through their presence.

This examination of the letter's connection to Wisdom literature and to an eschatological worldview has helped to identify its character while at the same time providing implications for the study of genre in general. As already argued, a genre is characterized by three elements: form, content, and function. I have illustrated that the letter of James belongs to that wider literary genre of Wisdom literature characterized by the subgenre of a protreptic discourse whereby it aims at providing moral exhortation in the form of a focused, sustained argument and demonstration. At the same time, the letter shows influences from an eschatological worldview, for the eschatological perspective provides the horizon in which the community instruction flourishes.

James is not just a collection of moral exhortations. It has a focus and an argument in which exhortations are used to demonstrate the lifestyle of his community. James is more concerned with the life of his own group as opposed to that of the wider society. His attitude to the

---

those who remain perfect. However, such apocalyptic images do not make the letter of James an apocalypse. George Nickelsburg characterizes some of the characteristic features of apocalyptic texts in this way: "The authors of apocalyptic texts, while they actually draw heavily on the Torah and the prophets, present new revelations, although they attribute them variously to pre-Mosaic authors (Enoch and Abraham), Moses himself, and post-Mosaic figures (Daniel, Ezra and Baruch). The sources of these new revelations are said to be cosmic journeys and dream visions, interpreted by angels" (George W. E. Nickelsburg, "Wisdom and Apocalypticism in Early Judaism: Some Points for Discussion," *Society of Biblical Literature Seminar Papers*, ed. Eugene H. Loverling [Atlanta: Scholars Press, 1994] 722–3). The function of apocalyptic texts is to provide a revealed message of comfort for readers who are enduring persecution. They are promised that the imminent judgment will remove all forms of oppression. James, on the other hand, does not give any centrality to a revelation of the future. The eschatological future acts in James as the horizon against which the present functions. All admonitions, moral exhortations, and demonstrations contained in the letter function as a call to remain true and to persevere in the rebirth that has occurred within them through the implanted word (1:21). The eschatological and apocalyptic elements within the letter of James function in the service of the protreptic discourse, and not as an end in themselves as occurs in apocalyptic texts.

world and the call specifically to "keep oneself unstained by the world" (1:27) illustrates this notion well. Further, James wishes to call his readers to the fullness of this new life, to authentic maturity as "the twelve tribes of the Dispersion." His argument presents those values necessary to identify the believer as part of a new social order. All the ethical instructions within the letter aim at the social formation of the group, giving them a specific identity and providing them with the guidelines necessary to maintain their new social order in its own distinctiveness as opposed to the wider society. As such these ethical instructions and values are countercultural. They define the community through their opposition to the world and through friendship with God. Seen in this way, the call to perfection that so characterizes this writing is directed to their present life. It is a call to lead their lives in an integral way as a new society, that of the eschatological twelve tribes of the Dispersion. As such the form of the writing serves its function admirably.

From its outward form as a letter one can say that this protreptic discourse is sent as a letter to a community that James is encouraging to embrace an authentic way of life. I turn now to examine how the concept of perfection unfolds within the letter of James and contributes to the very nature and purpose of the letter.

CHAPTER FOUR

Faith Perfected through Works: A Context for the Moral Instructions in the Letter of James

Importance of Perfection in the Letter of James

The examination of the nature of the letter of James has shown that it is not just a loose collection of moral statements, but a writing that calls the readers to embrace a particular way of life that sets them apart from the wider society. At the heart of this new social order that makes up James's community lies the call to embrace a way of integrity, authenticity, and perfection. This call to perfection gives direction to the whole writing and this chapter will illustrate the importance that perfection plays in expressing the lifestyle of the community of James.

The investigation of the concept of perfection in the world of classical Greek thought, the world of Judaism (as represented by the Hebrew Scriptures, the Septuagint, the writings of Philo and Qumran), and finally the world of the New Testament have provided a distinct background from which to begin examining the understanding of perfection in the letter of James. A noteworthy feature of this letter is the frequency with which the adjective "perfect" (τέλειος) occurs. It appears four times in the opening chapter (twice at 1:4 and at 1:17 and 1:25) and again at 3:2. The verb "to make perfect, to complete" (τελειόω) is used at 2:22, while the verb "to fulfill, to accomplish" (τελέω) is used at 2:8. This is remarkable given the shortness of the letter. The frequency of its use is testimony to the importance James gives to this concept.

Concern for the type of life that the community should adopt gives the context for examining the importance James gives to the concept of perfection. Attention will focus on three aspects of the letter where

perfection plays an important role: The letter opens with a call to perfection (1:2-4) that provides direction to the entire writing. Second, wisdom is the perfect gift (1:17) that comes from above and provides the horizon for the attainment of perfection in the present dispensation. Finally, James draws attention to the concept of "the perfect law" (1:25) that provides direction for the way the community of James should function: faith perfected through action is what characterizes the members of the community of James.

Having examined the concept of perfection within the letter of James, attention will then be given to drawing out its significance for all the moral teaching of the letter. Perfection emerges as the goal of a life of faith that expresses itself in action. A profession of faith in God with one's lips is not sufficient. Faith must be demonstrated by a lifestyle led in conformity with God's will. Wisdom and the law enable believers to lead the life that God wants of them.

In the Tradition of the Biblical Understanding of Perfection

The examination of the notion of perfection in the Hebrew Scriptures and the Septuagint has led to an identification of three aspects that give a specific biblical flavor to this concept distinguishing it from the wider Greek culture of the time. While the world of Greek philosophy tended to give attention chiefly to the characteristic of τέλειος as completeness in the sense of attaining the goal (τέλος) for which one was striving,[1] the biblical understanding went in a different direction. The following are the characteristics that have already been identified:

(1) The idea of wholeness or completeness whereby a being remains true to its original constitution. As observed, this is an idea shared with the wider Greek world. However, the origin of this concept was not that of the classical Greek or Hellenistic worlds. Its roots originated in the Jewish cult. Only that which lacks imperfection could be offered to the Lord.

(2) This wholeness is only attained through a wholehearted dedication to God. God demands exclusive worship and whatever takes one away from that relationship destroys that "perfection." This same idea is captured by another adjective, *saddiq* ("righteous"). A righteous person is one who leads a perfect relationship with God and with others. Here, a further dimension is introduced, namely one centered on a community.

---

[1] As F.M.J. Waanders (*The History of ΤΕΛΟΣ and ΤΕΛΕΩ in Ancient Greek* [Amsterdam: Grüner, 1983] 237) says: "All available evidence leads me to believe that the most frequent meaning of τέλειος ('having τέλος') is 'complete.'"

(3) Finally, this wholehearted devotion to the Lord is expressed through the fulfillment of the Torah and its stipulations, the commandments. The Torah itself is viewed as the will of the Lord, and one lives out the Lord's will through obedience to the Torah.

Against this background of the understanding of τέλειος in the biblical world, I now turn to examine the importance of this concept in the letter of James. In many ways, James is a unique writing. One of the most characteristic features is its concern to give its readers an ethical direction. Rather than offer heady reflections on the readers' faith, the writer offers them motivations and directions enabling them to remain in friendship with God (4:4) and to show concern for one another (1:27).

The ethical teaching of the letter can be understood more clearly when it is seen in the context of meta-ethical reflections on the nature of ethics. Ethicists draw a distinction between "ethics" and "morality."[2] The word "ethics," derived from the Greek word *ethos* (ἔθος), means "custom or habit."[3] Its Latin translation was *mos, mores*, from which the English words "moral, morality" are derived. While etymologically the two words meant exactly the same thing (custom, habit, an activity common to society), in the course of time these words began to be used for two different concepts. "Morality" referred to laws or rules of conduct, while "ethics" in a more general sense embraced a critical reflection on morality and ways of behavior.[4] On a practical level, ethics would embrace, for example, reflection on the value of life, the nature of goodness, principles that are basic to a whole moral system. Morality, on the other hand, is expressed by the concrete actions that one performs every day, for example, telling the truth in a particular situation.

[2] See the work of J. de Graaf, *Elementair Begrip van de Ethiek*, 2d ed. (Amsterdam: De Erven Bohn Bv, 1974) 1–2.

[3] See Liddell and Scott, "ἔθος," *An Intermediate Greek-English Lexicon*, 7th ed. (Oxford: Clarendon Press, 1968) 226. They quote the phrase from Thucydides: "ἐν ἔθει εἶναι, to be in *the habit*."

Johannes P. Louw and Eugene A. Nida, "ἔθος," (*Greek-English Lexicon of the New Testament Based on Semantic Domains*, vol. 1 [New York: United Bible Societies, 1988] 507, #41.25) are much more specific:

"a pattern of behavior more or less fixed by tradition and generally sanctioned by the society—'custom, habit.'

"ἔθος: καθὼς ἔθος ἐστὶν τοῖς Ἰουδαίοις ἐνταφιάζειν, 'as is the burial custom of the Jews' Jn 19:40.

"ἦθος: φθείρουσιν ἤθη χρηστὰ ὁμιλίαι κακαί, 'bad companions ruin good habits' 1 Cor 15:33."

[4] See de Graaf, *Elementair Begrip van de Ethiek*, 1.

This distinction is useful as we approach the letter of James. The morality of the letter emerges from the exhortations that dominate it. The various instructions related to rich and poor, to the control of one's tongue, to the avoidance of anger, etc., are all examples of morality, of moral injunctions. However, there is a further dimension to which attention needs to be devoted, namely that ethical dimension that reflects upon these moral instructions and asks what gives them meaning and direction. The concept of τέλειος is to be viewed as exercising an ethical role in that it provides the perspective for, and the motivation behind, the various moral actions. One is called to wholeness in one's relationship with God as well as with the community. The call or desire to remain in this relationship provides the motivation behind the individual instructions. The paraenesis of the letter gives expression to the underlying theme of τέλειος. This chapter will aim at showing that this ethical understanding of perfection provides the basis and direction for the moral instructions that make up the entirety of the letter.

Call to Perfection through Enduring Trials

The letter of James opens with a call to be perfect, lacking in nothing (1:4). This call is generated in the context of a consideration on the endurance of trials that come because of one's faith. On three occasions James turns attention to the positive value that enduring trials has in the life of the believer (1:2-4, 12-15; and 5:7-11).[5] Through these passages an understanding of the call to perfection emerges as an important theme within the letter.

Testing of Faith Leads to Perfection (1:2-4)

In this short writing, the noun "faith" (πίστις) occurs at least sixteen times.[6] Faith is just as central to this letter as it is in the writings of Paul. The importance of this concept is underscored even further when we note that it is the first theme introduced in this writing.[7] Faith

---

[5] Attention will be given to Jas 1:2-4 and 5:7-11 as these passages are the more significant ones for illustrating the theme of perfection.

[6] The noun πίστις occurs sixteen times (1:3, 6; 2:1, 5, 14 [twice], 17, 18 [three times], 20, 22 [twice], 24, 26; 5:15), while the verb πιστεύω occurs three times (2:19 [twice], and 23).

[7] I have argued elsewhere (*James and the Q Sayings of Jesus*, JSNTS 47 [Sheffield: Sheffield Academic Press, 1991] 26–33) that the function of the opening chapter is to introduce those themes that will be taken up again and developed further in the

that is tested and brought to perfection is the theme of the opening verses (1:2-4). As such, these verses set the direction for the rest of the letter. This theme of perfecting faith through trials also concludes the letter (5:7-11). It is not by chance that the opening and closing of the letter focus on a similar theme. To borrow a phrase from D. Edmond Hiebert: "'The testing of your faith' (1:3) seems to be the key which James left hanging at the front door, intended to unlock the contents of the book."[8]

The hearers should rejoice in trials because testing faith leads to endurance. This is the first premise in the line of argument in this passage. James opens his letter with a word of encouragement for his hearers. He is in effect saying: "Be happy, because our faith teaches us that sufferings and trials are good for us, they lead to endurance and further bring us to perfection." The thought is very clear: Sufferings and trials are a means of testing faith[9] and call for patient endurance.[10]

---

rest of the epistle. Douglas J. Moo (*The Letter of James: An Introduction and Commentary* [Grand Rapids, Mich.: Eerdmans, 1985] 39) compared the letter of James to a symphony indicating in this way the themes that recur throughout the letter. However, he does not see these themes developing or growing in intensity. As he says (*The Letter of James*, 39): "Several key motifs continually crop up, like musical motifs in a symphony or opera, but these are not dominant enough to serve as organizing heads."

[8] D. Edmond Hiebert, "The Unifying Theme of the Epistle of James," *Bibliotheca Sacra* 135 (1978) 224.

[9] This phrase "the testing of your faith . . ." (τὸ δοκίμιον ὑμῶν τῆς πίστεως . . . 1:3) can have a number of possible meanings. Some scholars have tried to understand it in the sense of "the genuineness of faith." This is in fact the way in which it is used in 1 Pet 1:7. For Peter, faith demonstrates its genuine character in the future through the way in which it has been preserved through suffering (see Rudolf Hoppe, *Der theologische Hintergrund des Jakobusbriefes* [Würzburg: Echter Verlag, 1977] 23). The focus in James, however, is not on the aspect of the genuine quality of faith, but rather on the way that faith is tested. In this sense, it is best to understand James as referring here to "the means of testing your faith" (Patrick J. Hartin, "Call to Be Perfect through Suffering [James 1,2-4]: The Concept of Perfection in the Epistle of James and the Sermon on the Mount," *Biblica* 4:77 [1996] 478–9).

[10] In much intertestamental literature, the theme of endurance through suffering surfaces frequently. For example, Sir 2:1-5 gives expression to this notion in a very similar way: "My child, when you come to serve the Lord, / prepare yourself for testing. . . . / Accept whatever befalls you, / and in times of humiliation be patient. / For gold is tested in the fire, / and those found acceptable, in the furnace of humiliation."

See also Sir 4:17-18: "For at first she will walk with them on tortuous paths; / she will bring fear and dread upon them, / and will torment them by her discipline

In referring to "the testing of your faith," James has in mind the faith of the community, rather than just the faith of the individual. The Greek pronoun "your" (ὑμῶν) is plural, not singular. This is the first indication that James's concern lies more with the community than with the individual. This is significant because the morality being advocated is chiefly a community oriented morality, rather than an individualistic one.

Endurance leads to a perfect work (1:4). The word "perfect" (τέλειος) occurs twice in this one verse: "and let endurance have its full effect [ἔργον τέλειον], so that you may be mature [τέλειοι] and complete, lacking in nothing."[11] The first part of the verse brings the thought of the previous verses to a climax with endurance leading to a "perfect work." The development of the phrases proceed in this way: trials of faith lead to endurance and ultimately to the perfect work. Later this thought is restated somewhat differently when reference is made to Abraham: "faith was brought to completion by the works" (2:22).[12] The

---

/ until she trusts them, / and she will test them with her ordinances. / Then she will come straight back to them again and gladden them, / and will reveal her secrets to them."

Wis 2:19 also speaks about the testing of the righteous: "Let us test him [the righteous person] with insult and torture, / so that we may find out how gentle he is, / and make trial of his forbearance."

The Testament of Job presents Job as an example of the way to act: "He will bring on you many plagues, he will take away for himself your goods, he will carry off your children. But, if you are patient, I will make your name renowned in all generations of the earth till the consummation of the age" (TJob 4:5-6). (The translation is taken from R. P. Spittler, "The Testament of Job," *The Old Testament Pseudepigrapha*, vol. 1, *Apocalyptic Literature and Testaments*, ed. James H. Charlesworth [Garden City, N.Y.: Doubleday, 1983] 841.) See also TJob 27:3-7.

This theme is also found in many writings from antiquity. For example, Seneca, *On Providence* 2:1-6: "You ask, 'Why do many adversities come to good men? . . .'" (John W. Basore, trans., *Seneca Moral Essays*, vol. 1, The Loeb Classical Library [Cambridge, Mass.: Harvard University Press, 1958] 6–11); *The Sentences of Sextus*, 7a: "In a trial of faith, a faithful person is a god in a living human body" (Richard A. Edwards and Robert A. Wild, trans., *The Sentences of Sextus* [Chico, Calif.: Scholars Press, 1981] 17); and The Shepherd of Hermas, *Mandates*, 5:1, 1-6: "'Be,' said he, 'long-suffering and prudent and you shall have power over all evil deeds and shalt do all righteousness. . . . You see that long suffering is very sweet, surpassing honey, and is valuable to the Lord and he dwells in it'" (Kirsopp Lake, trans., *The Apostolic Fathers*, vol. 2, *The Shepherd of Hermas*, The Loeb Classical Library [Cambridge, Mass.: Harvard University Press, 1970] 86–9).

[11] ἡ δὲ ὑπομονὴ ἔργον τέλειον ἐχέτω, ἵνα ἦτε τέλειοι καὶ ὁλόκληροι ἐν μηδενὶ λειπόμενοι (1:4).

[12] Here the verb τελειόω ("to make perfect") is used.

similarity in thought is clear: In 1:3-4, faith is perfected through works of trials and suffering, while in 2:22 faith is perfected through the works of Abraham whose testing was to offer his son in sacrifice. The meaning of "perfect" in these instances is that of "completeness, totality, or wholeness."

The second use of τέλειος is followed by two other phrases "complete in all parts, entire"[13] (ὁλόκληροι)[14] and "lacking in nothing" (ἐν μηδενὶ λειπόμενοι). These are synonyms expressing the completeness, the wholeness, of the members of James's community. The perfect work to which the first part of this verse referred is now identified as embracing the members of the community who have remained true to their faith through the trials they endured. As Martin Dibelius argues, James in effect says: "*You* are that perfect work."[15] They are complete persons who integrate their faith and actions. The opposite of the "perfect person" is "the divided person" to whom the following passage (1:5-8) gives attention. The perfection that is attained is that of completeness or wholeness. It is in line with the Old Testament ideas of "wholeness, completeness, without blemish." Such people now conform to their original constitution. The form of this sentence (1:4) is that of an exhortation, conforming to the paraenetical nature of the material. This exhortation carries through to the rest of the verse as Dibelius indicates: "Let what endurance produces be perfected, and thus you will be perfected."[16] Ultimately, this is a call to be perfect, in line with the call that occurs in Matt 5:48: "Be perfect, therefore, as your heavenly Father is perfect."

Adamson[17] makes a further interesting connection. He reads this understanding of the "perfect person" in reference to the opening verse of the letter where the writer identifies himself as a "servant" (δοῦλος), indicating his "wholehearted devotion, service and allegiance."[18] This

[13] Liddell and Scott, "ὁλόκληρος," *An Intermediate Greek-English Lexicon,* 552.

[14] Luke Timothy Johnson (*The Letter of James: A New Translation with Introduction and Commentary,* The Anchor Bible 37A [New York: Doubleday, 1995] 178) notes the health nuances of this particular adjective by referring to "'wholeness' or 'soundness' in contrast to disease (Acts 3:16)."

[15] Martin Dibelius, *James: A Commentary on the Epistle of James,* trans. Michael A. Williams (Philadelphia: Fortress Press, 1975) 74. Dibelius supports this understanding by going on to say: "Only this interpretation is justified both by the correspondence between 'perfect' [τέλειοι v4b] and 'perfect work' [ἔργον τέλειον v4a] and by the schema of the concatenation; furthermore, it creates no linguistic difficulties."

[16] Ibid.

[17] James B. Adamson, *James: The Man and His Message* (Grand Rapids, Mich.: Eerdmans, 1989) 269.

[18] Ibid.

is exactly what τέλειος refers to: such a person is whole and undivided in his or her allegiance to God. Faith in God is to be complete and undivided (perfect) and can be seen through the actions performed. It will be this faith in action that the rest of the letter will endeavor to illustrate.

This opening passage has set the tone for the entire writing with the central theme of perfecting faith. Faith reaches perfection through many trials. Faith is challenged by promoting an allegiance to the world that draws people away from their allegiance to God. Hence, Jas 1:27 defines true religion as keeping "oneself unstained by the world." Perfecting faith is clearly illustrated in the teaching on "faith and works" as seen in the examples of Abraham and Rahab (2:20-25) and Job (5:10-11). Finally, it is "the perfect law" (1:25), the law of liberty, that guides one to put faith into action. Through faith in action one comes to perfection and one's relationship with God is deepened.

Exhortation to Patience amid Trials (5:7-11)

James returns to the theme of patience and endurance amid trials and sufferings at the end of the letter. This conclusion establishes a close connection with the opening of the letter. The entire letter is placed between these two passages dealing with patience in the midst of trials. This is a common biblical stylistic pattern known as inclusion. Emphasis here lies on the call: "Be patient, therefore, beloved, until the coming of the Lord" (Jas 5:7). The Greek word for patience (μακρο-θυμία) used throughout 5:7-11 may be translated as "long-suffering." It is a virtue that expresses firm hope and certainty in the reversal of the situation.[19] The nearness of the parousia is an assurance in the minds of the believers that gives hope to their long-suffering as they await the Lord's coming. Just as the farmer can do nothing to hasten the arrival of the crops, so too the suffering community of James has to wait patiently. They know that their situation will change, but they cannot hasten it. All they can do is persist in their adherence to their faith and not despair. This does not mean a call to passivity, as our modern day notion of patience seems to imply. Instead, the future hope is an ever-present certain hope inspiring them to do everything to persevere so that their hope will be realized. Activity, rather than passivity, is what characterizes the community to whom James writes.

Those who persevere faithfully approach the "coming of the Lord" with confidence. At the same time the image of "the Judge standing at

---

[19] See Johannes Horst, "μακροθυμία, μακροθυμέω," *Theological Dictionary of the New Testament*, vol. 4, ed. Gerhard Kittel, trans. Geoffrey W. Bromiley (Grand Rapids, Mich.: Eerdmans, 1969) 385–6.

the doors" (5:9) is also introduced. Judgment holds no fears for one who has endured suffering and trials patiently. This concluding passage gives direction and perspective for those who are called to perfection. The eschatological age emerges as the culmination for patient endurance. The completeness of the life of faith is reached with the "coming of the Lord" and the reward of the "crown of life." This hope in the Lord's coming gives "value to situations where sufferings and trials are experienced."[20]

The ethical understanding of perfection of faith is the dominant motif of these passages. One strives for the completeness or wholeness of faith that finds expression in a relationship with God and with one another. This ethical perspective gives direction to the moral exhortations of the entire writing. The readers are challenged to remain firm in their relationships with God and with the community. In this way the ethical concept of perfection lays the foundation for the moral instruction of the entire writing.

Wisdom as the Horizon for Attaining Perfection

The significance of the concept of perfection for James emerges from another series of passages (1:5-8; 1:17; 3:13-18; and 4:1-10) that consider the theme of wisdom. An examination of these passages shows wisdom as the horizon for attaining perfection in the eschatological age. A number of interesting insights into the nature of perfection occur especially in identifying the life of a believer as an exclusive and enduring relationship with God.

The Gift of Wisdom (1:5-8)

In the development of the Wisdom literature of the Hebrew biblical and deuterocanonical traditions there arose a concern to provide a reflection on the nature of wisdom and its relationship with God. This is seen in such texts as Proverbs 8 and 9 and Sirach 24. One significant insight offered by such writings is that all wisdom is a gift from God (Jas 1:5-8). Jewish Wisdom literature accepted this idea of wisdom as God's gift as almost self evident (Prov 2:6; 8:22-31; Sir 1:1-4; 24:1-12; Wis 7:24-27; 9:4). The saying of the book of Wisdom—"For even one who is perfect among human beings / will be regarded as nothing without the wisdom that comes from you" (9:6)—is central to the Wisdom tradition to which James is heir. James introduces the need for the

---

[20] Hartin, "Call to Be Perfect through Suffering," 482.

gift of wisdom from above in the call to perfection which opens the letter. Consequently, Jas 1:2-4 requires the gift of wisdom in order to make up anything that may be lacking.

The thought of the opening passage (1:2-4) continues through the following verses (1:5-8). The author ended 1:4 with a call to wholeness. This prompted James to consider the possibility that the believer may lack something, particularly wisdom. James urges that person to turn to God with confidence knowing that God "gives to all generously and ungrudgingly" (1:5). Wisdom as God's gift is a practical gift, enabling one to know how to act in specific situations. In the Jewish traditions, the only truly wise person was God, and all human wisdom was but a gift from the divine wisdom.[21] Humanity cannot attain wisdom through its own efforts. The only way to acquire wisdom is to ask God. Solomon exemplified this spirit through his request for a mind that was able to discern (1 Kgs 3:5-15).[22]

Elsewhere, the Hebrew traditions draw a connection between wisdom and steadfast endurance.[23] The picture of wisdom supporting the individual in the midst of arduous times and trials is well captured by Sir 4:17-18:

> For at first she [Wisdom] will walk with them on tortuous paths;
>   she will bring fear and dread upon them,
> and will torment them by her discipline
>   until she trusts them,
> and she will test them with her ordinances.
> Then she will come straight back to them again and gladden them,
>   and will reveal her secrets to them.

---

[21] The book of Wisdom (8:21) expresses this well: "But I perceived that I would not possess wisdom unless God gave her to me— / and it was a mark of insight to know whose gift she was— / so I appealed to the Lord and implored him, / and with my whole heart I said . . . ."

[22] "Give your servant therefore an understanding mind to govern your people, able to discern between good and evil; for who can govern this your great people?" (1 Kgs 3:9).

[23] 4 Macc provides a good example that shows how wisdom is the path to overcome weakness and passions and enables one to lead one's life according to the Law of God. "Reason, I suggest, is the mind making a deliberate choice of the life of wisdom. Wisdom, I submit, is knowledge of things divine and human, and of their causes. And this wisdom, I assume, is the culture we acquire from the Law, through which we learn the things of God reverently and the things of men to our worldly advantage" (4 Macc 1:15-17; H. Anderson, trans., "4 Maccabees," *The Old Testament Pseudepigrapha*, vol. 2, ed. James A. Charlesworth [London: Darton, Longman & Todd, 1985] 545).

Yet, why did James single out wisdom as that gift that might be lacking? Wisdom, according to the biblical understanding (exemplified especially in the person of Solomon), is above all the gift of discernment, of knowing how to act in particular circumstances. Wisdom enables one to act when faced with trials, temptations, and suffering[24] and is the vital gift one needs to strive for perfection. Wisdom, then, is the context for the attainment of perfection. This request for wisdom provides the practical illustration of the Gospel injunction: "Ask and it will be given you" (Matt 7:7).

The letter of James opened on a note of joy. The reason for this joy now becomes clear. Wisdom is God's gift that enables believers to be steadfast amidst trials and sufferings, and to act in such a way that they can be perfect.[25] Wisdom provides the horizon for the moral action of believers as they look forward to the fulfillment of their hopes in the eschatological age.

In this passage, James goes further and introduces the example of the double-minded person, the one who doubts. Using a very graphic image, he compares the double-minded person to the waves of the sea that are driven back and forth at the impulse of the wind. Double-minded people[26] are unable to give allegiance to only one person. In the area of faith, too, they are seen to vacillate. This conforms to the same teaching of Jesus in the Sermon on the Mount where Jesus says to his disciples: "No one can serve two masters; for a slave will either hate the one and love the other, or be devoted to the one and despise the other. You cannot serve God and wealth" (Matt 6:24).

The book of Sirach had expressed a close connection between the fear of the Lord and wisdom: "To fear the Lord is the beginning of wisdom" (Sir 1:14). Later in the same chapter mention is made about betraying that fear of the Lord: "Do not disobey the fear of the Lord; / do not approach him with a divided mind" (1:28). Of significance here

---

[24] See J. A. Kirk, "The Meaning of Wisdom in James: Examination of a Hypothesis," *New Testament Studies* 16 (1969/70) 24–38.

[25] The connection between wisdom and perfection is well expressed in Wis 9:6: "For even one who is perfect among human beings / will be regarded as nothing without the wisdom that comes from you." In referring to this passage, Dibelius (*James*, 77) rightly notes that there is no mention here of a perfection that is the result of sufferings or afflictions. The significance of this passage lies precisely in the connection between wisdom and perfection. The gift of wisdom leads to perfection, enabling one to know how to act correctly. However, this passage does not pay attention to exactly what human actions are required on the path to perfection.

[26] The word used for double-minded, δίψυχος, is not found elsewhere in the New Testament. In fact, it is not found in Greek literature prior to the epistle of

is the similarity to the teaching of James: a divided heart or mind cannot claim to have a relationship with the Lord. Faith and doubt cannot coexist.

James ends with a harsh condemnation of the double-minded, the doubters: they "must not expect to receive anything from the Lord" (1:8). Being double-minded, they are in fact disloyal to the Lord. James's faith is a faith that requires single-minded devotion with absolute trust and faithfulness. Wholehearted allegiance is what this faith demands. This further illustrates the notion of perfection that was observed in the Old Testament characterization of perfection: God requires exclusive worship and trust. "Hear, O Israel: The LORD is our God, the LORD alone" (Deut 6:4). A double-minded person betrays this exclusivity. The notion of righteousness gives expression to this same idea because only the righteous person remains true to this exclusive relationship to the Lord. Wisdom is that much-needed gift showing how to place total and exclusive trust in the Lord. This is an underlying theme of the entire letter. The climax of this teaching is reached in Jas 4:4: "Whoever wishes to be a friend of the world becomes an enemy of God." There is no middle ground. The challenge James sets before his readers is to become a people whose total allegiance, total friendship, is with the Lord.

James. It appears in literature soon after James, namely, in *The Didache* 4:4: "Thou shalt not be of two minds whether it shall be or not" (οὐ διψυχήσεις, πότερον ἔσται ἢ οὔ), Kirsopp Lake trans., *The Apostolic Fathers*, vol. 1, *The Didache*, The Loeb Classical Library (Cambridge, Mass.: Harvard University Press, 1965) 315; *The Epistle of Barnabas* 19:5: "Thou shalt not be in two minds whether it shall be or not" (οὐ μὴ διψυχήσῃς, πότερον ἔσται ἢ οὔ), Lake, *The Apostolic Fathers*, vol. 1, 402–3; *1 Clement* 23:2: "Wherefore let us not be double-minded . . . " (διὸ μὴ διψυχῶμεν . . .), Lake, *The Apostolic Fathers*, vol. 1, 50–1; 2 Clem 11:2: "For the prophetic word also says: 'Miserable are the double-minded that doubt in their heart . . . .'" (λέγει γὰρ καὶ ὁ προφητικὸς λόγος· Ταλαίπωροί εἰσιν οἱ δίψυχοι), Lake, *The Apostolic Fathers*, vol. 1, 144–5; and some fifty occasions in *The Shepherd of Hermas* where this term or related terms occur.

However, all the uses of this word seem to be dependent upon James. While Dibelius (*James*, 83) and James H. Ropes (*A Critical and Exegetical Commentary on the Epistle of St. James* [Edinburgh: T. and T. Clark (1916), 1978] 143) both categorically deny that it could have been coined by James, I do not think that one can be so certain. Given the fact that no evidence exists for its usage prior to James, and that later Christian literature is dependent on James in this regard, there is at least the possibility that James was responsible for its construction. Be that as it may, at least the idea to which James draws attention is not novel. It is well attested to in the Hebrew writings. See, for example, Ps 12:2: "They utter lies to each other; / with flattering lips and a double heart they speak."

Every Perfect Gift Is from Above (1:17)

James 1:5-8 presented wisdom as God's gift enabling believers to attain perfection. Here, in 1:17, James develops his thought more fully. He says that every perfect gift has its origin in God—it comes from above. The notion of "perfect gift" again implies the basic understanding of wholeness or totality. Every gift that comes from God is in essence one that is complete, not lacking in anything. The significance of this emerges from the context. In the previous verses (1:12-16), James had discussed the nature of temptation and trials and had argued that God is not the source of evil. No temptations, nothing that is evil, comes from God. Instead, James proceeds to show in a very positive sense that everything that comes from God is perfect.

James goes further to present an insight into his understanding of God and the consequences this has for believers. As the "Father of lights," God is the creator of the universe.[27] Yet, God is not just the creator of the heavenly bodies, like the stars and sun and moon; God is also the creator of a new people. In 1:18, James uses the image of giving birth to show that God has brought the readers into being as "the first fruits of his creatures." This is one of the most significant phrases in the letter, and one that reveals so well the understanding James has of his readers. As those who are called to be perfect, they are God's first fruits. Just as the notion of perfection in the biblical world originated in the Jewish cult to refer to the offering that must be unblemished, so "the first fruits" imagery recaptures this cultic language. According to their tradition, Israel would offer a sacrifice to God from the first fruits of the land and of animals.[28] Nothing that was imperfect

---

[27] The phrase "Father of lights" refers to God in the role of creator of the sun and moon and stars. While this exact phrase is rare, the thought it expresses is at home in the Jewish traditions. In Job 38:28 reference is made to "the father of the rain" (ὑετοῦ πατήρ). The creation motifs present God as creator especially of the heavenly bodies. In Philo *De Specialibus Legibus,* I, 96 reference is made to the "Father of the world" (τῷ τοῦ κόσμου πατρί). Further, God is also pictured through the symbol of light. See, for example, Philo, *De somniis,* I, 75, "And it is easy otherwise by means of argument to perceive this, since God is the first light, 'For the Lord is my light and my Saviour,' is the language of the Psalms; and not only the light, but he is also the archetypal pattern of every other light . . ." (Charles D. Yonge, trans., *The Works of Philo* [Peabody, Mass.: Hendrickson, 1993] 372). See as well, the writings of John, for example, 1 John 1:5: "This is the message we have heard from him and proclaim to you, that God is light and in him there is no darkness at all."

[28] The first harvest of agriculture (Deut 26:1-11) and of food (Deut 18:4) and the first offering of animals (Deut 15:19-23) are consecrated and offered to the Lord.

could form part of that offering. By applying this image to his readers as the first fruits, James implies that they too must be unblemished. They are perfect, not through anything of their own doing, but through God's actions. As the creator, God has chosen them from all creatures. By rebirth they become the first-fruits of God's creatures.

The full significance of this rebirth as the first fruits emerges from the context of the letter's opening address: "To the twelve tribes in the Dispersion" (1:1).[29] As I have argued elsewhere,[30] the best approach in trying to understand this term is to read it against the background of the Israelite hope for the restoration of their nation. They saw this restoration occurring through the reconstitution of the twelve tribe kingdom. This hope is traceable back to the promise made by Nathan to David: "Your house and your kingdom shall be made sure forever before me; your throne shall be established forever" (2 Sam 7:16). Notwithstanding the destruction of both the northern and the southern kingdoms, this hope in a reconstituted twelve tribe kingdom endured. It persisted especially in the preaching and expectations of the prophets (Ezek 37:19-24 and Jer 3:18). The Qumran community also expressed great interest in this hope. In their own writings they went so far as to describe the reorganization of this twelve tribe kingdom as can be seen especially from the description of its battle order.[31]

These first fruits acknowledge God as the creator and giver of all harvests and flocks. This offering brings about God's blessing on the rest of the harvest (Prov 3:9-10). The first offering of animals is also offered to God: "But if it has any defect—any serious defect, such as lameness or blindness—you shall not sacrifice it to the LORD your God" (Deut 15:21).

[29] There is much dispute about the exact meaning of this phrase. See, for example, the views of Dibelius, *James*, 66–8; Sophie Laws, *A Commentary on the Epistle of James*, Black's New Testament Commentaries (London: Black, 1980) 47–9; Franz Mussner, *Der Jakobusbrief: Auslegung*, 4th ed. (Freiburg: Herder, 1981) 11–2; Peter H. Davids, *The Epistle of James: A Commentary on the Greek Text* (Grand Rapids, Mich.: Paternoster Press, 1982) 63–4; and Johnson, *The Letter of James*, 169.

[30] See Patrick J. Hartin, "'Who Is Wise and Understanding among You?' (James 3:13): An Analysis of Wisdom, Eschatology and Apocalypticism in the Epistle of James," *Society of Biblical Literature Seminar Papers* (Atlanta: Scholars Press, 1996) 483–503.

[31] For example, 1QM 2:1-2: "They shall arrange the chiefs of the priests behind the High Priest and of his second (in rank), twelve chiefs to serve in perpetuity before God. And the twenty-six chiefs of the divisions shall serve in their divisions and after them the chiefs of the levites to serve always, twelve, one per tribe" (Florentino García Martínez, ed., *The Dead Sea Scrolls Translated: The Qumran Texts in English*, trans. Wilfred G. E. Watson [Leiden: Brill, 1994] 96).

This same hope in a reconstituted twelve tribe kingdom provides much of the initial impetus behind the teaching and activity of Jesus. John the Baptist's mission was a preparation for the inauguration of this kingdom: "In those days John the Baptist appeared in the wilderness of Judea proclaiming, 'Repent, for the kingdom of heaven has come near'" (Matt 3:1-2). Jesus' choice of twelve disciples whom he instructed in the mysteries of the kingdom was no chance event. The Gospel writers present it as a type of acted out parable (Matt 10:1-4) where the twelve disciples are representative of the new twelve tribe kingdom. In a visible way they illustrate the initial constitution of the kingdom of God that Jesus came to inaugurate and which formed the center of all his preaching.

In Matt 15:24, Jesus says to the woman from the region of Tyre and Sidon: "I was sent only to the lost sheep of the house of Israel." Jesus' mission is seen by the tradition behind Matthew's Gospel to be directed initially and exclusively to the people of Israel. Furthermore, it is his task to bring together, to gather in, the tribes that had been lost. In sending out his followers, Jesus gives them the same task to perform. Their mission, like that of Jesus, is to focus on the people of Israel and to gather in the lost tribes. "These twelve Jesus sent out with the following instructions: 'Go nowhere among the Gentiles, and enter no town of the Samaritans, but go rather to the lost sheep of the house of Israel'" (Matt 10:5-6).

This role of gathering in the lost tribes reaches its fulfillment in the future eschatological age where the followers of Jesus are presented as sitting on twelve thrones judging the twelve tribes. "And I confer on you, just as my Father has conferred on me, a kingdom, so that you may eat and drink at my table in my kingdom, and you will sit on thrones judging the twelve tribes of Israel" (Luke 22:29-30; Matt 19:28-29). Here, they share in the role and actions of Jesus insofar as they gather in those who belong to the twelve tribes at the end of time.

By opening his letter in this way, James shows that he belongs to this tradition of gathering in the twelve tribes of Israel. He sees that these Jewish-Christians whom he addresses constitute that new twelve tribe kingdom for which the Israelites had been hoping for centuries. They are the start of something new, and "the first fruits of God's creatures" signifies this new beginning. The starting point for God's new creative activity begins with these Jewish Christians, but it is not meant to end there.[32] Ultimately, it is to embrace all humanity. The first fruits means that others will follow. The new Israel, the new twelve

---

[32] See Mussner, *Der Jakobusbrief*, 96.

tribe kingdom, will only reach perfection in the future eschatological age at the end of time. In the meantime, the readers of this letter are the first to form part of this new reconstituted people. All this occurs through the creative power of the God in whom they believe.

In a sense this is a confirmation of what James, the brother of the Lord, says in addressing the council at Jerusalem after Paul had spoken: "This agrees with the words of the prophets, as it is written, / 'After this I will return, / and I will rebuild the dwelling of David, which has fallen; / from its ruins I will rebuild it, / and I will set it up'" (Acts 15:15-16). In identifying his readers in this way, James sees them as the true Israel in its eschatological restoration.[33] Their community is a sign of the presence of the eschatological age.

Seen in this context, the perfect gift to which James makes reference in 1:18 is the gift of rebirth ("he brought us forth, he gave us birth," ἀπεκύησεν ἡμᾶς) as the reconstituted people of God, the twelve tribe kingdom. We are the beginning. As such God has perfected us, enabling us to become God's people and to ensure that we remain in this relationship with God. Once again, the notion of perfection includes within its scope the aspect of an allegiance to God that demands an enduring relationship. More importantly, it also points to the reconstitution of God's people to the original image for which they had been created.

The Gift of Wisdom from Above (3:13-18)

This section brings together James's thought on wisdom as discussed above. James 1:5 refers to the gift of wisdom that God gives to overcome whatever is lacking. This gift renders one "complete and whole," in other words, perfect. James 1:17 speaks about every perfect gift as coming from above. In this section (3:13-18) James gives specific attention to the true wisdom which comes from above as God's gift. "But the wisdom from above is first pure, then peaceable, gentle, willing to yield, full of mercy and good fruits, without a trace of partiality or hypocrisy" (3:17). This wisdom is both divine and practical. As a gift that comes from God, it flowers forth in a particular way of life.

James illustrates what wisdom is by contrasting two different lifestyles. Ultimately, the only way in which this contrast can be illustrated is by pointing to the ethical lifestyles that they produce. James first speaks against a lifestyle that is led without wisdom (3:14-16)[34]

---

[33] Ibid., 62.

[34] James operates here in the opposite way to other catalogues of ancient virtues and vices. James begins with the list of vices while, for example, 1QS 4 begins with the virtues.

and describes this in purely negative terms. In particular, three adjectives characterize it: "earthly, unspiritual, devilish."[35] Here an ever decreasing or ever worsening development is envisaged,[36] progressing from the earthly through the natural (seen in the negative sense of opposition to God) until the demoniac is attained. This description climaxes by showing this lifestyle in direct opposition to what true wisdom gives. Instead of coming from God, it comes from the devil.[37] We are not dealing here with two different wisdoms producing two different lifestyles. This lifestyle is not influenced by another type of wisdom,[38] rather it comes from the devil. It would be best to characterize it as "anti-wisdom."[39]

True wisdom is characterized in Jas 3:17-18 as coming from above (ἄνωθεν σοφία). In describing the qualities of a life led through the influence of wisdom, James places at the head the adjective "pure" (ἁγνή).[40] In classical Greek, purity originally had a cultic connection and took on the meaning of something that is unblemished. In the moral sphere it referred to whatever was without moral defect.[41] This is exactly what the adjective τέλειος has been used to indicate in other contexts. This word becomes an alternative for the moral perfection, the moral completeness, arising from the gift of wisdom and producing actions that are without defect, actions that are morally well intentioned and, in this sense, perfect.[42] James begins, then, his description

---

[35] ἐπίγειος, ψυχική, and δαιμονιώδης. These three adjectives are not frequently attested in ancient Greek literature.

[36] See Ropes, *A Critical and Exegetical Commentary on the Epistle of St. James*, 248.

[37] Davids (*The Epistle of James*, 153) opts for this understanding of δαιμονιώδης and translates it as "inspired by the devil." This obviously contrasts with being "inspired by the Holy Spirit."

[38] See Hartin, *James and the Q Sayings of Jesus*, 104; Laws, *A Commentary on the Epistle of James*, 162–3.

[39] Timothy B. Cargal, *Restoring the Diaspora: Discursive Structure and Purpose in the Epistle of James*, Society of Biblical Literature Dissertation Series 144 (Atlanta: Scholars Press, 1993) 153.

[40] ἁγνή is defined as a "pure, holy, cultic word, originally an attribute of the divinity and everything belonging to it" (William F. Arnt and F. Wilbur Gingrich, eds., *A Greek-English Lexicon of the New Testament and Other Early Christian Literature: A Translation and Adaptation of Walter Bauer's Griechisch-Deutsches Wörterbuch zu den Schriften des Neuen Testaments und der übrigen urchristlichen Literatur*, 4th rev. ed. [Chicago: University of Chicago Press, 1957] 11).

[41] Louw and Nida (*Greek-English Lexicon*, vol. 1, 746, #88.28) define ἁγνή in this way: "pertaining to being without moral defect or blemish and hence pure—'pure without defect.'"

[42] The term ἁγνή occurs elsewhere in the New Testament. For example:

of true wisdom by indicating that it is perfect, without moral faults or failings. It enables the recipients to lead their lives, to direct their actions, in a morally perfect way.

James continues to define this heavenly wisdom by means of a number of adjectives that are grouped in a threefold way:[43] (1) peaceable, gentle, willing to yield;[44] (2) full of mercy and good fruits;[45] and (3) without a trace of partiality or hypocrisy.[46]

In this description wisdom is presented as a moral virtue inspiring a particular way of life. Wisdom is demonstrated in action, just as faith is, and it involves the very life of the believer.[47]

The culmination of this description of true wisdom comes with the final verse of chapter 3: "And a harvest of righteousness is sown in peace for those who make peace" (3:18). Probably an isolated saying,[48] James has woven it into the context of this letter to capture the essence of his description of wisdom. At the same time it provides a link to what follows (4:1-10). The result of acting wisely, of acting according to God's will, illustrates that one is in a correct relationship with God, that one possesses righteousness.[49]

- 1 John 3:3: "And all who have this hope in him purify themselves, just as he is pure [καθὼς ἐκεῖνος ἁγνός ἐστιν]."
- Phil 4:8: "Finally, beloved, whatever is true, whatever is honorable, whatever is just, whatever is pure [ὅσα ἁγνά] . . ."
- 1 Pet 3:2: "when they see the purity and reverence of your lives [ἐποπτεύσαντες τὴν ἐν φόβῳ ἁγνὴν ἀναστροφὴν ὑμῶν]."

[43] Joseph Chaine, *L'Epître de Saint Jacques,* 2d ed. (Paris: Gabalda, 1927) 93.

[44] εἰρηνική, ἐπιεικής, εὐπειθής. These adjectives are joined together by means of alliteration (all begin with ε):

- "peaceable" (εἰρηνική) indicates that their lifestyle is incompatible with dissentions and strife (something that is taken up in 4:1-10).
- "gentle, willing to yield" (ἐπιεικής, εὐπειθής): "They may be seen as a complementary pair, two sides of a coin; wisdom is reasonable or gentle both in a dominant and a subordinate position" (Laws, *A Commentary on the Epistle of James,* 163).

[45] μεστὴ ἐλέους καὶ καρπῶν ἀγαθῶν. These are central virtues for the author because they illustrate well his definition of religion in 1:27.

[46] Finally, he introduces a set of adjectives that begin again with alliteration (this time with ἀ): ἀδιάκριτος, ἀνυπόκριτος. These adjectives express fundamental themes in the letter. The command "not to make distinctions" is central to the opening verses of chapter 2. Showing partiality runs counter to the whole spirit of the community that has a concern for the spiritual welfare of every member.

[47] See Hartin, *James and the Q Sayings of Jesus,* 111.

[48] See Dibelius, *James,* 214–5.

[49] According to Chaine (*L'Epître de Saint Jacques,* 94–5) the word δικαιοσύνη refers to that virtue of justice by which one conforms one's actions to the will and law of God.

James has used this verse in a masterful way as a hinge to connect the verses that proceed and the verses that follow.[50] In the subsequent verses (4:1-10) James's concern is with the evil consequences of jealousy and selfishness. The antithesis to these is "peace making." Consequently, he prepares for what follows by isolating the antidote to envy and jealousy. At the same time, peaceableness was presented in the previous description as one of the seven characteristics of wisdom. What he does now is lift this characteristic out and elevate it to the prime quality of all the characteristics of wisdom.[51]

The introduction of the concept of righteousness is important. Until now James has been considering the results of wisdom. Now he turns to speak about righteousness. Both aspects are in a way connected. For James "the harvest of righteousness" is the reward for peacemakers—those who make peace obtain the reward of righteousness. This is very similar to the promise in Matthew's beatitudes: "Blessed are the peacemakers, for they will be called children of God" (Matt 5:9). In both, the results of peacemaking bring one into a relationship with God. James's argument is clear: because wisdom is peaceable, those who make peace are the ones who possess wisdom. At the same time, those who make peace also obtain the reward of righteousness. This ultimately means that wisdom brings the reward of righteousness.[52]

Once again, the notion of perfection shines through. Perfection is understood as the quality of a relationship with God that demands allegiance in an exclusive way. Righteousness is undoubtedly that quality which shows the exclusive bond existing between God and the believer. The wise are indeed "the perfect" because they acknowledge their exclusive relationship with God and allow that relationship to influence all their actions.

Friendship with God (4:4)

James 4:1-10[53] presents a consideration of a life led without wisdom

[50] This is contrary to Dibelius (*James,* 214–5), who views it as an isolated saying and does not see any connections to the context.

[51] See Laws, *A Commentary on the Epistle of James,* 165.

[52] As Laws (*A Commentary on the Epistle of James,* 166) expresses it: "James's argument, assuming this connection, would run as follows: there is no wisdom where there is divisiveness, for wisdom is peaceable [cf. Prov. iii.7, 'her paths are peace']; it is the peacemakers, then, who possess wisdom, which is the *fruit of righteousness.*"

[53] Scholars disagree about how to understand this section (4:1-10). Is it to be taken as a unity with the preceding (3:13-18), or is it to be viewed independently?

and dominated by envy and jealousy.[54] I do not intend to consider this whole passage in detail,[55] but there is one verse that is important to examine within this context because it shows what is at stake with the two contrasting lifestyles, one led with wisdom and one led without wisdom: "Adulterers! Do you not know that friendship with the world is enmity with God? Therefore whoever wishes to be a friend of the world becomes an enemy of God" (4:4).

James again reminds his readers that there is a sharp dichotomy between the two lifestyles. Previously he had described the lifestyle led without wisdom, as inspired by the devil. Already in the opening verses of the letter, he had painted the picture of the double-minded person and showed that such a person could not have faith: one either had full allegiance to the Lord or one did not. To vacillate meant that one had deserted one's allegiance to the Lord. There is no middle ground. Here, James returns to the same theme, but this time he expresses it in terms of friendship. His readers are offered a clear choice between friendship with the world and friendship with the Lord.[56]

That the world is evil and opposed to God has been previously emphasized.[57] Consequently, the person who wishes to remain true to the relationship with God has to separate from the world and its evil influences. The double-minded are those who do not wish to choose: they want to live by both standards. However, it is impossible to lead a life that is simultaneously inspired by God, on the one hand, and the devil on the other.

The reference to "Adulterers!" is very apt. In the world of Israel those who went astray and abandoned their relationship with God

---

Hartin (*James and the Q Sayings of Jesus*, 30) and Laws (*A Commentary on the Epistle of James*, 166–7) see 4:1-10 as an independent set of exhortations. Dibelius (*James*, 208), on the other hand, sees 4:1-10 as forming part of the wider section 3:13–4:12. Luke Timothy Johnson ("James 3:13–4:10 and the *topos* περὶ φθόνου," *Novum Testamentum* 25 [1983] 332; and *The Letter of James*, 268) views James 3:13–4:10 as belonging to one closely knit section.

[54] Johnson (*The Letter of James*, 276) characterizes this section as a *topos* in which James emulates the Hellenistic *topos* on envy.

[55] Further attention will be devoted to the contrast between friendship with God and friendship with the world in the section of chapter 5 entitled "A Spirituality of Friendship with God," p. 106.

[56] Johnson (*The Letter of James*, 288) illustrates how this language of friendship is so disconcerting given the background of its usage in the Hellenistic world.

[57] As expressed in the definition of religion in Jas 1:27, "Religion that is pure and undefiled before God, the Father, is this: to care for orphans and widows in their distress, and to keep oneself unstained by the world."

were referred to as adulterers. Adultery was used as a symbol, especially by the prophets, to indicate idolatry[58] and the turning away from allegiance to the one God. Those who are double-minded are indeed adulterous—instead of abiding in the exclusive relationship with the Lord, they have tried to embrace other opposing relationships. The ultimate consequence of a lifestyle led without wisdom is a friendship with the world, with those forces opposed to God.

Summary

The one "who is wise and understanding" (3:13) seeks God's friendship through a life inspired by the gift of God's wisdom. Friendship with God is another dimension of the experience of God's righteousness. Those who seek the friendship of God open their lives up to the influence of the perfect gift of wisdom from above that brings the reward of righteousness. James calls for total allegiance to the Lord, an allegiance that keeps one unstained from the world. The heart of the theological understanding of the letter of James is this: allegiance to God knows no compromise.

Important aspects of the notion of perfection have emerged from the examination of these four passages. The reflection on the nature of wisdom as God's gift is not undertaken in an abstract way. Rather, this reflection has urgent significance for the believer. The gift from above results in the rebirth of the believer: "so that we would become a kind of first fruits of his creatures" (1:18). This takes place through "the implanted word that has the power to save your souls" (1:21). The wisdom from above is a gift directed not just to a specific moral type of life; it also accomplishes regeneration and rebirth.[59]

This brings us to the heart of James's understanding of his call to perfection. This call is clearly not to a natural type of perfection, as was the case with the teaching of the Stoic philosophers. Perfection is the outcome of the gift of wisdom implanted within the souls of the believers. This implanted word changes one internally and has the power to save from death (1:21). As the first fruits of God's creatures, one is

---

[58] See, in particular, the prophet Hosea 1–3.

[59] Cargal (*Restoring the Diaspora*, 90) makes an important distinction between the way wisdom is seen to function in the Wisdom literature of the Old Testament and the way in which wisdom operates here in James. "The solution is indeed 'wisdom,' but this wisdom is not gained by 'enduring' and learning from God's 'reprimands.' Wisdom is 'generously' given by God to those who ask with 'faith.' It is a 'good and perfect gift,' 'implanted' within them and 'able to save [their] souls' from death."

reborn to a new existence which has already occurred. In this sense, the call to perfection is realized in the present. One is called to actualize this gift, implying that the eschatological has already begun: the gift of wisdom brings about regeneration and rebirth and makes of them "the first fruits of God's creatures" (1:18). God reconstitutes a people to conform to the image God had in the beginning. This gift of wisdom is identified as "the perfect gift" that renders us whole and complete, lacking nothing (1:5), restoring us as first fruits to the image of God's people. More especially, this completeness flowers forth in establishing right relations with God. Friendship with God is the privilege not just of a few, but the experience of all who receive God's gift of wisdom. This friendship embraces an enduring and exclusive relationship to the Lord.

Perfection and the Law

Besides wisdom, James connects perfection with another theme in his letter, namely the law. An examination of the significance of the law for James is vital because it gives a unique understanding to the nature of that community to whom James writes and shows how the law enables the community to maintain its identity as those who are called to perfection as God's twelve tribe kingdom.

James discusses the law in three passages 1:25; 2:8-12; and 4:11-12. The important question here is: What does James understand by "the law"? While James nowhere provides a clear and concise answer, the distinctive Christian-Jewish character and theology of the epistle argue for an interpretation that identifies the law with the biblical Torah that expresses God's will for God's people.[60]

The first reference to the law in the letter of James occurs in the context of the image of a mirror (1:23-25). This little parable provides the challenge to the believer not to act like those who look in a mirror and

---

[60] Robert W. Wall (*Community of the Wise: The Letter of James*, The New Testament in Context [Valley Forge, Pa.: Trinity Press International, 1997]) provides one of the more insightful discussions on the concept of law as Torah in James in his "Excursus: 'The Perfect Law of Liberty' (James 1:25)" (pp. 83–98). In deliberately using the term "Torah" in this context to reproduce James's term "law" (νόμος), I acknowledge my debt to Wall's insight.

The Torah is the expression of God's will and instruction for God's people as contained in the first five books of the Bible. It provides God's instruction and guidance for Israel. The Torah is the essential means by which they are constituted as God's people. It has a vital role to play in the socialization process of the people of Israel as a nation distinct from the other peoples of the world.

go away and forget what they look like. The believer looks into the mirror of the law and sees reflected there the way she or he is to act. Consequently, the law becomes a mirror reflecting the moral life of a believer. True to his Jewish background, James sees the biblical Torah as important for those who belong to his community. Further, for James the whole Torah demands adherence (2:10) since it expresses God's will for God's people (4:11-12).

Observance of the Torah is vital, for it provides the way James's community maintains its existence. The Torah acts as a guide giving direction to the members of the community. The aspect of the law that concerns James is not so much the ceremonial and ritual laws of the Torah, but the moral laws. As Robert Wall says:

> Especially important to James is the social role of the law, which draws moral boundaries around the faith community to keep it pure from outside contaminants (1:27), especially those that afflict the wealthy outsiders (2:1-7). The biblical Torah also provides the community's social boundaries, to facilitate acts of mercy toward its poor and powerless membership.[61]

The Torah provides a means of social identification for the members of James's community as the "twelve tribes in the Dispersion" (1:1). The Torah acts as a moral standard which identifies the way of life that separates this community from the wider society.

In describing the Torah, James uses a number of adjectives that continue to reflect his heritage and at the same time deepen his understanding of the Torah and the role that it plays within the socialization of his community. In this way the Torah contributes to the very nature and genre of the letter of James as a protreptic discourse.[62]

The Perfect Torah (1:25)

In reflecting on the relationship between wisdom and perfection in James, I argued for an association between the two concepts because the wise were considered to be "the perfect" in that their wisdom came from God and gave direction to their every action. Now, the same adjective "perfect" is identified with the Torah, thus providing a close

---

[61] Wall, *Community of the Wise*, 87.

[62] As noted in the previous chapter, one of the functions of protreptic discourse was to provide a means of social identification for those entering the community. The Torah exercises this function in the letter of James. The Torah gives direction for what they must do to identify with the community and to maintain their relationships with one another and with God.

connection between the Torah and wisdom. The book of Sirach was the first to identify the Torah as wisdom and in doing so expressed a long tradition that brought these themes together. For example, "Whoever fears the Lord will do this, / and whoever holds to the law will obtain wisdom" (Sir 15:1).[63]

One of the clearest illustrations of the connection between the Torah and wisdom occurs in 1 Kgs 2:1-9 where prior to his death David gives a farewell speech to his son, Solomon. In his advice, David urges Solomon to abide by the Torah: "Be strong, be courageous, and keep the charge of the LORD your God, walking in his ways and keeping his statutes, his commandments, his ordinances, and his testimonies, as it is written in the law of Moses" (2:2-3). Finally, David says that Solomon must act according to his wisdom (2:6) adding this theme of wisdom to that of obedience to the Torah. Later, in 1 Kgs 3:1-14, when Solomon is promised wisdom at the beginning of his rule, God instructs him: "If you will walk in my ways, keeping my statutes and my commandments, as your father David walked, then I will lengthen your life" (3:14). The gift of wisdom enables him to fulfill the Torah.

Like wisdom, the Torah is a perfect gift. The idea of the Torah leading to perfection is not new to the letter of James. James owes this thought to his Jewish heritage, for example, Ps 19:7-8:

> *The law of the LORD is perfect,* [64]
>   reviving the soul;
> the decrees of the LORD are sure,
>   making wise the simple;
> *the precepts of the LORD are right,*
>   rejoicing the heart,
> the commandment of the LORD is clear,
>   enlightening the eyes.

Here, the concepts of perfection and law unite.[65] A synonymous parallelism is established in the two verses with the phrases: "The law

---

[63] Sir 6:23-37 also speaks of the connection between wisdom and the observance of law: "Reflect on the statutes of the Lord, / and meditate at all times on his commandments. / It is he who will give insight to your mind, / and your desire for wisdom will be granted" (Sir 6:37). Sirach 6:31 identifies wisdom as "a splendid crown" again using language that is regal in its reference.

[64] Note that the Septuagint translates the Hebrew *"temimah"* (תמימה, "perfect") by "ἄμωμος" ("unblemished"). However, it still reproduces and connects to that conceptual meaning of perfection that expresses wholeness and completion.

[65] Another Psalm worth noting in this context is Psalm 119, a hymn of praise to the law of God. "Oh how I love your law! / It is my meditation all day long. / Your

of the LORD is perfect . . . the precepts of the LORD are right."[66] The adjectives "perfect" and "right" are synonymous. This conforms to ideas encountered before. Perfection is an aspect that calls for total allegiance to the Lord and expresses this allegiance in a right relationship with the Lord. In James, the Torah is perfect in that it is a gift from God, just as wisdom is. Observance of the Torah leads to the establishment of a wholehearted relationship with the Lord. But, it is especially on the community level that the Torah is seen to be perfect; it establishes the moral boundaries that are essential for the community to maintain itself as God's twelve tribe kingdom. The law establishes the identity of the members of this community in relationship with one another and in relationship with God as their creator.

The Law of Freedom (1:25)

The law of freedom is another description that James adds to his definition of the Torah. While it is true that this concept is found in Stoic writings and philosophy,[67] it is not necessary to resort to the Stoics to explain the origin and meaning of this expression. It is far more likely that James uses a phrase that is part of the common heritage and language of his age which the Stoics had also adopted and interpreted in their own way. Before resorting to a Stoic influence on James, one would have to find a concrete and specific connection between the two traditions. However, this is not possible. James does not betray any of the typical Stoic concepts such as the natural law or the specific Stoic attitude to ethics. Rather, he is at home, as I have consistently argued, within the world of Judaism.[68]

For James, then, "the perfect law, the law of liberty" gives expression to his understanding that the Torah furnishes the means of

---

commandment makes me wiser than my enemies, / for it is always with me" (Ps 119:97-98). The themes of wisdom and the law come together in this beautiful meditation on God's law.

[66] Here the word "right" translates the Hebrew *"yesarim"* (ישרים, Ps 19:9).

[67] Dibelius (*James*, 116–20) gives a very detailed examination of the phrase "the perfect law of freedom" and provides many examples from the world of the Stoics to illustrate their understanding of the freedom brought by the law. Dibelius sums up their position as follows: "But insofar as the true wisdom consists in obedience to that cosmic Reason which governs all and the neglect of which can only lead men into foolish and destructive conflicts, the ethical preaching of Stoicism (especially popular Stoicism) indeed demands an obedience which brings with it the state of utmost inner freedom" (116–7).

[68] See Davids, *The Epistle of James*, 99.

socialization for the community. The Torah provides guidelines on how their behavior should identify them as belonging to this particular society, created as God's first fruits. As such, the Torah liberates them from the world that is considered evil and destructive to God's new society. The Torah is perfect and frees the community to achieve its identity and true relationship with God and one another.

James demonstrates an attitude to the Torah that is distinctively different from that of Paul. For Paul, belief in Christ actually frees one from the law (Rom 6:15-23; 7:6–8:2; Gal 2:4; 4:21-31; 5:1, 13). Central to Paul's theology is the thesis of the opposition between two ways of life. One way is centered on faith in Jesus, the other is centered on observance of the Torah. While James is not entering the conflict in which Paul is involved,[69] he does show that he is heir to traditions within early Christianity that still preserve a very positive understanding to the Torah. The same positive approach to the Torah is identified by the Sermon on the Mount (Matt 5:17-20). Both James and the Jesus of the Sermon on the Mount portray the Torah as providing the social fabric of norms that enable those who belong to that new society to remain in relationship with one another and with God. In effect, James is saying to his community: this is who we are and the Torah frees us to maintain this relationship.

The Royal Law (2:8)

James 2:8-12 provides a further description of the Torah where the Torah is identified as "the royal law": "You do well if you really fulfill the royal law" (2:8). The term "law" and the verb "to fulfill, to bring to an end" (τελέω) forge a connection with the consideration of the law that has preceded in Jas 1:25. The law referred to here must be interpreted consistently, as it has been previously, as referring to the biblical Torah. The law is not to be restricted to just one command or instruction, otherwise the Greek word *"entole"* (ἐντολή, injunction or commandment) would have been used.[70]

The significance of the expression "the royal law" emerges when one sees it in the context of the entire passage (Jas 2:1-12). The royal (βασιλικὸν) law must refer back to Jas 2:5 where James uses similar vocabulary to speak about a kingdom: "Has not God chosen the poor in the world to be rich in faith and to be heirs of the kingdom [βασιλείας] that he has promised to those who love him?" The Torah is aptly de-

---

[69] See n. 85 below for a brief consideration of the relationship between James and Paul.

[70] See Davids, *The Epistle of James,* 114.

scribed as the "royal Torah," for it is the Torah that gives social identification to the members of the kingdom. The Torah is the means for the socialization of the group of believers whom James has described in 2:5 as members of the "kingdom."

Here, the letter of James reflects the theological horizons of the wisdom traditions with their view that the fulfillment of the law is the path to follow in order to attain perfection. The book of Wisdom develops this consistently:

> The beginning of wisdom is the most sincere desire for instruction,
> and concern for instruction is love of her,
> and love of her is the keeping of her laws,
> and giving heed to her laws is assurance of immortality,
> and immortality brings one near to God;
> so the desire for wisdom leads to a kingdom (6:17-20).

Love of wisdom is demonstrated through the keeping of her laws which leads to a relationship with God. This relationship brings immortality as well as the inheritance of a kingdom. This is similar to James's concept of fulfilling the "royal law" (2:8). By observing the requirements of the Torah, one inherits a kingdom and comes into a relationship with God.

The Law of Love (2:8)

James 2:8 goes on to argue that this royal Torah is encapsulated in the command of love, "You shall love your neighbor as yourself," which comes from Lev 19:18c.[71] The significance of Lev 19:18c appears from a close examination of its context within the entire chapter. Leviticus 19 is concerned with providing the social identification for the Israelites as to how they are to lead their lives according to the Torah. In the context of Leviticus 19, the author has given explicit attention to the poor: "You shall not render an unjust judgment; you shall not be partial to the poor or defer to the great" (Lev 19:15). James illustrated this very point in his parable on the discrimination that is made between rich and poor within the community. For James, this illustration is a way of showing that discrimination between rich and

---

[71] James also shows an influence and usage here of Leviticus 19. His statement, "You shall love your neighbor as yourself" (Jas 2:8), is a direct quotation of the Septuagint text of Lev 19:18c. Johnson has made a thorough and masterful examination of the use of Leviticus 19 in the Epistle of James (Luke Timothy Johnson, "The Use of Leviticus 19 in the Letter of James," *Journal of Biblical Literature* 101 [1982] 391–401).

poor cannot exist within that kingdom where God has chosen the poor to be its heirs (2:5). The law of love concerning one's neighbor is the embodiment of the royal Torah that the members of James's community are to embrace. Love of the poor is the identification marker that shows the type of society they are. For James, the notion of love is the heart of the Torah which the community is called to obey. Here, James is close to the teaching of Jesus which brought together the twofold expression of the law of love as embracing all the commands.[72]

The reference to the royal law and the law of love all occur within the context of this passage that opens with a reference to professing a faith in Jesus Christ[73] that demands a way of life opposed to every form of social discrimination.[74] The identifiable nature of this new society is its egalitarianism where no distinctions are made among its members.

Johnson[75] stresses that James's consideration of the law (2:8-12) is not a new topic, but one that must be seen to continue the discussion already initiated in 2:1-7 about the social equality that is demanded from members of this new society. The Torah provides the direction pointers for the way in which that society is to organize itself in remaining true to the image of this new kingdom of the poor that God has created.

The command to love one's neighbor operates as the embodiment of the Torah. It does not replace the Torah, but gives expression to the pulsating heart and direction of the Torah as God's will for God's people. Just as the law of love embraces the ethos of Jesus' moral teach-

---

[72] Practically every tradition in the New Testament gives expression to the law of love as the basic requirement for the lifestyle of the follower of Jesus. See, for example, Matt 19:19; 22:39; Mark 12:31; Luke 10:27; Rom 13:9; Gal 5:14; John 15:12; 1 John 3:11. Jesus raised the law of love to prime position in his ethical teaching as the way to sum up the entirety of the Torah. James shows he is heir to another tradition that gives a similar importance to the law of love.

[73] This is one of only two references to Jesus by name and title in this letter (1:1 and 2:1).

[74] I agree with Robert Wall's understanding of the appeal that is made to Jesus in this passage. It is not to Jesus as the new interpreter of the Torah, but rather as the one who lives out the Torah in an authentic and integral way in his life. As Wall says: "Again, I do not suppose that James's appeal to Jesus' faith in 2:1 is as authoritative interpreter of wisdom or a new Torah. Rather, the reference to 'the faith of our glorious Lord Jesus Christ' in 2:1 cues up the memory of his ministry among the poor [cf. Jas 2:2-4 par. Luke 14:7-14; Jas 2:5 par. Luke 6:20(-36)] alluded to in the following passage, a ministry that demonstrates his exemplary obedience to the 'royal Torah' of love (2:8)." (Wall, *Community of the Wise*, 96).

[75] Johnson, *The Letter of James*, 235.

ing, so too the law of love becomes for James the central focus expressing the royal Torah. The Torah is not limited to the law of love, but the law of love gives expression to the mind and heart of the lawgiver as contained in the Torah. James's thought parallels that of Leviticus 19. As part of the Torah, these various laws of Leviticus 19 are designed to express the way the members of the community of Israel are to lead their lives. These laws identify the members of the community and show how they are to maintain their relationship with one another and with God. At the heart of these instructions lies the command: "You shall love your neighbor as yourself." In like manner, James, following the example offered by Leviticus 19, calls on his readers to see the Torah as providing the signposts that they as a community must follow in order to function effectively as that new society of the poor living in relationship with one another and with God. The law of love, as in Lev 19:18c, provides the focal point for the way James's community must maintain its social fabric and identity.[76]

Summary

The law in James is the biblical Torah. The function of the Torah for James's community is a way to maintain the common moral and social boundaries that separate them from the wider world and at the same time orient them with a specific social concern for the poor within their midst. The law of love is at the heart of this Torah observance.

Faith Perfected through Works (2:22)

Wisdom as practical advice on how to lead one's life centers upon the conviction that faith must be demonstrated by actions. If it is to flower forth into action, faith has to be inspired by wisdom from above. Only through works, through action, can faith be brought to perfect completion: "You see that faith was active along with his works, and faith was brought to completion by the works" (2:22). This section (2:14-26) is a continuation of the thought expressed in 1:22-24. In the latter, James had expressed his basic theme: "Be doers of the word not hearers only." Now in 2:14-26 James continues this theme by developing the understanding of faith being put into action. Once again the structure of the letter of James is evident: a theme announced in the opening chapter (1:22-24) is developed further in the body of the letter (2:14-26).

---

[76] See Wall, *Community of the Wise,* 122.

James opens with a rhetorical question that goes to the heart of the issue: Can faith without works save you (2:14)? To illustrate this perspective James provides a hypothetical example (2:15-16): responding to the need of a brother or sister (their nakedness or lack of food) with words without actions is useless. He summarizes his argument with the statement: "So faith by itself, if it has no works, is dead" (2:17).[77]

James presents his argument in two parts (2:18-19 and 20-26). The first part of the argument (2:18-19) contrasts a faith "apart from works" and a "faith with works." The absurdity of a faith without works is forcefully illustrated by the idea that demons do believe in God as one.[78] The demons demonstrate the same basic Jewish belief in God as one which is made in the Jewish profession of faith: "Hear, O Israel: The LORD is our God, the LORD alone" (Deut 6:4). This very knowledge or understanding of God does not bring them salvation. Instead, it produces the opposite effect: they are afraid, "they shudder" (2:19). As Dibelius says: "Whoever acknowledges that the content of his faith is 'that God is one' [ὅτι εἷς ἐστιν ὁ θεός] must also admit that he shares this faith with the demons. Therefore, since the demons will be destroyed at the End, this faith is not a faith which 'can save.'"[79]

The second part of the argument is based upon two biblical examples, Abraham and Rahab (2:20-26). The example of Abraham argues the point that faith needs works to be a saving faith. "Was not our ancestor Abraham justified by works when he offered his son Isaac on the altar?" (2:21). The works that James mentions are plural and hence refer to more than just the binding of Isaac. Jewish tradition described many trials and tests to which Abraham was subjected. The greatest of these trials was the binding of his son Isaac: "Was not Abraham found faithful when tested, and it was reckoned to him as righteousness?" (1 Macc 2:52). The tradition that Abraham was tested by God developed into a teaching about the ten trials of Abraham.[80] Throughout all the trials, Abraham persevered and remained true to God. The idea of the trials of Abraham illustrates the opening theme of the letter which focused on the trials to which his readers were subjected. The point is clear: Abraham had faith; but he also had deeds that originated in this faith. Because of the actions that followed from his faith, God declared

---

[77] See Johnson *The Letter of James*, 246.

[78] In the Gospels, the demons acknowledge Jesus as the Son of God: For example, Mark 5:7: "What have you to do with me, Jesus, Son of the Most High God? I adjure you by God, do not torment me."

[79] Dibelius, *James*, 160.

[80] These ten trials are described in different ways in the Jewish tradition. See Dibelius's discussion in his excursus on "The Abraham Example" in *James*, 168–74.

Abraham as righteous (2:23). An important dimension of biblical perfection is that the believer is brought into a relationship with God which demands total allegiance to God. Abraham exemplifies this aspect of faith completely: through his belief in God his actions demonstrate the importance of God in his life and the relationship he enjoys with God.

"Faith was active along with his works, and faith was brought to completion [ἐτελειώθη] by the works" (2:22). The verb "to make perfect" (τελειόω) is introduced here. Abraham's actions bring his faith to completeness and maturity. This reflects the opening of the letter (1:2-4) which spoke about the testing of faith leading through endurance to perfection. The example of Abraham shows how his faith has come to perfection through patient endurance in the midst of many trials. This perfection embraces the idea of completeness and establishes a relationship with God as the only true God. James illustrates this relationship with God further through the reference to the fact that "he was called the friend of God" (2:23). Later, in 4:4 James shows that a choice is set before everyone: to choose between friendship with the world or friendship with God. Such a choice knows no compromise: it is either/or; it cannot be both. Abraham has shown that he has chosen to be a friend of God. The values that are indicative of this friendship guide his every action.

As a friend of God, Abraham sees the world through the eyes of God. He sees the world in the way in which God sees it. God is the giver of all good gifts, of every perfect gift (1:5, 17). Isaac was God's gift to Abraham and in offering Isaac on the altar Abraham was in effect returning God's gift. In this way, his faith was being perfected: he was brought into the right relationship with God.[81]

Rahab is the second of the biblical examples and is presented as a parallel to the example of Abraham.[82] Rahab is mentioned in only one verse and her significance is not developed. While her hospitality is praised, nothing is said of her faith. Different reasons are advanced to explain this, however it seems that James refers to her because she was an established figure in the Jewish tradition, often mentioned alongside Abraham in lists of people whose faith was worthy of note.[83] In referring to her hospitality, her faith can be deduced from the context. The example of Abraham shows that her works must have been inspired by her faith.[84] The book of Joshua singles out the profession of Rahab's faith: "The Lord your God is indeed God in heaven above and

[81] See Johnson, *The Letter of James*, 248.
[82] See Dibelius, *James*, 166.
[83] See Laws, *A Commentary on the Epistle of James*, 138.
[84] Ibid.

on earth below" (Josh 2:11). James shows in 2:25 that Rahab's faith is expressed in the act of welcoming and saving certain Israelites in Jericho, an action illustrating that she is "also justified by works" (2:25).

Finally, James repeats the thought expressed in 2:17 by means of a comparison: "For just as the body without the spirit is dead, so faith without works is also dead" (2:26). The dominating concern in this whole section is that faith without works is dead. The contrast is not between faith and works, but between "a faith that has no works" and "a faith with works."[85]

[85] Most treatments of this particular passage (2:14-26) focus on its relationship to the teaching of Paul, in particular Paul's consideration of justification through faith alone. More recent considerations, particularly commentaries such as those of Laws (*A Commentary on the Epistle of James*), Davids (*The Epistle of James*), and Johnson (*The Letter of James*), have rightly refused to read James through the eyes of Paul, but have argued that James must be read through his own eyes. "The important point is that one must not read this verse [namely, 2:24] with Pauline definitions in mind, but rather must allow James to speak out of his own background" (Davids, *The Epistle of James*, 132).

The following passages are the ones that bear some similarities. This gave rise to the thesis of an opposition between Paul and James.

> James 2:21: "Was not our ancestor Abraham justified *by works* when he offered his son Isaac on the altar?"
> Galatians 2:16: "Yet we know that a person is justified not *by the works of the law* but through faith in Jesus Christ. And we have come to believe in Christ Jesus, so that we might be justified by faith in Christ, and not by doing *the works of the law*, because no one will be justified *by the works of the law*."
>
> James 2:24: "You see that a person is justified *by works* and not by faith alone." Romans 3:28: "For we hold that a person is justified by faith apart from *works prescribed by the law*."

The closest similarity between James and Paul lies in the use of the word "works" (ἔργα). James uses it on two occasions in the above verses, while Paul uses it four times. However, Paul always uses the phrase "works of the law" (ἔργα νόμου). Despite the similarity, there is certainly a different thought intended in each of these uses. The works which Paul rejects are simply works of the law. James, on the other hand, is not referring to works of the law. He has in mind works as the outgrowth of faith. They are indeed works of faith. The conclusion arrived at by Ropes (*A Critical and Exegetical Commentary on the Epistle of St. James*, 35) is therefore unfounded, namely that James quotes Paul's formula exactly. James and Paul do in fact agree upon their notion of faith. It is actually their expression that is different. For James, faith, to be truly alive, must always express itself in action, in works. Whereas for Paul, faith must incorporate within its very notion an action of response. The example to which they both refer, namely Abraham, bears this out.

In reality, James and Paul clearly stress different aspects. Both converge in their notion of faith as being active, an idea common to first-century Judaism. As such,

Conclusion

"Faith perfected through works" is a phrase that summarizes well the message of the letter of James. Faith comes to completion through one's actions; and faith expresses the fullness of a righteous relationship with God through actions. James's practical wisdom advice is directed by the one aim of putting faith into action. For James, faith has first to be inspired by wisdom in order to flower forth in action. Wisdom is the fulcrum holding faith and works together, thereby producing a faith that is alive. The above examination has shown that perfection is an overarching theme giving direction to the thought and teaching of the entire letter. James's concept of perfection conforms to the threefold notion of perfection as expressed throughout the Jewish traditions and heritage to which the letter is heir. That traditional notion of perfection included wholeness, and a wholehearted dedication to the Lord that is expressed in obedience to the law.

Perfection as Wholeness

The idea of wholeness or completeness, whereby a being remains true to its original constitution, is the fundamental understanding of the meaning of perfection in James. Christian believers hold a special position in God's creation. Not only are they part of God's creation, but they are also the first fruits of God's creatures (1:18), God's perfect gift (1:17). As first fruits offered to God, they are without blemish, complete, whole. As the "twelve tribes in the Dispersion" they conform to the original constitution of God's people and are the first to begin the reconstitution of God's people. The community is now the reconstituted people of God, conforming to the image God had of God's people at the very beginning. The call to perfection is a call for the individuals to attain perfection as part of this reconstituted people of God.

When their faith is faced with trials and temptations, they are called to endure so that they may be perfect, lacking in nothing (1:5).

---

one does not have to argue for a dependence of thought of the one on the other. In accepting this fundamental insight of faith as the starting-point, James wishes to teach that faith is only really true if it demonstrates itself by means of works: it must bear fruit, must show what type of faith it is. Good works are essential and are a result of one's faith: they are works of faith. Paul, on the other hand, attacks those who say that faith is a result of works of the Law. For Paul, faith is a gift from God and no person can demand this gift as a result of producing good works of the Law.

Yet, should anything be lacking, God's gift of wisdom from above accomplishes their complete restoration.

The theme of perfection as overcoming whatever is lacking occurs in another passage in the context of the use of one's tongue (3:1-12). James acknowledges that as humans we all tend to fail in different ways, however, "Anyone who makes no mistakes in speaking is perfect . . ." (3:2). Those who can control their speech act according to the way in which God has created them in God's own likeness, and they use the gift of speech to bless God and one another (3:9-10).[86] Misuse of the gift of speech was also judged to be at the root of much evil in the world.[87]

Wholehearted Dedication to the Lord

Again it is God who has begun the work of re-creating the community as the "first fruits of God's creatures" (1:18). Together with the other members of the community they live in friendship with God as opposed to friendship with the world (4:4). As a community they are called: "Submit yourselves therefore to God. . . . Draw near to God, and he will draw near to you. . . . Humble yourselves before the Lord, and he will exalt you" (4:7-10). Perfection is what constitutes this total dependence upon God.

A righteous person leads a perfect relationship with God and with others. Central to the letter of James has been the call to be friends with God and to avoid friendship with the world. There is an exclusivity in the relationship to God. It is an "either/or" situation. No compromise is possible. Perfection lies in acknowledging dependence upon God

---

[86] In his criticism, James attacks those who misuse the gift of speech. Their use of the tongue does not conform to its nature and the way in which God has created it: "With it we bless the Lord and Father, and with it we curse those who are made in the likeness of God. From the same mouth come blessing and cursing. My brothers and sisters, this ought not to be so" (3:9-10).

[87] This was a very common teaching of the Greek moralists who tried to educate about the correct use of speech. See, especially, Plutarch, *The Education of Children*, 14: "The control of the tongue, then, still remains to be discussed of the topics I suggested. If anybody has the notion that this is a slight and insignificant matter he is far from the truth. For timely silence is a wise thing, and better than any speech . . . " (Frank Cole Babbitt, trans., *Plutarch's Moralia*, vol. 1 [Cambridge, Mass.: Harvard University Press, 1960] 50–1); and Plutarch, *Listening to Lectures*, 4: "But those who instantly interrupt with contradictions, neither hearing nor being heard, but talking while others talk, behave in an unseemly manner; whereas the man who has the habit of listening with restraint and respect, takes in and masters a useful discourse . . ." (Babbitt, *Plutarch's Moralia*, vol. 1, 214–5).

and in leading a life committed to this exclusive relationship. So much of the teaching of James revolves around this exclusive commitment: religion is defined as keeping "oneself unstained by the world" (1:27). Perfection is the theme that gives expression to this total dependence upon God. The image of the double-minded person gave full expression to the failure to give total allegiance to God (1:6-8). Control of the tongue (3:1-12) leads to perfection because the tongue acknowledges this relationship and praises God in whose likeness the believer has been created.

Perfection Leads to Obedience to the Law

In the Hebrew traditions, a person strove to fulfill the Torah accurately and completely. James remains true to these traditions. For him the Torah continues to remain valid. As the expression of God's will for God's people, the Torah is the essential means by which the socialization process continues. The members of James's community identify themselves with a specific way of acting based upon their interpretation of the Torah. At the same time, the Torah maintains the bonds between the members of the community and with God. The community to whom James writes is one that shares common bonds, a common way of life. The values of the community become the values of the individual—they are the values that separate them from the rest of the world. Just as Israel as a community strove to remain true to the Torah and to carry it out as fully as possible, so now in line with their heritage the new "twelve tribe kingdom" strives to fulfill the entirety of the law as epitomized by the traditions of Jesus in the law of love.

The ethos of the letter of James is one of perfection that gives direction to the paraenesis of the letter. The moral instructions are illustrations of how to live out that perfection in daily life: they give expression to what it means to be part of the twelve tribe kingdom. Perfection is a search for wholeness as a community in relationship with the one God who leads and guides them by the law. That perfection is attainable now "so that you may be mature and complete, lacking in nothing" (1:4). The wisdom advice provided by the letter promotes a way of life that strives for the socialization of a community of believers. The community instructions identify the members of the community as people whose faith informs every action. They are motivated not by the values of the wider society, but by those that come from their faith.

The ethics of the letter of James is not underpinned by the death and resurrection of Jesus, as is the case with Paul and the rest of the

New Testament writings. James is distinct in this regard. Like the Sayings Gospel Q, it is not the death and resurrection that provide the driving force for action, but the parousia, the coming of the Lord.[88] The parousia gives motivation to the ethics of James so that one will encounter the Judge standing at the doors, not in a fearful way, but in a joyful spirit, for there one is found to be perfect and there one attains "the crown of life" (1:12). Active endurance is the virtue characteristic of the life of James's community. By enduring in the midst of trials and sufferings, they preserve their relationship of friendship with God and ultimately are found to be perfect to the end.

The ethical perspective of perfection has been the focus of this chapter insofar as it gives meaning to the paraenetical teaching of the letter. The next chapter will show how this moral teaching is spelt out. The search will be for the spirituality of the letter of James as a practical guide for the believer's way of being in the world.

---

[88] See Jack Dean Kingsbury, *Jesus Christ in Matthew, Mark and Luke* (Philadelphia: Fortress Press, 1981) 5–7.

CHAPTER FIVE

A Spirituality of Authentic Perfection

What Constitutes Spirituality?

The letter of James takes seriously the call to put faith into action. The previous chapter has shown how the concept of perfection gave expression to the main spiritual impulses of the letter of James as it attempted to translate faith into action. This chapter examines these spiritual impulses to see how ultimately a spirituality emerges from the letter giving direction to the community to whom it is addressed.

The term "spirituality" is used ever more frequently in today's world. Every person, group, organization, religion claims to have their own spirituality. But, what exactly is meant by the term? The moment we try to define spirituality we encounter difficulties. We face the same problem when we try to define concepts such as love, truth, beauty, etc. We all have an understanding of what these concepts are, but when it comes to defining them we run out of words because they are intangible. A story, provided by Anthony de Mello, illustrates this elusive nature of spirituality:

> The disciples were absorbed in a discussion of Lao-tzu's dictum:
>   "Those who know do not say;
>   those who say do not know."
> When the Master entered, they asked him exactly what the words meant.
> Said the Master, "Which of you knows the fragrance of a rose?"
> All of them knew.
> Then he said, "Put it into words."
> All of them were silent.[1]

---

[1] Anthony de Mello, *One Minute Wisdom* (New York: Doubleday, 1986) 137. I am indebted to Ernest Kurtz and Katherine Ketcham, eds., *The Spirituality of Imperfection: Storytelling and the Journey to Wholeness* (New York: Bantam Books, 1992) 15, for drawing my attention to this story.

Spirituality, like the smell of a rose, is something with which we are all familiar, but somehow we struggle to give expression to it. For this reason, the term "spirituality" is used in a variety of ways. Some people view spirituality as referring to their religious experience that is expressed chiefly through their life of prayer. Others use the term to embrace their way of life as it incorporates their work, their interactions, and their relationships with others. Some more recent works on spirituality have defined it this way:

> Christian spirituality is the daily, communal, lived expression of one's ultimate beliefs characterized by openness to the self-transcending love of God, self, neighbor, and world through Jesus Christ and in the power of the Spirit. . . .[2]

> For Christians, [*spirituality*] means one's entire life as understood, felt, imagined, and decided upon in relationship to God, in Christ Jesus, empowered by the Spirit.[3]

The best way to define spirituality is to see it as a way of being in the world.[4] We lead our lives in particular ways that are influenced by our beliefs and ultimate convictions. Two poles operate in spirituality: our belief system and our actions. However, these do not exist independently of each other. The one flows from the other and back again. Our belief systems, our ultimate convictions, encapsulate our lives in such a way that to be true to ourselves we have to live out these convictions. Our actions, our way of life, give expression to who we are and to the principles of our convictions. This is expressed so well in the letter of James in the connection he forges between faith and works: "I by my works will show you my faith" (Jas 2:18). In a sense, the best way to characterize the spirituality of the letter of James is to label it "faith in action." Using this insight into spirituality, this study will examine how James presents this way of being in the world. Attention will be given to both aspects of spirituality, namely its belief

---

[2] Elizabeth Dreyer, "Christian Spirituality," *The Harper Collins Encyclopedia of Catholicism*, ed. Richard P. McBrien (New York: HarperCollins, 1995) 1216.

[3] Joann Wolski Conn, "Spirituality," *The New Dictionary of Theology*, ed. Joseph A. Komonchak, Mary Collins, and Dermot A. Lane (Wilmington, Del.: Michael Glazier, 1987) 972.

[4] As Kurtz and Ketcham (*The Spirituality of Imperfection*, 16) state: "Like 'love,' *spirituality* is a *way* that we 'be.' This *way of be-ing* defies definition and delineation; we cannot tie it up, in any way package it or enclose it. Elusive in the sense that it cannot be 'pinned down,' spirituality slips under and soars over efforts to capture it, to fence it in with words. Centuries of thought confirm that mere words can never induce the experience of spirituality."

system and the actions that it calls forth. James's understanding of perfection will be seen to characterize both dimensions of spirituality.

Faith

An investigation of the vocabulary in the letter shows that James is greatly concerned with faith. As has already been noted, the noun "faith" (πίστις) occurs sixteen times,[5] while the verb "to believe" (πιστεύω) occurs three times.[6] James's interest in faith is not in developing a theoretical understanding of faith, but rather in its practical workings.[7] As Hiebert says: "His purpose is practical rather than doctrinal."[8]

Many scholars question whether James does indeed have a belief system.[9] Those scholars, who categorize James as a paraenetic writing, deny that there is any overarching theme to the letter, let alone a pulsating heart that gives direction to the ethical instruction. For them paraenesis (defined as "moral exhortation, advice, instruction") is characterized by its being a presentation of a miscellaneous collection of exhortations. For example, Goodspeed defined James as "a handful of pearls, dropped one by one into the hearer's mind."[10] As I indicated in a previous chapter, the commentary of Martin Dibelius championed

---

[5] James 1:3, 6; 2:1, 5, 14 (twice), 17, 18 (three times), 20, 22 (twice), 24, 26; 5:15.

[6] 2:19 (twice) and 2:23.

[7] As R.C.H. Lenski (*The Interpretation of the Epistle to the Hebrews and of the Epistle of James* [Columbus, Ohio: Lutheran Book Concern, 1938] 538) says: "This entire epistle deals with *Christian faith,* and shows how this faith should be genuine, true, active, living, fruitful."

[8] D. Edmond Hiebert, "The Unifying Theme of the Epistle of James," *Bibliotheca Sacra* 135 (1978) 223.

[9] Sophie Laws ("The Doctrinal Basis for the Ethics of James," *Studia Evangelica,* vol. 7, Papers Presented to the Fifth International Congress on Biblical Studies Held at Oxford, 1973 [Berlin: Akademie-Verlag, 1982] 299–305) raises the issue of the doctrinal or theological foundation for the ethics in James: "It is similarly generally accepted that the epistle of James, while containing a proportionately greater amount of ethical material than any other document in the New Testament, is doctrinally the most attenuated: the faith would seem to have insufficient content to characterize the ethics" (p. 299). Ultimately, she sees James's ethics being founded upon the idea of the imitation of God: "What I have suggested so far is that the ways in which James speaks of God and of human conduct are so similar as to be likely to be connected, and that the connection would most easily be understood in terms of human conduct being ideally the imitation of God" (p. 304).

[10] Edgar J. Goodspeed, *An Introduction to the New Testament* (Chicago: University of Chicago Press, 1937) 290.

this approach to the letter of James.[11] Dibelius classified the letter of James as paraenetic literature whereby "the admonitions in Jas do not apply to a single audience and a single set of circumstances; *it is not possible to construct a single frame into which they will all fit.*"[12] This view led Dibelius to deny further that it was possible to construct any theological framework for the letter of James.[13] Instead, I have argued that the category of protreptic discourse, rather than that of paraenesis, applies to the letter of James.[14] As such, it does betray a uniformity of perspective whereby it wishes to provide a sustained argument to convince the readers. It presents a vision that projects a lifestyle for its readers to embrace. In the ethical advice one is able to see reflected an inner belief system that gives meaning to the ethical argumentation.[15] The belief system of James emerges only indirectly from the letter. Yet, it does provide a way of being in the world, giving expression to the way in which believers are called upon to lead their lives. This can be seen from an examination of the way in which the concept of God operates within the letter of James.

[11] See my discussion on the notion of paraenesis in the section of chapter 3 entitled "The Paraenetic or Protreptic Nature of This Wisdom Advice," p. 45. Martin Dibelius's commentary on James, *Der Brief des Jakobus,* originally appeared in German in September 1920. After ten editions, it was reprinted in June 1964 as a revised edition by Heinrich Greeven. This revised edition was translated into English by Fortress Press as part of their Hermeneia Series in 1975 (Martin Dibelius, *Der Brief des Jakobus,* rev. ed. [Göttingen: Vandenhoeck und Ruprecht, 1964]; English translation: *James: A Commentary on the Epistle of James,* trans. Michael A. Williams [Philadelphia: Fortress Press, 1975]).

[12] Dibelius, *James,* 11.

[13] As Dibelius (*James,* 47–8) says: "The manner in which Jas is tied so closely to the tradition makes it difficult to recognize what he himself believed, intended and taught. . . . But given this presupposition, one must also forego any attempt to bring into relief a 'theology' of Jas."

[14] See the section in chapter 3 entitled, "The Paraenetic or Protreptic Nature of This Wisdom Advice," p. 45.

[15] As Luke Timothy Johnson ("Friendship with the World/Friendship with God: A Study of Discipleship in James," *Discipleship in the New Testament,* ed. Fernando F. Segovia [Philadelphia: Fortress Press, 1985] 167) says: "It would be inappropriate to deny that part of Dibelius's great achievement which was correct, but it is important to recognize that wisdom writings, too, have their own inner coherence and that it is hazardous to move rapidly from general characterization to exegetical fiat."

God

James bases his exhortations on theological principles rather than christological ones.[16] While the name of Jesus is used directly only twice in the letter (at 1:1 and 2:1), the reference to God is far more frequent: sixteen times with "God" ([ὁ] θεός),[17] eight times with "Lord" (κύριος),[18] and three times with "Father" (πατήρ).[19] God is also referred to as "lawgiver and judge" (νομοθέτης καὶ κριτής, 4:12).

James is clearly monotheistic.[20] Even demons acknowledge God by the traditional Jewish confession that God is one: "You believe that God is one; you do well. Even the demons believe—and shudder" (2:19). This provides a very clear definition of God showing that God desires exclusive loyalty. Just as in the Israelite profession of faith, the Shema Israel, the Israelites are called to give exclusive worship and allegiance to their God: "Hear O Israel: The LORD is our God, the LORD alone . . ." (Deut 6:4). James expresses this theme through the opposites that he contrasts: ". . . friendship with the world is enmity with God. Therefore whoever wishes to be a friend of the world becomes an enemy of God" (Jas 4:4).

James upholds the basic goodness of God. For this reason, James warns against wrong ideas concerning God's relationship to evil and sin. "No one, when tempted, should say: 'I am being tempted by God'; for God cannot be tempted by evil and he himself tempts no one" (Jas 1:13). Two aspects of James's understanding of God are important. First, "God cannot be tempted by evil."[21] Second, God tempts no one. The logic of this is clear: God cannot be the author of temptation since God cannot be tempted by evil. As Laws explains: "What must be understood is that temptation is an impulse to sin, and since God is not

---

[16] See Luke Timothy Johnson, *The Letter of James: A New Translation with Introduction and Commentary*, The Anchor Bible 37A (New York: Doubleday, 1995) 164.

[17] Jas 1:1, 5, 13 (twice), 20, 27; 2:5, 19, 23 (twice); 3:9; 4:4 (twice), 6, 7, 8.

[18] Jas 1:7; 4:10, 15; 5:4, 10, 11, 14, 15.

[19] Jas 1:17, 27; 3:9.

[20] See Franz Mussner, *Der Jakobusbrief: Auslegung*, 4th ed. (Freiburg: Herder, 1981) 97.

[21] The word ἀπείραστος ("not tempted") appears in the New Testament only at this place. It is also virtually unknown in Hellenistic or classic Greek. For this reason its meaning is disputed. However, as Sophie Laws (*A Commentary on the Epistle of James*, Black's New Testament Commentaries [London: Black, 1980] 70–1) indicates, James has an affinity for playing with words. Consequently, one perhaps should see this term as a word coined by James in the context where he has been using the word πειρασμός (1:12) to show that God is "not tempted" by evil.

susceptible to any such desire for evil he cannot be seen as desiring that it be brought about in man."[22] Briefly stated, God has nothing to do with temptation or with evil.[23] The clarity and directness of this statement about God's nature as regards temptation is unique in the Bible.

For James, evil and sin are clear realities in the world, which are totally opposed to God. Nowhere does James speculate on the origin of evil, but what he is clear about is God's distinction from and opposition to evil. In effect, James makes a plea for a correct understanding of God.[24] As Frank Stagg says: "Against this false theology he sets forth a strong theodicy, negatively denying that God is behind temptation and sin and positively tracing all good to God."[25]

James's basic understanding of God is that God is transcendent and gives all gifts to those who ask. In particular, God is the source of all wisdom (1:5). This conforms to the Jewish notion of wisdom where God alone is wise. To become wise one must turn to God to receive that wisdom from God.

God's gift of wisdom is given "generously and ungrudgingly" (ἁπλῶς καὶ μὴ ὀνειδίζοντος) (1:5). The adverb "generously" (ἁπλῶς) appears only here in the New Testament. In this context of God's action of giving, it takes on the meaning of God giving single-mindedly or without reservation.[26] Added to this is the adverb "ungrudgingly" (ὀνειδίζοντος) (Jas 1:5). The *Sentences of Sextus* (339) contain a saying that comes close to James's meaning: "Whoever combines gift-giving with reproach acts insultingly."[27] Any gift that bears with it some insult is regarded as being less than generous.[28] The giving of God is totally generous and unconditional.

---

[22] Laws, *A Commentary on the Epistle of James*, 71.

[23] Johnson (*The Letter of James*, 193) draws attention to the closeness in thought to the *Sentences of Sextus:* "The sentiment here is crisply stated by *Sentences of Sextus*, 30: God is 'the wise light that has no room for its opposite.'"

[24] See Mussner, *Der Jakobusbrief*, 90.

[25] Frank Stagg, "Exegetical Themes in James 1 and 2," *Review and Expositor* 4:66 (1969) 395–6.

[26] See James B. Adamson, *James, the Man and His Message* (Grand Rapids, Mich.: Eerdmans, 1989) 349. Johnson (*The Letter of James*, 179) translates it as "simply," while Mussner (*Der Jakobusbrief*, 97) understands it as "without reckoning."

[27] *The Sentences of Sextus* are a collection of 451 sayings compiled in Egypt in the second century C.E. The translation used here is from Richard A. Edwards and Robert A. Wild, eds. and trans., *The Sentences of Sextus* (Chico, Calif.: Scholars Press, 1981) 57, # 339.

[28] See Johnson, *The Letter of James*, 180.

James returns to the theme of God, the generous giver, later at 4:6. "But he gives all the more grace; therefore it says, / 'God opposes the proud, / but gives grace to the humble.'" This is the only place in the letter where James uses the noun "grace" (χάρις), probably because of the quotation from Prov 3:34. God is seen to give "all the more grace" which illustrates again God's generosity: God gives to humanity that which surpasses what they deserve or hope for. The Lord is defined as being "compassionate and merciful" (Jas 5:11).[29] This understanding of God gives direction to the spirituality James calls for in his readers. Since God is the giver of every perfect gift, everything that one lacks is to be sought from God. It is a call for a dependency upon God, who will bring one to perfection.

Not only is God the giver of wisdom, but God is also the source of every "perfect gift" in that every gift from God is complete and total, lacking in nothing. God is "the Father of lights" (1:17), the creator of the world, the creator of the stars and sun. God is also the re-creator in the order of the spirit. Through the power of God the believer becomes "a kind of first fruits of his creatures" (1:18). Another important consideration of God as the perfect giver of gifts is that there is no exclusivity in God's generosity. As "the Father of lights" God appears in the role of creator of the universe.[30] Every gift traces its origin back to God as creator. The image of God as the "Father of lights" stresses the nature of God as the one whose generosity never wavers or changes. This is indicated through the further addition to the explanation "with whom there is no variation of shadow due to change" (1:17). The passage intends to contrast God's steadfastness with the changing nature of creation.[31] This must be read in its context where God's generosity is once more the center of attention. God's act of giving never fluctuates, but continues steadfastly. As Ropes expresses it:

> The affirmation is that to send good gifts belongs to God's unvarying nature. In this he is unlike the sun, which sends now the full light of noon, now the dimness of twilight, and which at night sends no light at all. God's light ever shines; from him proceeds no turning shadow.[32]

---

[29] See Mussner, *Der Jakobusbrief*, 97–8.

[30] The plural "of lights" clearly suggests "the heavenly lights," and in particular the sun and the moon. In this way, God is seen as the creator of the heavenly bodies. This conforms to the basic Israelite belief that God is the creator of the heavenly bodies: Gen 1:14-16; Ps 36:9.

[31] See Johnson, *The Letter of James*, 196–7.

[32] James H. Ropes, *A Critical and Exegetical Commentary on the Epistle of St. James* (Edinburgh: T. and T. Clark, [1916] 1978) 161.

The Imitation of God

Since we are created in "the likeness of God" (3:9), the implication is that we must act like God.[33] The concept of the imitation of the actions of God is not directly stated, but it can be deduced from the arguments of the letter. God is one and single minded, which is contrasted to the person who is double-minded: "For the doubter, being double-minded and unstable in every way, must not expect to receive anything from the Lord" (1:7-8). On the one hand, there is God who is one and single-minded, and on the other there is the doubter, who is fickle and double-minded.[34] The ethical implications of the belief that God is one demands that the human person act to maintain this unity.[35]

God desires social justice.[36] The definition of religion calls one to act in like manner by showing concern for the marginalized of society, the widow and orphan (1:27). God hates social injustice (5:1-6). Moreover, the understanding that "the Lord is compassionate and merciful" (5:11) especially forms the basis for this imitation of God. In implementing the perfect law of love, one is in fact emulating the God of mercy and compassion. Every ethical theme bears out this stamp of love, compassion, and mercy: concern for the poor (5:1-6), the avoidance of discrimination (2:1-13), not speaking evil of others (4:11), concern for the sick (5:13-18), the bringing back of a wandering brother (5:19-20). The very definition of religion expresses this concern well: "Religion that is pure and undefiled before God, the Father, is this: to care for orphans and widows in their distress, and to keep oneself un-

---

[33] It is debated whether the notion of the imitation of God *(imitatio Dei)* is a theme found in the Hebrew writings. There are a few passages where the imitation of God seems to underlie an Old Testament passage, but on deeper examination one discovers that this is not the case. This is an aspect that I will examine later in greater length in ch. 6. In particular, I shall examine the connections between James's understanding of perfection and that of Matthew in the Sermon on the Mount and what this implies for the notion of the imitation of God. See Laws, *A Commentary on the Epistle of James*, 30–2.

[34] Ibid., 30. I think, however, that this insight can be further strengthened by referring to the description James gives of the human person as created in "the likeness of God" (3:9).

[35] As Adamson *(James, the Man and His Message*, 349) says: "True, these two ideas, the human disunity and the unity of God, are never spelled out; rather, they are set in implicit contrast (see Dt 6:4f.). 'That God is one' (2:19) is expressly affirmed and its ethical implications are everywhere implied in the Epistle (e.g., 4:2)."

[36] See Mussner, *Der Jakobusbrief*, 98.

stained by the world" (1:27). Consequently, these actions imitate the actions of God.

Again, the notion of perfection plays a key role in the definition of God and the way one is called to be in the world. Every perfect gift comes from God, and the perfect law of love is the principle guiding every action. If we are created in the likeness of God, does this not reflect the statement in Matthew's Gospel: "Be perfect, therefore, as your heavenly Father is perfect" (5:48)?[37] In all that God does, God acts with integrity: God is consistent in all God's actions and is true to the very nature of God. The believer is called upon to act in like manner.

Faith in Action

The letter of James does not set out to present a theological treatise or philosophical argument. Its main concern is with the life of the community and with the socialization of the members of the community. He wishes to remind his readers how this life of faith is lived out in reality in the context of their society as the "twelve tribes in the Dispersion." The advice provides them with the way they can identify and maintain their communal bonds. The actions to which believers are called stem from their faith perspective, from their understanding of who the God is in whom they believe.[38] There is, as has been shown, a theological underpinning for the lifestyle that they adopt and their way of being in the world. The values that come from their faith motivate the community. Among the spiritual values and impulses of the community to whom James writes the following are certainly the most significant.

A Spirituality of Integrity

If spirituality is, as we have defined it, a way of being in the world, then one of the key characteristics of this way of life is to be a person or a community of integrity. This concept of integrity comes close to expressing the concept of perfection which, it has been argued, gives direction to all the ethical instructions of the letter. The Shorter Oxford English Dictionary defines "integrity" this way:

> 1. The condition of having no part or element wanting; unbroken state; material wholeness, completeness, entirety. 2. Unimpaired or uncorrupted state; original perfect condition; soundness . . . . 3. a. Innocence,

---

[37] See ch. 6.

[38] See Laws, "The Doctrinal Basis for the Ethics of James," 299–305.

> sinlessness . . . . b. Soundness of moral principle; the character of un-
> corrupted virtue; uprightness, honesty, sincerity . . . .[39]

This definition of integrity comes very close to the notion of perfection as has been described in previous chapters. In the threefold description of perfection, it is particularly the first (and original biblical)
notion that the concept of integrity captures, namely: the idea of wholeness whereby a being remains true to its original constitution.[40] Again,
the direction of integrity includes both a personal and a community
dimension.[41] How does James envisage that his readers should
demonstrate that they are persons of integrity?

Integrity Comes from Suffering (1:2-4)

Contrary to the experience of the world today, James, in agreement
with other early Christian traditions,[42] does not view suffering as
something to be avoided, but as something to be embraced. James 1:2-
4, as we have seen,[43] argues that the attitude of endurance, or of active
resistance in the midst of suffering, leads one to perfection: ". . . let
endurance have its full effect, so that you may be mature and complete, lacking in nothing." The example of Job, to which James refers
at the end of the letter (5:11), shows how this works itself out in practice. Job struggles with his suffering. He struggles to make sense of it
and to integrate it into his life and his worldview. He never gives up
his quest for meaning. Ultimately, in his suffering he experiences the

---

[39] *The Shorter Oxford English Dictionary on Historical Principles,* 3d ed., prepared
by William Little, H. W. Fowler, and Jessie Coulson; rev. and ed. C. T. Onions, completely reset with etymologies revised by G.W.S. Friedrichsen and with revised addenda, vol. 1 (Oxford: Clarendon Press, 1986) 1088.

[40] Both Laws ("Trial and Integrity," *A Commentary on the Epistle of James,* 49–61)
and Elsa Tamez ("Integrity," *The Scandalous Message of James: Faith without Works Is
Dead* [New York: Crossroad, 1992] 56–69) make this association between integrity
and perfection.

[41] My aim here is not to repeat the extensive consideration already given to the
notion of perfection. Instead, I draw from that consideration to show how it
emerges as a guiding, spiritual principle for the personal lives of the believers as
well as of the community, making sense for their way of being in the world.

[42] See the Synoptic traditions: "If any want to become my followers, let them
deny themselves and take up their cross and follow me. For those who want to
save their life will lose it, and those who lose their life for my sake, and for the sake
of the gospel, will save it" (Mark 8:34-35). See as well Paul's account of his sufferings on behalf of Christ and the gospel message in 2 Cor 11:16-29.

[43] See the section of chapter 4 entitled "Testing of Faith Leads to Perfection (1:2-4),"
p. 60.

mystery of God and abandons himself to that mystery. In this way, he attains his perfection and is finally restored to wholeness, and completeness, to the person he was in the beginning. In the same way all believers are perfected through endurance in the midst of suffering. Through persistent struggles with trials and difficulties and by never giving up, they grow in awareness of who they are and of their relationships with others and with God. Their faith acquires a wholeness and completeness through their allegiance to God and to one another.

As Dibelius observes,[44] James ends this consideration with an exhortation. He does not conclude his discussion with a statement, but rather with an appeal to his readers: "Let what endurance produces be perfected, and thus you will be perfected."[45] "Become a person of integrity," is what James in effect is saying. But, James's appeal is not to be read in an individualistic mode. James began this section with an address to all the members of the community, "my brothers and sisters" (ἀδελφοί μου [1:2]). In the call to be perfect, to be a people of integrity, they are called to integrate within themselves and their community their understanding of the trials and sufferings they are experiencing. As a group, they are all enduring and experiencing similar sufferings, and the call is also to be aware of the similar situations of one another—not just to be focused upon oneself.[46] Through common experiences of testing and suffering the socialization process continues. They discover their unity and identity with the other members of the community. Their endurance ultimately shows that as a community they are faithful to and trust in the God who called them.[47] God's "perfect work" ultimately results in a community of integrity that has conformed to God's plan for them. They become a community that is the "first fruits of God's creatures" (1:18).[48]

Integrity Demands Single-Mindedness

To maintain the integrity of their society and community requires God's action. Hence, James instructs them to pray (1:5-6), especially

---

[44] Dibelius, *James,* 74.

[45] This is the way in which Dibelius (*James,* 74) paraphrases the verse.

[46] As Tamez (*The Scandalous Message of James,* 58) expresses it: "Integralness, then, does not occur only in the body of one member of the community, but rather in the entire community, in which everyone becomes sensitive to the pain of the others within the community and outside of it. To feel what the other feels is truly a gift that should cause us to rejoice."

[47] Johnson (*The Letter of James,* 184) emphasizes this community dimension of this fidelity to God.

[48] Ibid.

for wisdom when they know that this integrity is lacking. Those who have not achieved complete integrity are told to pray for the wisdom that will guide them to become people of integrity. Of greatest concern to James are those who are "double-minded" (δίψυχος [1:7-8]) because they have deserted their firm adherence both to God and to the community. A complete person, someone with integrity, is the exact opposite of the divided person.[49] God is single-minded in God's attitude to humanity, and it is this same attitude that God requests of humanity. A double-minded person has a destructive influence on the community. People who vacillate find it difficult to choose between friendship with the world and friendship with God (Jas 4:4). Not only are they divided within themselves, but they are also a force for splitting the community apart.[50] The community's very existence is based upon people who have a like-minded faith perspective that gives direction to their way of being in the world.[51] One bears a responsibility for the members of the community. This explains the letter's concluding concern for bringing back a wandering member of the community (5:19-20). The whole letter strives to uphold the integrity of the community and every member in it. All the advice that is given reflects this basic concern that they remain a people of integrity.

A spirituality of integrity leads people to strive to be single-minded in motivation and allegiance to God and to one another. This has community consequences. People who are not divided within themselves do not divide the community. Because they are inspired by the same perspective and outlook on reality, such members of the community work together to foster and maintain their bonds with God and with the community. James's ethical instructions provide the guidelines on how the community should function. Every individual contributes to the identity and integrity of the community by honoring those values that maintain the nature of the community.

Integrity in Speech

The theme of speech runs throughout the letter of James. As is his custom in the opening chapter, James introduces this theme (1:19) and then returns to it on three occasions in the body of the letter (3:1-12; 4:11-12; and 5:12). James 1:19 first announces this theme: "You must understand this, my beloved: let everyone be quick to listen, slow to speak, slow to anger." Then, a few verses later he says: "If any think

---

[49] See Laws, *A Commentary on the Epistle of James*, 54.
[50] See Johnson, *The Letter of James*, 184.
[51] See Tamez, *The Scandalous Message of James*, 60.

they are religious, and do not bridle their tongues but deceive their hearts, their religion is worthless" (1:26).

James 3:1-12 returns to the theme of speech by presenting what could be called a "lament to the tongue." The image of "bridling the tongue" (found previously at 1:26) gives James the opportunity to develop a reflection on the control of speech (3:1-12). James acknowledges that we all make many mistakes, but it is the person who makes no mistakes in speaking who is perfect (3:2). A person who does not err or sin in speech is truly a person of integrity.[52] By failing to control one's speech, the integrity of the person is undermined. The same tongue which blesses God also curses fellow humans who are created in God's image (3:9-10). Once again, people who act in this manner fluctuate like the waves that are tossed by the wind (1:6). Such people are not people of integrity nor of single-mindedness. They do not value God's creation, and they do not treat God's creatures (created in God's likeness) with the respect they are due.

The real evil of the duplicity of the tongue emerges through the identification of the source from which that evil stems: "The tongue is placed among our members as a world of iniquity; it stains the whole body, sets on fire the cycle of nature, and is itself set on fire by hell" (3:6). Evil inspires the tongue, an evil that comes from the very source of all evil, Gehenna. Once again, we encounter the worldview of James where one is called to lead life according to the outlook and vision of God as opposed to that which comes from the world. It is a further illustration of the dichotomy between friendship with God and friendship with the world. To attempt to embrace both is not an option. One's double-mannered speech shows that one is acting like the double-minded person. This demonstrates an abandonment of God's vision and a capitulation to the allure of the manners of the world.[53] Integrity demands attention be paid to speech, for it demonstrates a basic commitment either to God or to the world.

James returns to the theme of speech on two further occasions: Jas 4:11-12 and 5:12. In 4:11-12, James urges his community not to speak evil of one another. By doing so, they are in fact breaking the law, the Torah, and in this way they set themselves above the Torah, making themselves judges, deciding what laws to obey and what to ignore.[54]

---

[52] This truly conforms to the definition of integrity given above: the person is complete and whole who shows soundness of character and is sincere and honest in what is said.

[53] See Johnson, *The Letter of James*, 265.

[54] Ibid., 293.

No society can function if its members lay claim to pick and choose among the various laws directing the good of the society.

In Jas 5:12, the issue of honesty in speech emerges. The simplicity of one's speech is stressed in opposition to any form of duplicity whereby one professes to take an oath and yet either does not carry it out or, perhaps worse, tries to manipulate the divine for one's own ends. Honesty in speech is required in order to uphold all relationships within the community. The very life of any society depends on its members telling the truth. Honesty in speech affects both the integrity of the individual as well as the integrity of the community. It is vital if the socialization process within James's community is to continue. By witnessing to the truth, the individual identifies with the values of the society and ensures that the bonds within the community are upheld.

A Spirituality of Friendship with God

Among the spiritual values that James's community is encouraged to embrace is the call to maintain friendship with God. This expresses the very identity of the community. James 4:4 is one of the central verses to the entire letter; it captures the main thrust of the letter's central argument.[55] "Adulterers! Do you not know that friendship with the world is enmity with God? Therefore whoever wishes to be a friend of the world becomes an enemy of God." The letter of James is characterized by a dualism of contrasts: for example, those who act with wisdom and those who act without wisdom (3:13-18), the rich and the poor (5:1-6), etc. This verse presents another series of contrasts: friendship with the world and friendship with God. However, this set of contrasts is undoubtedly the most fundamental of all, giving rise to all the other contrasts.[56]

James 4:4 fits into a context that has numerous disputed questions.[57] Probably the most discussed issue has been that of the unity of the verses making up the context. Attention has already been given to

---

[55] Ibid., 84–7.

[56] Timothy B. Cargal (*Restoring the Diaspora: Discursive Structure and Purpose in the Epistle of James,* SBL Dissertation Series 144 [Atlanta: Scholars Press, 1993] 229–32) gives a whole list of "oppositions of actions," although he does not list Jas 4:4 among them. Johnson (*The Letter of James,* 14, n. 45) also notes this discrepancy.

[57] Johnson ("Friendship with the World/Friendship with God," 168) notes three basic issues: "Questions concerning the proper text, the meaning of words and the way to punctuate abound."

the divided opinions of scholars regarding the unity of 4:1-10 with the preceding verses 3:13-18.[58] While I hold that Jas 4:1-10 is an independent set of exhortations,[59] nevertheless these verses take up the issues of peace with which 3:18 ended. James 4:1 begins by asking the question: "Those conflicts and disputes among you, where do they come from?" This leads James to give attention to failings within the community and to issue an appeal to overcome these failings.[60] The failings that Jas 4:1-10 has in mind are of a specific type. They touch the essence of the community's relationship with and commitment to God. The very harsh phrase "Adulterers" (μοιχαλίδες) with which Jas 4:4 opens shows the seriousness of breaking this commitment. Using prophetic language,[61] James continues the metaphor that the Old Testament prophets used by applying the marriage image to the relationship between God and Israel. When this covenant bond was broken, the image of adultery was used to represent the rupture of Israel's relationship with God (Hosea 1–3). James sees some members of the community to whom he writes having ruptured the bond God had established with them.[62] This breaking of the divine covenant is a very serious charge leveled against them.[63]

Friendship with the World Is Enmity with God

Herein lies the heart of the accusation. Friendship with God and friendship with the world cannot coexist. The same contrast is expressed in a different way by Matthew's Gospel when Jesus says: "You

[58] See the section of chapter 4 entitled "Friendship with God (4:4)," p. 75.

[59] Patrick J. Hartin, *James and the Q Sayings of Jesus*, JSNTS 47 (Sheffield: Sheffield Academic Press, 1991) 30.

[60] See Patrick J. Hartin, "James: A New Testament Wisdom Writing and Its Relationship to Q," D.Th. Dissertation (University of South Africa: Pretoria, 1988) 380.

[61] Dibelius (*James*, 220) argues that the use of the feminine gender here comes from its connection with the metaphor of the "sacred marriage" that was used to explain the relationship between Israel and God.

[62] This is the commonly held interpretation. The marriage image is taken over by the Christian community from the Old Testament metaphor of Israel as the "faithful/unfaithful wife" of God. The Christian community then applied it to their own relationship with God. See, for example, Cargal, *Restoring the Diaspora*, 159–60; Joseph Chaine, *L'Epître de Saint Jacques* (Paris: J. Gabalda et Fils, 1927) 99–100; Peter H. Davids, *The Epistle of James: A Commentary on the Greek Text* (Grand Rapids, Mich.: Paternoster Press, 1982) 160–1; Dibelius, *James*, 220.

[63] As Johnson ("Friendship with the World/Friendship with God," 170) says: "The first part of this verse places us rather squarely, therefore, in the context of idolatry and covenant fidelity."

cannot serve God and wealth" (6:24).[64] God demands total allegiance. A divided allegiance is not possible. This reflects again the image of the "double-minded person" James used at the opening of the letter (1:7-8). James reinforces this image again at 4:8: "Cleanse your hands, you sinners, and purify your hearts, you double-minded." There is no possibility of divided loyalty: there is a clear cut choice between friendship with God or with the world. However, to explain James's intent regarding these differing friendships, an understanding of the meaning of the terms "friendship" and "the world" in the context of James's society must be gained.

Friendship: One of the more serious difficulties with this term "friendship" is that people mistakenly understand it as having the meaning our modern world associates with it. Nothing could be further from the truth. In our society, the term "friend" can be used to embrace almost any acquaintance. However, this was not the situation in the ancient world. The notion of friendship in the ancient world was much more restrictive and had a deeper application. In ancient Greek and Roman societies, friendship was greatly prized and formed the topic of much reflection and discussion in the writings of their great thinkers.[65] Aristotle devoted much attention to the nature of friendship showing the different levels of friendship. He argued that true friendship was difficult to attain, and that it was not possible to maintain friendship with many people at the same time.[66]

---

[64] 1 John 2:15-17 has a close parallel to the thought of James: "Do not love the world or the things in the world. The love of the Father is not in those who love the world; for all that is in the world—the desire of the flesh, the desire of the eyes, the pride in riches—comes not from the Father but from the world. And the world and its desire are passing away, but those who do the will of God live forever." While John uses the image of the love of God, James has used the image of friendship. Both, however, attribute to "desire" the cause for the shift in allegiance to God.

[65] Note the saying of Epicurus ("Principal Doctrines," 27): "Of all the things which wisdom acquires to produce the blessedness of the complete life, far the greatest is the possession of friendship" (Cyril Bailey, *Epicurus: The Extant Remains with Short Critical Apparatus, Translation and Notes* [Oxford: Clarendon Press, 1926] 100–1).

[66] Aristotle, *Nicomachean Ethics,* Book 8. Aristotle distinguished three kinds of friendship based either on utility or pleasure or virtue. For Aristotle, friendship based on virtue was the more perfect friendship: "The friendship of the good and of those who are alike in virtue is perfect; for these wish good to one another in the same way, so far forth as they are good; . . . their friendship, therefore, continues as long as they are good; and virtue is a permanent thing" (Book 8, 3.7). This type of friendship is very rare because much time is needed to be invested in the relationship: "Moreover, it requires time and long acquaintance, for, according to the

The real significance of friendship was that friends looked on reality in the same way. They had the same shared vision and embraced
the same values.[67] The two were bonded together in a very special
way, being united above all on the spiritual level. Euripides, a Greek
dramatist of the fifth century B.C.E., used the phrase "one soul" to define friends.[68] Cicero, the great Roman orator and statesman of the first
century B.C.E., called a friend a "second self."[69] In particular, in his
work *On Friendship,* Cicero had Laelius describe his renowned friendship with Scipio in this way: ". . . we shared the one element indis-
pensable to friendship, a complete agreement in aims, ambitions, and
attitudes."[70] Cicero developed this thought further when he wrote:
"Now friendship is just this and nothing else: complete sympathy in
all matters of importance, plus goodwill and affection, and I am inclined to think that with the exception of wisdom, the gods have given
nothing finer to men than this."[71]

This understanding of friendship in the context of the ancient
world helps to explain why friendship with the world cannot coexist
with the friendship of God. God and the world are diametrically opposed to each other, and it is not possible to share two completely

---

proverb, it is impossible for men to know one another before they have eaten a
stated quantity of salt together. . . . This species of friendship, therefore, both with
respect to time and everything else, is perfect" (Book 8, 3.9–10). Aristotle went on
to argue that since true friendship was limited to a few, it was impossible to be
friends with many people at the same time: "For it would seem impossible to be a
very strong friend to many. . . . So it seems to be in real fact: for in friendship between companions, many do not become friends; and those friendships which are
most celebrated, are between two only" (Book 9, 10.5–6). (R. W. Browne, trans., *The
Nicomachean Ethics of Aristotle* [London: Henry G. Bohn, 1950]).

   [67] See Johnson, *The Letter of James,* 288.

   [68] Euripides, *Orestes,* 1046: "Dearest, who bear'st a name desirable and sweet on
sister's lips!—one soul with mine! [καὶ ψυχὴν μίαν]" (Arthur S. Way, trans., *Euripides,* vol. 2, The Loeb Classical Library [Cambridge, Mass.: Harvard University
Press, 1939] 216–7).

   [69] Cicero, *On Friendship,* 21.80: "For a man loves himself not in order to exact
from himself some pay for his affection, but simply because every man is by his
very nature dear to himself. Unless this same principle is transferred to friendship,
a man will never find a true friend, for the true friend is, so to speak, a second self"
(Frank O. Copley, trans., *Cicero: On Old Age and On Friendship* [Ann Arbor: University of Michigan Press, 1967] 80).

   [70] Cicero, *On Friendship,* 4.15 (translation from Copley, *Cicero,* 52).

   [71] Cicero, *On Friendship,* 6.20 (translation from Copley, *Cicero,* 54–5). Among the
characteristics of friendship, Cicero lists steadfastness, loyalty, and trust as the
most basic qualities of all (Cicero, *On Friendship,* 18.65).

contrary visions. As a friend of God, one shares the same vision, the same values God has—one trusts God fully and sees reality as God would.

The world: The Scriptures use the term "world" (κόσμος) in many different and divergent ways. Basically, three different understandings emerge from the New Testament writings: (1) the universe or the totality of all created beings, (2) the earth or world where human history unfolds, (3) unredeemed creation that is opposed to God.[72]

The term "world" (κόσμος) occurs five times in James (1:27; 2:5; 3:6; 4:4 [twice]) and its meaning generally conforms to the third usage noted above, namely that which is opposed to God. This understanding emerges clearly from James 1:27 where religion is defined in terms of keeping "oneself unstained by the world." Here the world and God are opposed to each other: the values of God and the world are incompatible. Again the negative association of the term is found in 3:6 where James describes the tongue as "a world of iniquity": the world is the cause of evil. In 2:5, James again uses the term in an interesting way: "Has not God chosen the poor in the world to be rich in faith and to be heirs of the kingdom that he has promised to those who love him?" In the midst of unredeemed creation stand the poor who acknowledge their need of God's transforming power. Consequently, the world and the kingdom are contrasted to each other, and God's activity brings the poor from the world into God's kingdom.

This understanding of the world represents a vision, or an outlook, that is completely at odds with that of God. It implies that friendship with the world would result in living by the standards of the world and adopting a hostile attitude to God. By means of this contrast, James calls on his readers to exercise their freedom and to make a choice either for or against God.[73] Once again, this duality reflects the distinction between two contrasting societies: the one that embraces the values of God and the other that adopts the values of the world. James's nature as a protreptic discourse is very evident here whereby the readers are urged to embrace a new social order. At the center of this new order is God. This relationship of friendship with God is the motivating force inspiring all the members of this new society to identify with one another in embracing these values that come from God and to maintain their bonds with one another.

---

[72] Hermann Sasse, "κόσμος," *Theological Dictionary of the New Testament*, vol. 3, ed. Gerhard Kittel, trans. Geoffrey W. Bromiley (Grand Rapids, Mich.: Eerdmans, 1972) 868–98.

[73] See Johnson, "Friendship with the World/Friendship with God," 174–5.

A Spirituality that Embraces God's Vision

The spirituality of friendship with God is basic to the perspective of the whole letter. The readers must have their outlook on reality imprinted by the vision of God; they must make the perspective, the values, the vision of God their own. This in turn demands a specific approach to the society outside, namely the world. They are to avoid as harmful and deadly whatever does not share that vision and is in effect opposed to God. Ultimately, it results in choosing. To which society does one belong? Does one live life according to God's standards or the world's standards?

This is undoubtedly the pulsating heart of the spirituality of James. God's vision must be that of the believer. No compromise is possible. The letter of James exhorts Christians to reaffirm their commitment to God and to guard against compromising God's values in place of the world's values. A single-minded devotion to God must dominate the lives of believers and give direction to their every action. In all the specific advice that James gives throughout the letter, he is urging his readers to see reality as God would. In this way, one becomes a friend of God as Abraham did (2:23).

The consequence of leading a life in friendship with God means that one belongs to a community, to a society, very different from the wider world. Those who belong to this community embrace values and norms that set them apart from the wider society and distinguish them from the society in which they live. Friendship with God gives an identity to all those who have embraced the same way of living out their faith. As observed before, this does not mean that the community retreats from the world. The community continues to live in the world, but its values help maintain their identity as God's friends. All the members of this new society share this same ethos and strive to uphold it in all their actions. The spirituality of the letter of James presents a way of being in the world, whereby its community still lives in the world, but their values do not receive their inspiration from the world.

A Spirituality Permeated by Love of Neighbor

James's spirituality is also stamped by a specific attitude to the law, which James understands as the biblical Torah that embodies God's will for God's people.[74] Here, I intend to develop that teaching briefly as part of the overall vision of the spirituality of this letter. The way of

---

[74] See the section of chapter 4 entitled "Perfection and the Law," p. 78.

life that James presents for his readers embraces the Torah as the corner-stone. The call to be a friend of God demands that one appropriate God's vision and God's standards as one's own. As such, the Torah be-comes the fundamental vision directing the lives of all believers. It has that important social function of giving direction to the members of James's community and setting the boundaries distinguishing the com-munity of James from the outside world.[75]

The community of James must show consistency between their faith, their vision, and the way this faith-vision is put into action. James's discussion on the fulfillment of the law in 2:8-13 continues the argument he began in 2:1-7. In the opening of the chapter (2:1), James was above all concerned that actions be consistent with faith. To show partiality or to discriminate against certain members of the commu-nity was inconsistent with a profession of faith in Jesus as Lord. Faith in Jesus should bring a specific vision of reality which demands that one take seriously God's choice of the poor to become members of God's kingdom (2:5). This should lead believers to use God's outlook as the way they act—they are to treat the poor consistently in the same way that God treats them.[76]

Like Jesus, James proclaims the importance of love of neighbor (2:8).[77] For James, the command to love one's neighbor becomes the embodiment of the Torah. It does not replace the Torah, but gives ex-pression to the very essence and heart of the Torah.

James upholds the wholeness and the completeness of the Torah (2:10). At the same time, James makes no mention of circumcision or of the food, the ceremonial and ritual laws of Judaism.[78] This shows that when James speaks about keeping "the whole law" (2:10) he has in mind the essence of the Torah that provides a moral vision for those who accept God's will for them.

---

[75] Robert W. Wall, *Community of the Wise: The Letter of James*, The New Testament in Context (Valley Forge, Pa.: Trinity Press International, 1997) 87.

[76] Johnson (*The Letter of James*, 235) rightly notes that James's concern here is not to deliver a philosophical consideration on the nature of law, but to stress the unity between what one believes and what one does.

[77] See Matt 22:34-40; Mark 12:28-34; Luke 10:25-28. Almost all the other New Testament traditions (Rom 13:9; Gal 5:14; John 15:12; 1 John 3:11) make reference to the law of love.

James 2:8 speaks about the one aspect of the law of love, namely "love of one's neighbor." However, the other aspect of the law of love, namely love of God, is re-ferred to in the previous section in Jas 2:5. This is a further argument for consider-ing Jas 2:1-7 and 8-13 together.

[78] Wall, *Community of the Wise*, 87.

James's spirituality does not countenance a legalism with regard to the law.[79] When James says, "For whoever keeps the whole law but fails in one point has become accountable for all of it" (2:10), he is not advocating a legalistic fulfillment of the minute stipulations of laws. Rather, James is concerned with upholding a specific attitude to the Torah. If the Torah is God's vision for humanity, one is to embrace that vision in its entirety through the observance of its commands. One infraction of the command to love one's neighbor, such as showing partiality or discriminating (2:9), is in effect an illustration that one is not upholding the heart of the Torah. James gives further illustrations of how one cannot say one is keeping the Torah if one violates one aspect of its vision, for example, by committing adultery or murder.[80] James once again endorses a perspective that he emphasizes throughout the letter: consistency between word and action. In Jas 1:21, believers receive the "implanted word" which gives direction to their action, whereby they become doers of the word and not just hearers (1:22). The stress in James on keeping the entire law is "not on the observance of a sum total of minutiae, but on the maintenance of a complete integrity of word and deed."[81]

God's perspective should be the driving force for the implementation of the law of love. The final verse of this section echoes this: "For judgment will be without mercy to anyone who has shown no mercy; mercy triumphs over judgment" (2:13). God is a God of mercy and compassion (5:11). This is the stance that God adopts toward creation, and if one claims to be a friend of God, one must embrace the same stance. This is a further appeal to take God as the model for action and to view reality with the same vision and outlook as God. The focus here rests on the community's way of action, rather than on God's. One of the concrete ways in which the community fails to show mercy would be to fail to show concern for the poor. Those who follow the vision of God in their lives show a concern for the poor, for they are "heirs of the kingdom" (2:5) and become participants in the divine mercy.[82] Love of neighbor is the essential signpost directing the com-

---

[79] See Laws (*A Commentary on the Epistle of James*, 112–3), who says that at first sight James seems to be asserting the Jewish approach of a legalistic fulfillment of law. But, she goes on to show that this is not exactly the approach James intends.

[80] See Johnson, *The Letter of James*, 236.

[81] Laws, *A Commentary on the Epistle of James*, 116.

[82] As Cargal (*Restoring the Diaspora*, 118) says: "Those who have been transformed by the 'implanted word' will desire to 'perform mercy' just as God does by identifying with and 'choosing the poor with respect to the world.'"

munity to the way they are to fulfill God's will and function as the new society of the poor in relationship with God and one another.

A Spirituality of the Poor

James introduces the theme of rich and poor in his introductory chapter (1:9-11) and returns to that theme again in the body of the letter (2:1-7 and 5:1-6).[83] An examination of this theme shows a definite spirituality arising with regards to poverty and a consequent attitude adopted toward the rich. Attention will be given to each of these passages to discover James's spirituality of the poor.

The Reversal of Situations (1:9-11)

James draws a sharp contrast between rich and poor. In the society of God's kingdom, their situations are reversed. God will raise up the poor to the exalted status as Christians despite their lowly status in the world. On the other hand, the rich may appear important now because of their wealth, but ultimately God will bring them low. This envisages a reversal of situations and positions.[84]

In recent studies, particularly of an anthropological or sociological nature, poverty has been shown to be above all a matter of what affects one's honor.[85] Besides an obvious lack of economic resources, poverty was the result of a lack of status, a lack of power, that would ultimately result in oppression. This is particularly evident in this passage which concerns the status of the rich versus the poor. Their roles will ultimately be reversed, because the poor will find their status, honor, and power in God, who will raise them up.

[83] As I have argued (*James and the Q Sayings of Jesus,* 26–35), all the themes addressed in the body of the letter are introduced first of all in the opening chapter. See also Fred O. Francis, "The Form and Function of the Opening and Closing Paragraphs of James and 1 John," *Zeitschrift für die neutestamentliche Wissenschaft und die Kunde der älteren Kirche* 61 (1970) 110–26.

[84] This reversal of situations is without doubt a typically Christian perspective. In particular, the Gospel of Luke gives great weight to it, as is evident in the Magnificat (Luke 1:46-56; see especially, "He has brought down the powerful from their thrones, and lifted up the lowly" [Luke 1:52]) and in the beatitudes (Luke 6:20-26), especially the contrast between the poor and the rich: "Blessed are you who are poor, for yours is the kingdom of God . . . " (Luke 6:20) and "But woe to you who are rich, for you have received your consolation" (Luke 6:24).

[85] See Bruce J. Malina, "Wealth and Poverty in the New Testament and Its World," *Interpretation* 41 (1987) 354–67.

I would agree with Maynard-Reid, who argues that the discussion as to the "Christian" status of the rich is not the main issue.[86] James is more interested in presenting a contrast between the future status of the poor and rich. The contrast of humiliation-exaltation dominates (1:9-11)[87] and envisages a reversal of situations. When will this reversal take place? Most scholars see this referring to the future eschatological age when God's judgment on the world is meted out (5:1-6).[88] Maynard-Reid, on the other hand, opts for a perspective that includes both a present and a future reversal.[89] Again, I think the issue of when is not the main focus of James in this passage. He is again ambiguous. Certainly, from the references to reversal of fortunes elsewhere in this letter (especially 5:1-6), James has in mind the future eschatological end-time intervention of God in judgment.

Central here is the wisdom instruction contrasting two different responses to reality. The rich trust and glory in themselves, their achievements, and the world. The poor, having nothing within themselves to trust, place their confidence in God and in God's kingdom. Those who have adopted God's outlook on reality will ultimately be exalted, for they exalt in God. The others, who exalt at present in the world, will experience a reversal and will be humbled. This is the same contrast

---

[86] Pedrito U. Maynard-Reid (*Poverty and Wealth in James* [Maryknoll, N.Y.: Orbis Books, 1987] 44) says: "The issue of whether the rich person is a Christian or not actually has no relevancy in this context. Nowhere in the epistle does James make such a distinction clear. To him all rich fall in the same category."

The section here (1:9-11) is somewhat ambiguous. Scholars argue extensively about whether the rich person is a brother or not. The two ways of interpreting actually revolve around whether the word "brother" (ἀδελφός) should be attributed to the rich (ὁ πλούσιος).

Those who add the word "brother" to "the rich" interpret the rich as members of James's community. This means that the lowliness that the rich now experience is a result of becoming members of the Christian community and they are able to glory and boast in this new status (see Ropes, *A Critical and Exegetical Commentary on the Epistle of St. James*, 145–6; and Davids, *The Epistle of James*, 76–7).

Those who interpret it without the reference to "brother" understand that the rich are not "Christians"—they are not members of the community of James. James is then writing ironically (see Dibelius, *James*, 85).

[87] See Mussner, *Die Jakobusbrief*, 76.

[88] See, for example, Dibelius, *James*, 84; Davids, *The Epistle of James*, 77–8; Mussner, *Der Jakobusbrief*, 76; all of whom interpret the references in an eschatological end time perspective.

[89] As Maynard-Reid (*Poverty and Wealth in James*, 45) says: "In this pericope the time of the reversal is not made clear, and it is possible that he had in mind a present reversal as well as an eschatological reversal."

that James draws later between friendship with the world versus friendship with God (4:4).

The spiritual principle underlining this passage is James's conviction that the vision of the world is very different from that of God.[90] The worldly outlook gives importance to status, position, and wealth; the vision of God shows that such things are fleeting. Those who trust in God will be the most blessed. James presents a spirituality that calls on the reader to see reality through the eyes of God. The poor are those truly blessed for they are promised an eternal reversal of their situation and will enjoy an exaltation with the Lord forever.

Discrimination against the Poor (2:1-7)

James argues that faith in Jesus excludes every form of discrimination (2:1). By means of a graphic example, which is much like one of Jesus' parables, James portrays a gathering of the assembly (συναγωγή). The use of this term in this particular context has provoked much discussion among scholars because it can be used to refer to many aspects of the gathered assembly. More recently, scholars, following the evidence amassed by Roy Bowen Ward,[91] understand this assembly as a judicial court.[92] The rabbinical evidence shows very striking examples of similarities between James's descriptions here and those found in rabbinic documents describing judicial assemblies.[93] Consequently, it seems best to understand the assembly as a judicial assembly. The two people who enter are strangers to the process (2:2).[94] The point of the illustration focuses on the way the assembly reacts to these two strangers: the one who is poor is made to stand or to sit at the judges' feet, while the one who is finely dressed and is obviously rich is given a seat (2:3). Surely the poor person has been discriminated against in favor of the rich person (2:4)!

James contrasts this treatment of the poor to the way God views the poor: "Has not God chosen the poor in the world to be rich in faith and to be heirs of the kingdom that he has promised to those who love

---

[90] See Johnson, *The Letter of James*, 191.

[91] Roy Bowen Ward, "Partiality in the Assembly: James 2:2-4," *Harvard Theological Review* 62 (1969) 87–97.

[92] See Davids, *The Epistle of James*, 109; Johnson, *The Letter of James*, 227; Maynard-Reid, *Poverty and Wealth in James*, 57.

[93] Maynard-Reid (*Poverty and Wealth in James*, 57) gives two very good examples from Rabbinic texts to illustrate the similarities with James.

[94] The New Testament gives a number of examples where synagogues are presumed to hold a judicial function: For example, the flogging in the synagogue implies the carrying out of a judicial decision (Matt 10:17; 23:34; Mark 13:9; Acts 26:11).

him?" (2:5). James had indicated this same perspective earlier (1:9-11) in referring to God's reversal of the lot of the poor. God's viewpoint is to bring the poor into God's kingdom: hence members of James's community must take God's viewpoint as their own and treat the poor in a similar way. Their community must create that new society where the poor will be at home.

Further, the rich are rejected by God for three reasons: they oppress the members of the community,[95] they take them to court, and, finally, they blaspheme (2:6-7). Here again the honor-shame dimension is evident. Because the rich possess honor, they have status and power. Instead of using their power positively to protect the powerless, they exercise their positions for their own ends. Obviously, this is an abuse of their power. However, the final charge against them is the worst of all: they blaspheme. The name of Jesus is insulted whenever those who bear his name are insulted (Acts 5:41).[96] By bringing the poor to court, the rich insult not just the poor, but the name of Jesus that was invoked over them in baptism. By showing preference for the rich, the community was in fact supporting blasphemers.[97] These are the very reasons why the community should not show deference for the rich over the poor. As Maynard-Reid says: "According to James, then, anyone who honors the rich at the expense of the poor discriminates against those whom God has elected."[98]

James's example is specific and graphic. However, it also serves as a universal example for people of every age concerning two issues: the value of the poor in God's eyes and the avoidance of any form of discrimination. Once again, James portrays a spirituality that is founded on the way God looks upon reality. As a friend of God (4:4), one sees reality in the same way, with the same perspective. The poor are special in God's sight. God has made a special choice in favor of the poor.[99] This is a message that the Scriptures teach with unanimity.[100] To be a member of James's community means that one must value the

---

[95] "Is it not the rich who oppress you?" (ὑμεῖς δὲ ἠτιμάσατε τὸν πτωχόν) (Jas 2:6). The term "oppress" (ἀτιμάω) is also used in the Septuagint for the oppression of the poor (Prov 14:21; Sir 10:23).

[96] See Laws, *A Commentary on the Epistle of James,* 105–6.

[97] See Davids, *The Epistle of James,* 114.

[98] Maynard-Reid, *Poverty and Wealth in James,* 67.

[99] The Psalms in particular proclaim God's care for the poor and afflicted. See, for example, Pss 9:12, 18; 10:2, 9; 12:5; 14:6; 34:6; 35:10; 40:17; 68:10; 70:5; 82:1-4; 107:41; 109:31; 113:7-8; 140:12.

[100] The prophets especially champion the poor and oppressed because they are seen as God's chosen ones (see, for example, Amos 2:6-7; 5:10-13; 8:4-6).

poor in exactly the same way. Inconsistency between faith and actions is not acceptable.

The example also provides a challenge to abstain from any discrimination in their actions. Discrimination is inconsistent with their faith in Jesus Christ (2:1). While this example focuses on showing partiality for the rich over the poor, it is not meant to be restricted to this category. James calls for a spirituality that takes seriously the equality of all people and demands that their actions bear this out. Inspired by their faith in Jesus (2:1) and their friendship with God (4:4), the members of the community are called to act in a way that demonstrates their equality.[101]

The Arrogance of the Rich (5:1-6)

In this final passage that gives attention to the rich and the poor, James (5:1-6) presents a picture of the arrogance of the rich that lies in stark contrast to the attitude of James's community toward the poor. The style of this section, particularly in describing the last times, resembles that of the Old Testament prophets.[102] For example, the call to the rich to "weep and wail" (5:1) and to prepare themselves for a "day of slaughter" is reminiscent of Jer 25:34:

> Wail, you shepherds, and cry out;
>   roll in ashes, you lords of the flock,
> for the days of your slaughter have come—and your dispersions,
>   and you shall fall like a choice vessel.

These descriptions of woes against the rich were also very common in intertestamental literature, for example, 1 Enoch: "Woe to you, fools, for you shall perish through your folly! You do not listen to the wise, and you shall not receive good things. And now do know that you are ready for the day of destruction."[103] As with the prophets,[104] the woes

---

[101] It also shows the type of life they are to avoid.

[102] James's language and imagery is indebted to that of the Old Testament prophets, but he shows little development or reflection upon it. This supports an early date for the letter of James.

[103] 1 Enoch 98:9-10 in E. Isaac, trans., "1 Enoch," *The Old Testament Pseudepigrapha,* vol. 1, ed. James H. Charlesworth (Garden City, N.Y.: Doubleday, 1983) 79. See the entire section referred to as the letter of Enoch 92–105. For a discussion on the significance of 1 Enoch for the letter of James see Patrick J. Hartin, "'Who Is Wise and Understanding among You?' (James 3:13): An Analysis of Wisdom, Eschatology and Apocalypticism in the Epistle of James," *Society of Biblical Literature Seminar Papers* (Atlanta: Scholars Press, 1996) 483–503.

[104] See, for example, the oracles of Isaiah, such as those addressed against Egypt (Isaiah 19) and against Babylon, Edom, Arabia (Isaiah 21).

addressed against the rich do not really intend to convert the rich to change their ways of life. Their purpose is more for the community: to offer them comfort by showing them what will happen to the rich who had oppressed them. As with the great prophets of Israel's past, James is concerned about social injustices, and he sees God intervening to right these injustices.[105]

Using the rich as a foil to comfort his community, James describes the fate of their wealth: "Your riches have rotted, and your clothes are moth-eaten. Your gold and silver have rusted, and their rust will be evidence against you, and it will eat your flesh like fire" (5:2-3). What is condemned is not the fact that they possess wealth, but rather the evil ways in which they have accumulated this wealth: through fraud (5:4) and murder (5:6). The irony of this whole description lies in the great reversal that the rich will encounter. In the final days, everything they trusted in will be destroyed: it will be for them a "day of slaughter" (5:5). Ironically, they are the ones who have killed to get what they wanted, yet on the last days they will be the ones who are slaughtered.

This example of the rich illustrates well what James said earlier: "Those conflicts and disputes among you; where do they come from? Do they not come from your cravings that are at war within you?" (4:1). The avarice and greed of the wealthy ("their cravings") led them "to murder the righteous one" (5:6). They placed their trust in the world and sought friendship with the world. This brought them alienation from God and led them to produce more and more evil. In illustrating what is in store for the rich, James shows the ultimate consequences of sharing the vision of the world in opposition to sharing God's vision. They will experience that God's power is truly a reality, and God will ultimately reverse the situations of injustice.[106] Once again the honor-shame tension reveals itself. The wealth the rich amass is largely due to the power and status they possess. The end of time will bring about a reversal of fortunes because their power will be no more. When faced with the power of the Lord of hosts, their power fades into insignificance.

---

[105] A graphic example of the social injustices and the punishment that is to befall the perpetrators can be seen in the prophet Amos: "Thus says the LORD: / For three transgressions of Israel, / and for four, I will not revoke the punishment; / because they sell the righteous for silver, / and the needy for a pair of sandals— / they who trample the head of the poor into the dust of the earth, / and push the afflicted out of the way" (Amos 2:6-7).

[106] See Johnson, *The Letter of James*, 309.

A Spirituality of Social Concern

The above detailed examination reveals a spirituality that is on the one hand opposed to friendship with the world, while on the other hand is actively concerned about the social evils of the world. In considering the end of this age and its destruction, the words of James are meant for this present world.[107] James's spirituality is concerned with the social situations of our world and he speaks out (as the prophets of the Old Testament did) in condemnation. He identifies areas where injustices have occurred (fraud of wages due to daily laborers in 5:4 and murdering the righteous in 5:6) and calls for their reversal.

Yet, it is more than a spirituality of condemnation—it is also a spirituality of comfort for the poor and the oppressed. The tirade against the rich, as was indicated, was not issued to provoke the rich to change their ways. Instead, it was to give the poor and the oppressed the assurance that God was on their side, and that ultimately God would right the injustices. Faced with unjust situations the poor are urged to cry out to the Lord who hears their cries: "The cries of the harvesters have reached the ears of the Lord of hosts" (Jas 5:4).[108] The very fact that they cry out and their voices are heard shows that they have a right to make their injustices known to the Lord and to call upon him to redress their wrongs. This spirituality allows believers to place themselves in God's care. They do not resort to violence; rather, they leave the redress to the Lord.

In 1:27, James had defined religion as having a social concern: "Religion that is pure and undefiled before God, the Father, is this: to care for orphans and widows in their distress, and to keep oneself unstained by the world." In this understanding, religion calls upon believers to have a concern for the powerless ones in society. The terms "widow and orphan" were the traditional designations in the Old Testament for those who were powerless to ensure their own survival (Deut 24:17). They were part of that group in society who experienced

---

[107] See Maynard-Reid, *Poverty and Wealth in James*, 97.

[108] This is very similar to the cries for vengeance in the book of Revelation. For example, "You are just, O Holy One, who are and were, / for you have judged these things; / because they shed the blood of saints and prophets, / you have given them blood to drink. / It is what they deserve!" (Rev 16:5-6). The Psalms show that the poor and afflicted can call upon the Lord for help, simply because they are poor: "Incline your ear, O LORD, and answer me, / for I am poor and needy. / Preserve my life, for I am devoted to you; / save your servant who trusts in you. / You are my God; be gracious to me, O Lord, / for to you do I cry all day long" (Ps 86:1-2).

poverty in reality. In the passages that consider the rich and the poor, James shows how one's religion embraces this social concern. A religion that does not have such concerns cannot be called "religion." James shows how close he is to the vision Jesus expressed throughout his life. The final parable in Matthew's Gospel articulates this social dimension of religion (25:31-46). Jesus sees that at the end of time a distinction is made between those who have embraced a concern for the needs of others and those who have not. Only those with a social awareness will be admitted to his kingdom: "Truly I tell you, just as you did it to one of the least of these who are members of my family, you did it to me" (Matt 25:40).

This concern for the poor is a further demonstration of James's message concerning faith expressed in action. James's spirituality continues to call for adopting God's vision to give direction to one's whole existence. The Scriptures present God's vision as a basic "option for the poor."[109] James has embraced this option for the poor, and throughout the letter appeals to his community to make that choice their own. The social equality of all members of James's community is what distinguishes them from the wider world. Concern for the poor and equality for all are significant social boundary markers that identify James's community. James endorses a spirituality that takes seriously the equality of all and that avoids every form of discrimination.

A Spirituality of Prayer

Prayer is an essential dimension for every community of faith, touching the lives both of the individual and of the community. It is one concrete way in which the individual's life meshes with that of the community, hence it is fitting that James returns to this several times throughout this brief letter. He adopts a specific attitude toward prayer, which contributes to the spirituality of this letter.

Erroneous Prayer

True prayer should be offered in faith with the confidence that "God, who gives to all generously and ungrudgingly," will grant the request (1:5). Contrasted with this is the double-minded person who cannot pray in the correct manner because of a divided heart. This reveals a divided allegiance and loyalty. Once again the tension between being friends with God and friends with the world is evident. Only those who are sincerely friends of God are able to pray correctly, for in

---

[109] See Maynard-Reid, *Poverty and Wealth in James*, 98.

the act of prayer one worships God and acknowledges one's relationship with God. True prayer demonstrates absolute confidence and trust in God, and as such it exercises a marked influence on the life of the believer. True prayer also brings with it a firm understanding of God and of religion.

James 4:3 continues the thought of praying in the wrong manner: "You ask and do not receive, because you ask wrongly, in order to spend what you get on your pleasures." This reflects again the context of the double-minded person torn between friendship with the world and friendship with God (4:4). Those who are double-minded are only concerned with their own desires. No wonder they will not receive what they request.

Authentic Prayer

Prayer is treated extensively in the concluding section of the letter (5:13-18).[110] Nowhere does the need for prayer emerge more critically than in situations of suffering (5:13). There the believer places trust in God by praying. However, prayers should not be offered just in moments of illness, but also at times of joy and happiness when one may turn to give praise to God.[111]

Prayer is not only an individual experience, but also has a definite community dimension. For the first time in this short letter, James introduces the word "church" (ἐκκλησία [5:14]) to refer to the followers of Jesus.[112] In doing so, James challenges the body of believers to demonstrate their Christian identity and existence through the way they treat the sick. The response to sickness should be a communal one where they all rally together to show support for the sick person. Nowhere is

---

[110] Davids (*The Epistle of James*, 191) notes that James takes up the topic of prayer at this point because normally letters ended with some form of greeting whereby the recipients are wished God's blessing and good health. This ending can be seen to fulfill this dimension.

[111] "They should sing songs of praise [ψαλλέτω]" (Jas 5:13). The verb ψάλλω originally meant singing accompanied by a harp. Here it refers generically to any form of singing (see Johnson, *The Letter of James*, 329–30).

Paul gives some excellent illustrations of prayer offered during all moments of life. Paul's arrest in Philippi during his second missionary journey (Acts 16:11-40) is an excellent example. After being arrested, flogged, and thrown into prison, "about midnight Paul and Silas were praying and singing hymns to God, and the prisoners were listening to them" (Acts 16:25). Experiences of both trials and joys are occasions for praying to the Lord.

[112] Paul uses the term "church" (ἐκκλησία) frequently in this way, particularly in his opening address, for example, 1 Cor 1:2; 2 Cor 1:1; Gal 1:2.

this more forcefully demonstrated than by uniting in prayer with and for the sick person.[113] In situations of illness, the sick should invoke the prayer of the community with the firm assurance that through this prayer the sick will be restored to health (5:14-15). The sick are encouraged to pray both for spiritual healing as well as for bodily health.[114] All prayer, however, is "prayer of faith" (5:15), prayer that demonstrates a total commitment to the Lord. Such prayer shows that the community is committed to the Lord.

The community dimension of prayer is further emphasized in this section when James instructs the members of the community: "Confess your sins to one another, and pray for one another, so that you may be healed." This reference to the confession of sins again continues a custom within the Jewish community of acknowledging one's sins to the Lord. This is particularly evident on the Day of Atonement.[115] The acknowledgment of guilt occurs not just in the interior recesses of the soul, but also in the context of the community. Through the self-condemnation and the communal prayer for forgiveness, the grace of forgiveness is experienced and the sick person is restored to both spiritual and physical health. As Tamez says: "The community that accepts this challenge will enter into the deep process of integrity to which it is invited."[116]

The final verses of the letter describe the qualities that prayer should embrace: all prayer should be fervent and constant (5:17-18).[117] Elijah, the greatest of the prophets, is invoked as an example of a person at prayer. Elijah is presented as "a human being like us" (5:17). Thus, Elijah's actions can and should be imitated by all. His fervent prayer becomes the mark for imitation and also reveals the tremendous power

---

[113] Johnson (*The Letter of James*, 343) notes that there are two possible responses that a community can make to sickness. The community could expel the sick member, as occurred in the biblical cases where lepers are expelled from the community. Or, the community could embrace the sick and help them to deal with and overcome their affliction. It is the latter response that should mark the identity of a Christian community.

[114] Tamez, *The Scandalous Message of James*, 71.

[115] The Israelite religion knew of a confession of sins that was both personal and community based. For example, a more personal and individual confession is observed in the following instances: Lev 5:5; Num 5:7; Pss 32:5; 51:3-5. A more community-oriented dimension of the confession of sins is observed in the following: Lev 16:21; 26:40; Dan 9:4-10.

[116] Tamez, *The Scandalous Message of James*, 72.

[117] Davids (*The Epistle of James*, 198) sees these final verses as an expression of the author's intention, namely "turning or preserving people from error" (cf. the similarity in 1 John 5:21).

of prayer. The fervent prayer of the community also brings back those who stray from the community (5:19-20). The final picture of the letter is that of a community united in prayer and accepting responsibility for one another, particularly for those who have strayed away from the community.[118]

A true spirituality of prayer emerges from the pages of this letter. This spirituality expresses the tremendous confidence in the power of prayer to heal spiritually and physically, both as individuals as well as communally.[119] It is a confidence born of the gospel injunction: "Ask, and it will be given you; search, and you will find; knock, and the door will be opened for you" (Matt 7:7). Prayer offered in faith identifies the believers as those who share a common friendship with God. Every moment of life gives reason for turning to prayer, whether in joy or in sorrow. The true qualities of prayer offered in faith are those that demonstrate persistence, fervor, and constancy. Most noteworthy is the community dimension of prayer that helps to restore the members to health physically and spiritually. At the same time, prayer enables the community to discover its true identity as a Christian community. Prayer is another social marker identifying the members of James's community and separating them from the wider society. Prayer empowers both the individual as well as the community to maintain integrity and identity.

Conclusion: A Spirituality of Authentic Perfection

The spirituality of James is clearly a spirituality where the belief system influences the ethical perspective. As noted, one's belief system gives impetus to one's way of being in the world. James shows that an understanding of God ultimately influences the way in which his readers are to lead their lives. James imagines the whole life of the believer to be in a relationship with God and with a community.[120] This is seen from James's first description of God as the one "who gives to all generously [ἁπλῶς]" (1:5). The expression "wholeheartedly" probably captures the meaning more accurately.[121] This indeed approaches more

---

[118] See Laws, *A Commentary on the Epistle of James*, 241.

[119] See Johnson, *Letter of James*, 344.

[120] This conforms to the definition of spirituality as defined by Conn, "Spirituality," 972.

[121] As Otto Bauernfeind ("ἁπλοῦς," *Theological Dictionary of the New Testament*, vol. 1, ed. Gerhard Kittel, trans. Geoffrey W. Bromiley [Grand Rapids, Mich.: Eerdmans, 1969] 386) argues: "In Jm 1:5 . . . the meaning might well be 'kind' or 'generous.' Yet the sense of 'wholehearted' is perhaps nearer the mark." See also Laws, "The Doctrinal Basis for the Ethics of James," 300.

closely the definition of perfect whereby one is complete and whole. As such, God is perfect and this expression illustrates God's integrity.

Contrasted to this wholeheartedness and integrity of God stands the human person whom James describes as "double-minded" (1:8). Double-mindedness is most evident when one tries to remain friends with the world and with God at the same time (4:4). The human person is called to overcome this divided state by striving for wholeness, perfection, and integrity.

James grounds his call to perfection ultimately in the imitation of God.[122] This can be seen from the contrasting parallelism of Jas 1:4 and 1:5. In verse 4 the human person is called upon to attain perfection and completeness, while in verse 5 God is described as the one who is perfect because God can supply whatever is lacking. The person is called to be like God since the person is created in the likeness of God (3:9).[123] This likeness is to be expressed in ethical action, which is inspired by the desire to emulate the action of God. In this way, the person attains wholeness, perfection, and integrity. The letter of James differs from the distinctively New Testament emphasis on the imitation of Jesus with its own perspective on the imitation of God. This again makes the spirituality of James unique because it grounds its approach in what is common to all religions, a belief in God, rather than in what is specific to Christianity, namely, in a confession to Jesus.[124] In this way, James reminds Christians that there is much they have in common with others who do not profess a belief in the person and significance of Jesus. In union with both Judaism and Islam, the spirituality of James embraces a confession in the oneness of God.[125] This theological confession gives impetus to the life and way of being in the world that is so characteristic of James and yet it is also one that can find a resonance among people of other faiths.[126]

[122] Laws draws attention to the importance of the theme of the imitation of God for the ethical life of the believer (Laws, "The Doctrinal Basis for the Ethics of James," 299–305).

[123] I shall examine further this question of imitating God through one's actions when I consider Matthew's call to be perfect (Matt 6:48: "Be perfect, therefore, as your heavenly Father is perfect") and its similarity to James's understanding of perfection in ch. 6.

[124] See Johnson, *The Letter of James,* 164.

[125] Ibid.

[126] In this James differs from the emphasis in the rest of the New Testament which generally speaks about the imitation of Jesus, rather than the imitation of God (Laws, "The Doctrinal Basis for the Ethics of James," 304).

Yet, what does it mean to imitate God? God's way of acting becomes the basis for the moral action of the person.[127] Concretely, this can only be answered from the situations to which James draws attention. In the situations of unfair discrimination (2:1-7), of inconsistent speech (3:1-12), of putting word into action (1:22-23; 2:14-22), of showing a preference for the poor and the oppressed (5:1-6), James shows that one is called to act as God would act.

Ultimately, the spirituality of James is a spirituality of authentic perfection. This spirituality embraces a way of being in the world that is characterized by people who form part of communities who strive for integrity. One of the ways in which this integrity is demonstrated is through the approach to suffering. Believers are seen to be perfected through endurance in the midst of suffering. They integrate within themselves and their community their understanding of the trials they are experiencing. The endurance they demonstrate testifies to their fidelity and trust as a community in the God who created and called them.

A further distinctive aspect of James's spirituality is that it embraces a community morality. The instructions of the letter are based upon an ethics that gives direction to the moral relationship between the community and God, or between individuals with one another or with God. Striving for integrity impacts both on the individual and the community. The life and vitality of the community depends upon the integrity of its members. The individual is an essential part of the community and is never viewed in isolation from the community. Even where individuals are addressed, they are seen as members of the community. The closing scene of the letter is that of a community united in prayer and accepting responsibility for one another, especially for those members who have wandered away both literally and physically.

James's concern is above all with the moral and social implications of the actions of both the individual and the community.[128] James 1:27 defined religion as having a social responsibility. James distinguishes himself from the wisdom advice of the time by propounding a spirituality of the poor, of those who are the outcasts of society. Whereas much of the wisdom of the ancient world was directed toward the at-

---

[127] Ibid.

[128] What is distinctively missing in James is what often occurs in wisdom considerations, namely a focus *on customs* that bear no specifically moral implications. For example, the book of Proverbs abounds in advice of this nature: "When you sit down to eat with a ruler, observe carefully what is before you, and put a knife to your throat if you have a big appetite" (Prov 23:1-2).

tainment of status, the spirituality of James is countercultural, just as that of Jesus was.[129] James's spirituality is an appeal to see reality through the eyes of God, rather than through the eyes of the world. The world gives importance to wealth, status, power. God gives importance to the poor, to those who place their trust in God. The poor are those who are in the end most blessed, for they will experience a reversal of situations and will encounter an exaltation with the Lord. James's teaching on the poor speaks to people of every age. The value of the poor in the eyes of God as well as the avoidance of every form of discrimination are values that the Christian community is to appropriate at every age. James calls for a way of acting that takes seriously the equality of all and avoids every form of discrimination. These values are the distinctive social markers that set James's community apart from the rest of the world.

While the spirituality of James may be termed countercultural, James does not propose a spirituality that involves a flight from the world as occurred with the community of Qumran.[130] James's community still lives in the world. What drives and motivates their activities in the world are the values of their own faith community, not the values of the world.[131] Specifically, James urges a close harmony between faith and action. Nothing could be more important for Christians today than to keep before them the unity of their faith and its implications for their lives. Without doubt, the spirituality of James is timeless. It is a spirituality that avoids the worldliness that threatens every generation, and one that is especially relevant for our own time.

---

[129] As Luke Timothy Johnson ("The Social World of James: Literary Analysis and Historical Reconstruction," *The Social World of the First Christians: Essays in Honor of Wayne A. Weeks,* ed. L. Michael White and O. Larry Yarbrough [Minneapolis: Fortress Press, 1989] 195–6, n. 80) remarks: "That one of the motivations for being 'wise' is to be a greater success in the world than others is frequently implied, but nowhere more obvious than in Pseudo-Isocrates, *To Demonicus* 2, 3, 13, 15, 17, 21, 24, 26, 32, 33, 35, 38; nothing could be at greater odds to such 'pursuit of nobility' than the 'lowly-mindedness' encouraged by James (4:7-10)."

[130] See Johnson, "Friendship with the World/Friendship with God," 172–3.

[131] For example, James distances himself sharply from the attitudes of the landowners (Jas 5:1-6) and merchants (Jas 4:13-17).

CHAPTER SIX

Perfection in the Letter of James and the Sermon on the Mount

The examination of the spirituality of perfection found in the letter of James reveals that this letter grounds moral action in the imitation of God rather than in the imitation of Jesus. While this is a distinctive feature of James, he is not alone in advancing this perspective. Another important tradition of early Christianity, Matthew's Sermon on the Mount, also presents a similar understanding. This chapter[1] will examine Matthew's call to perfection that lies at the heart of the Sermon on the Mount ("Be perfect, therefore, as your heavenly Father is perfect" [Matt 5:48]) with the intention of showing how similar the letter of James and Matthew's Sermon on the Mount are in their understanding of perfection. Seeing these similarities will help situate James's thought and spirituality within the context of the emerging traditions of early Christianity. James's thought is not to be relegated to the margins of early Christianity. It lies close to a tradition that is at the heart of the early Christian movement as witnessed by the Sermon on the Mount.

The Call to Perfection in the Letter of James and the Sermon on the Mount

An examination of Matthew's call to perfection in the context of the Sermon on the Mount reveals how close this concept comes to its use in the letter of James. As with James, the Gospel of Matthew bears witness to its heritage in the world of Judaism. The Gospel of Matthew

---

[1] The substance of this chapter formed part of a paper entitled "'Be perfect, therefore, as your heavenly Father is perfect' (Mt 5:48): An Examination of the Call

was particularly concerned with defining the relationship of the teaching of Jesus to Judaism.[2] Just as the concept of perfection in the letter of James can only be understood against the background of the Jewish world, so too does Matthew's concept of perfection conform in large measure to that world of the Jewish Old Testament and the Septuagint.

"Be Perfect, Therefore, as Your Heavenly Father Is Perfect" (Matt 5:48)

The occurrence of the adjective "perfect" (τέλειος) in the letter of James has proved to be significant in unfolding the thought and message of this writing. The same is true for its appearance in Matthew's Sermon on the Mount. In fact, the attributive use of "perfect" (τέλειος) is very rare in the Synoptic Gospels, occurring only three times, on all occasions in the Gospel of Matthew (twice in Matt 5:48 and once in 19:21). Matthew 5:48 ("Be perfect, therefore, as your heavenly Father is perfect") occurs within the context of the Sermon on the Mount.[3] The verse is found at the culmination of a series of six antitheses (5:21-47) that contrast the traditional interpretation of the law with Jesus' interpretation: "You have heard that it was said. . . . But I say to you . . ." (5:21-22). Matthew 5:48 brings the first part of the sermon (5:1-48) to a climax.[4] The Gospel of Luke also contains a sermon (The Sermon on the Plain, 6:20-49), but its climax is very different: "Be merciful, just as your Father is merciful" (Luke 6:36). It is hard to decide which of the

---

to Imitate God in Matthew's Sermon on the Mount," presented to the Pacific Northwest Region Annual Meeting of the Society of Biblical Literature (1–3 May 1997) held at Trinity Western University, Langley, British Columbia, Canada.

[2] See Anthony J. Saldarini, *Matthew's Christian-Jewish Community* (Chicago: University of Chicago Press, 1994); J. Andrew Overman, *Matthew's Gospel and Formative Judaism: The Social World of the Matthean Community* (Minneapolis: Fortress Press, 1990).

[3] See the outline and division of the sermon in Hans Dieter Betz, *The Sermon on the Mount* (Minneapolis: Fortress Press, 1995). It is not my intention here to examine the relationship between Matthew's Sermon on the Mount and the letter of James. This I have done elsewhere (*James and the Q Sayings of Jesus*, JSNTS 47 [Sheffield: Sheffield University Press, 1991] 144–72).

[4] One of the stylistic ways in which Matthew draws attention to the development of his thought, particularly in the context of his sermons, is by means of central verses which hold an important position in the unfolding of the sermon's thought. Other such verses in the Sermon on the Mount, in addition to 5:48, are: 5:17, 20; 6:1; and 7:12, 21. Ulrich Luz calls such a verse "a *kelal*, a summarizing transitional verse" (*Matthew, 1–7: A Commentary*, trans. Wilhelm C. Linss [Minneapolis: Augsburg Press, 1989] 338). See, as well, Luz's definition of *"kelalim"*: "Such verses or texts are distinguished by their position; they open up larger contexts. They are

two represents the more original saying.[5] However, since the word "perfect" (τέλειος) only occurs among the Synoptic Gospels in the Gospel of Matthew and since it is clearly redactional at 19:21, it seems logical to conclude that it is also redactional here at 5:48.[6] The text of Luke 6:36 would be seen to reflect the original form in the Sayings Gospel Q.[7] It seems distinctly possible, as Davies and Allison have so well argued,[8] that Matthew transformed this verse through the influence of Deut 18:13: "You must be perfect before the LORD your God."[9] The influence of Deuteronomy is evident throughout the whole section of the antitheses (Matt 5:21-47) that precede Matt 5:48, and this lends further support to see the influence of Deut 18:13 at this point.[10]

---

not simply titles but rather combinations of materials and generalizations at the beginning or end of a section, often with explicit transitional function" (p. 39). Such verses either opening or concluding a section have the intention of providing a transition as well as a means of stressing the thought. Matthew 5:48 employs both functions—it provides a focus upon the main aspect of the preceding argument while also offering a transition to some new aspect or dimension. The phrase "your heavenly Father" (ὁ πατὴρ ὑμῶν ὁ οὐράνιος) achieves this twofold connection very well. Looking back over the sermon, this title recapitulates the reference to God in the previous verses (being used in a similar way at 5:16 and 5:45). At the same time, the phrase invites a transition to the next section on prayer (6:1-15) where the thought again occurs at 6:1 and 9.

[5] See Joseph A. Fitzmyer, *The Gospel according to Luke (I–XI)*, vol. 1, The Anchor Bible 28 (New York: Doubleday, 1981) 640–1.

[6] See W. D. Davies and Dale C. Allison, *A Critical and Exegetical Commentary on the Gospel according to Saint Matthew*, The International Critical Commentary, vol. 1 (Edinburgh: T. and T. Clark, 1988) 560.

[7] It is my presupposition that Matthew and Luke drew upon an existing sermon, found in the Sayings Gospel Q, which they have each redacted in their own way. This Sayings Gospel Q is the source for both the Sermon on the Mount and the Sermon on the Plain. In particular, Luke's saying: "Be merciful, just as your Father is merciful" (3:36) probably lies closest to the Q Sermon; Matthew's sermon shows evidence of greater redactional development. See as well the reconstruction of this verse by the International Q Project which supports Luke's reading as the more original: "[[γίν]]εσθε οἰκτίρμονες ὡς . . . ὁ πατὴρ ὑμῶν οἰκτίρμων ἐστίν" (Milton C. Moreland and James M. Robinson, "The International Q Project: Work Sessions, 6–8 August, 18–19 November, 1993," *Journal of Biblical Literature* 113 [1994] 497).

[8] Davies and Allison, *The Gospel according to Saint Matthew*, 560.

[9] This is my translation. The Septuagint text of Deut 18:13 reads: "τέλειος ἔσῃ ἐναντίον κυρίου τοῦ θεοῦ σου." Note that the Greek τέλειος once again reproduces the Hebrew תמים.

[10] As Davies and Allison (*The Gospel according to Saint Matthew*, 560) note: "If, as we have tentatively suggested, the first three paragraphs in 5.21-48 take up teaching from Deuteronomy while the second three paragraphs cite texts from Leviticus,

A noteworthy development is evident in Matthew's construction of the saying. Despite the richness of the language of perfection throughout the Old Testament and the Dead Sea Scrolls, no single attribution of this quality is made to God.[11] Even within the New Testament only at Matt 5:48 is God so designated as perfect.[12] While God is not defined in terms of perfection, nevertheless there are some instances where the notion of perfection is indirectly attributed to God. For example, the name Jotham ("Yôtam") means "Jahweh [is] perfect" (Judg 9:5).[13] The actions and the ways of God are also described as being perfect. For example, "The Rock, his work is perfect, / and all his ways are just. / A faithful God, without deceit, / just and upright is he" (Deut 32:4). "With the loyal you show yourself loyal; / with the blameless you show yourself blameless . . . . / This God—his way is perfect; / the promise of the LORD proves true; / he is a shield for all who take refuge in him" (Ps 18:25-30). Job 37:16 says: "Do you know the balancings of the clouds, / the wondrous works of the one whose knowledge is perfect?"

In contrast to this lack of direct attribution of perfection to God in the Old Testament, the Gospel of Matthew attributes the quality of perfection directly to God. In Matt 5:43-47, God bestows the good things of creation on good and evil alike. God does not distinguish between them with regard to the gifts of creation. The purpose of God's gifts is not to convert the wicked. The presumption is that even though God bestows these gifts upon the wicked, they still remain steadfastly opposed to God. God's kindness far supersedes that of God's enemies, for they still remain God's enemies.[14] In Matt 5:48 the example of God's action is provided as the motivation for the way in which one

---

it is satisfying to discover in the final verse of 5.21-48 the influence of both Leviticus and Deuteronomy."

[11] Ibid., 563.

[12] Rudolf Schnackenburg conjectures that this is because no defect in God's nature was possible "so that the predicate 'perfect' becomes for him superfluous and hardly meaningful" ("Christian Perfection according to Matthew," *Christian Existence in the New Testament*, vol. 1 [Notre Dame, Ind.: University of Notre Dame Press, 1968] 166). To my mind this is an essentialist argument that would correspond better to Greek than to Hebrew thought.

[13] See Leopold Sabourin, "Why Is God Called 'Perfect' in Mt 5:48?" *Biblische Zeitschrift, Neue Folge* 24 (1980) 266. See also 2 Kings 15:32.

[14] As Betz says: "This is God's perfection. His treatment of his enemies is not to be taken as a sign of his weakness, or, indeed, of his indifference to good and evil among human beings. Justice, as God represents it, is above all that, but never indifferent to it" (Betz, *The Sermon on the Mount*, 324).

should act. In particular, the context of the love of enemies provides the basis for the call to imitate God's action. The example of God's action provides the reason for extending love to enemies: "For he makes his sun rise on the evil and on the good, and sends rain on the righteous and on the unrighteous" (5:45). Because God is kind to all no matter whether they are good or evil, the disciples of Jesus must emulate this action through kindness to all, irrespective of who they are or what they do. One emulates not the being of God, but the action of God.

Matthew's focus in 5:48 is on human action and conduct. The description of God is understood in the context of moral human action, rather than on theological reflection.[15] One is to act in the way in which God acts.

A Threefold Understanding of the Nature of Perfection

An examination of the meaning of the concept of perfection in Matthew's Sermon on the Mount shows that all three ideas noted previously in examining the Old Testament and the Septuagint understanding of perfection are found here as well. At the same time, the sermon comes very close to the understanding of perfection expressed in the letter of James.

Perfection as Wholeness

In a sense, Jesus' call in the Sermon on the Mount to "be perfect" is a call to wholeness, to attain God's original intention or will. This comes across clearly in the third antithesis related to divorce. In distinction to the attitude of Moses who permitted divorce, Jesus returns to the original idea of creation (Gen 1:27; 2:24) and calls for a return to God's original will whereby the union of man and woman must be upheld.[16] The disciple attains this completeness and wholeness through the imitation of the Father's action. The Father's love embraces all humanity, and so the believer attains completeness through a similar imitation of God's action of unconditional love.[17]

This same concept of wholeness whereby a being remains true to its original constitution remains the basic understanding of perfection in the letter of James. The readers are referred to as "the first fruits of

---

[15] See Jacques Dupont, "L'Appel à imiter Dieu en Matthieu 5,48 et Luc 6,36," *Rivista Biblica* 14 (1966) 154.

[16] See Schnackenburg, "Christian Perfection according to Matthew," 174–5.

[17] Ibid., 175–6.

God's creatures" (1:18); they are God's perfect gift (1:17). As the first fruits they are without blemish, complete, whole. They are also the "twelve tribes in the Dispersion," representing the reconstitution of God's people. As such, the concept of perfection truly applies to them. They are called to remain true to that completeness to which God has called them. Should their faith meet trials and temptations, they are called to endure so that they may remain perfect (Jas 1:5). If anything is lacking, they are to call on God who will grant it to them (Jas 1:6).

Perfection Demands Wholehearted Dedication to the Lord

The Sermon on the Mount also gives expression to the aspect of completeness as a right relationship with God. It is a call to discipleship that gives expression to one's relationship with God as Father. The phrase "your heavenly Father" is deliberately chosen by Matthew as his central image for God throughout the sermon. Matthew 5:48 recapitulates the description of God used at 5:16 and 5:45. At the same time, it prepares for the way in which God is to be addressed during prayer in 6:9. This concept attempts to capture the closeness of the relationship between God and the believer. If God is Father, it is possible for the believer to imitate God.

James also identifies God by this title of Father in 1:17, where God is described as "the Father of lights." Faith demonstrates the fullness of a righteous relationship with God through actions. The letter of James centers on maintaining a right relationship with God. Central to the letter is the call to be friends with God and to avoid friendship with the world (4:4). Perfection emerges from acknowledging this relationship of dependence upon God and in leading a life that gives expression to this relationship. "Submit yourselves therefore to God. . . . Draw near to God, and he will draw near to you. . . . Humble yourselves before the Lord, and he will exalt you" (4:7-10).

Perfection Leads to Obedience of the Law

In the Sermon on the Mount, Matt 5:20 and 5:48 parallel each other. The call to perfection is essentially a call to exceed the righteousness of the scribes and Pharisees. The righteousness of which Matthew speaks corresponds to that Old Testament idea of the right "behavior commanded by God in his covenant."[18] A righteous person is one who carries out the behavior commanded by God. This conduct is expressed

---

[18] See Luz, *Matthew 1–7*, 238. His focus lies on human behavior. Luz (*Matthew 1–7*, 237) investigated three possible meanings of righteousness, namely "(1) human behavior, (2) a divine gift or God's power, (3) a combination of the two,

through a life of obedience to the Torah, to the laws of the Lord.[19] In the context of discipleship, the righteousness to which Jesus calls his followers is a way of acting that conforms itself to Jesus' instructions.[20] Matthew 5:17-20 provides the direction for this behavior. The type of right behavior that the followers of Jesus are to embrace goes beyond that of the scribes and Pharisees: "For I tell you, unless your righteousness exceeds that of the scribes and Pharisees, you will never enter the kingdom of heaven" (5:20). This "higher righteousness"[21] requires that the disciples carry out the law to a greater degree than the scribes and Pharisees do. Each one of the six antitheses that follow stresses this contrast: "You have heard that it was said . . . . But I say to you . . . ." In Matt 5:48, the one who is perfect is the one who has been obedient to God's will and has carried out all God's commands to the fullest possible extent.[22] This "higher righteousness" that believers embrace in their actions (5:20) is characterized as "perfection" (τέλειος) (5:48),[23] which believers are to exercise in carrying out God's will.[24]

God's covenant order as gift and task." He concluded that the consistent interpretation of the early Church should be followed, namely the first interpretation that sees righteousness as human behavior that conforms itself to God's law or will.

[19] Among the community of the Dead Sea Scrolls, perfection, as the goal of the community, demanded an obedience to the laws of the community (W. D. Davies, *The Setting of the Sermon on the Mount* [Atlanta: Scholars Press, 1989] 209–15). This is similar to Jesus' requirement here in the Sermon on the Mount to obey all his laws: "Therefore, whoever breaks one of the least of these commandments, and teaches others to do the same, will be called least in the kingdom of heaven" (Matt 5:19) (Davies and Allison, *The Gospel according to Saint Matthew,* 562).

[20] As Davies and Allison say: "'Righteousness' is therefore Christian character and conduct in accordance with the demands of Jesus—right intention, right word, right deed. Hence 'righteousness' does not refer, even implicitly, to God's gift. The Pauline (forensic, eschatological) connotation is absent" (*The Gospel according to Saint Matthew,* 499).

[21] As Luz (*Matthew 1–7,* 340) refers to it.

[22] The Didache has a similar notion of perfection: "For if thou canst bear the whole yoke of the Lord, thou wilt be perfect (τέλειος ἔσῃ)" (6:2) (Kirsopp Lake, trans., "The Didache," *The Apostolic Fathers,* vol. 1 [Cambridge, Mass.: Harvard University Press, 1965] 318–9).

[23] As Davies and Allison (*The Gospel according to Saint Matthew,* 502) state: "As the πλεῖον of 5.20 and the περισσόν of 5.47 imply, Christian righteousness means doing more. It means, in fact, as 5.48 plainly states, a quest for 'perfection'; and such a quest was not in Matthew's eyes, equally enjoined by Moses."

[24] Betz, *The Sermon on the Mount,* 324.

Luz presents a somewhat similar understanding of perfection when he says: "Two elements belong to perfection: as *a subjective element* the idea that the heart must not be divided and that obedience must be entire; as *an objective element* the complete fulfilling of all demands of the law."[25]

The followers of Jesus adopt an inner attitude that transforms the whole person as she or he carries out God's will as expressed in the law.[26] This is contrasted with the attitude of the Pharisees that was concerned with the fulfillment of the external observance of laws. For Jesus' disciples, perfection is their characteristic mark, distinguishing them by a behavior of obedience to the law of God and total commitment to God's will.[27]

The attitude to the law functions in a very similar way to that of the letter of James. The law for both Matthew and James is the Torah, that gives expression to God's will for God's people. Both traditions show concern for upholding the Torah in its totality. As James says, "For whoever keeps the whole law but fails in one point has become accountable for all of it" (2:10). Jesus says prior to the antitheses in the sermon: "Therefore, whoever breaks one of the least of these commandments, and teaches others to do the same, will be called least in the kingdom of heaven" (Matt 5:19). The Torah in its entirety gives direction for the way in which believers are to lead their lives. The social boundaries that the Torah defines are equally important for both James and Matthew. The laws help give identity to those who belong to a particular community. These same laws are necessary for the community to function as a society that is distinct from the world around them. Matthew's Sermon on the Mount shows this clearly. It takes the various commands from the Decalogue and illustrates how they are to be carried out within Matthew's community. Those who belong to Matthew's community show a specific way of understanding these commandments that distinguishes them from other societies. For both Matthew and James, the Torah enables the socializing process of their respective communities to continue whereby the members of the community maintain their bonds through their common understanding of the Torah and its implementation within their society. The Torah provides them with the means for their community to function and to maintain the distinctiveness of its way of life.

For James, the love of neighbor operates as the epitome of the Torah—it is the heartbeat of the Torah. The same can be said for

---

[25] Luz, *Matthew 1–7*, 346. The italics are my own.

[26] See Schnackenburg, *Christian Perfection according to Matthew*, 178.

[27] Sabourin, "Why Is God Called 'Perfect' in Mt 5:48?" 268.

Matthew's interpretation of the Torah within the Sermon on the Mount. In particular, the context of Matt 5:48 bears this out. The love command in the Sermon on the Mount is the last of the six antitheses (Matt 5:43-47). As such, it is the climax of the antitheses and is given a prime place of importance.[28] The love command becomes the very center of the "higher righteousness" that is demanded of believers. To walk in the way Jesus outlined demands an unconditional love for all people. As an all-encompassing command, nothing is lacking from it; it is perfect. To be perfect means that one is to love perfectly.[29] With this focus upon the love of neighbor, the Sermon on the Mount has developed further the understanding of perfection and given it a distinctiveness not found elsewhere in the Gospels. Jesus' disciples must not limit their love to their friends as the scribes and Pharisees do; rather, they must embrace everyone, including their enemies.[30] Their behavior is driven by their desire to imitate the actions of God. At the same time, such persons demonstrate that they are whole by remaining true to the way in which God has created them.

Finally, for both James and the Sermon on the Mount, perfection is a reality to be attained in the present. The whole purpose of the Torah was to provide a direction for the way the society should act in the present. Characteristic of the sermon is the view that salvation is a reality experienced in the present, not simply a promise for some distant future.[31] The sermon believes in the real possibility of perfection, of righteousness, in the present.[32] For Matthew, perfection has little to do with a state of perfection. Instead, perfection is a call to a discipleship that recognizes relationships with God and others and acknowledges what those relationships demand.[33] It is perhaps best to characterize Matthew's notion of perfection as being "in process," as Thurston has

[28] See Davies and Allison, *The Gospel according to Saint Matthew,* 549.

[29] As Davies and Allison (*The Gospel according to Saint Matthew,* 562–3) argue: "To obey Jesus' words, his law, is therefore, to love utterly: no more can be asked. And in this lies perfection: love of unrestrained compass lacks for nothing. It is catholic, all-inclusive. It is perfect."

[30] E. Yarnold, "Τέλειος in St. Matthew's Gospel," *Studia Evangelica,* Papers Presented to the International Congress on "The Four Gospels" in 1957, 102:4 (Berlin: Akademie-Verlag, 1968) 270.

[31] See Rudolf Schnackenburg, "The Sermon on the Mount and Modern Man," *Christian Existence in the New Testament,* vol. 1 (Notre Dame, Ind.: University of Notre Dame Press, 1968) 143.

[32] Jennifer DeWeerth, "Perfection, Righteousness and Justice in the Sermon on the Mount," *Criterion* 35 (1996) 24.

[33] Bonnie Bowman Thurston, "Matthew 5:43-48: 'You, therefore, must be perfect,'" *Interpretation* 41 (1987) 171.

expressed it.[34] In this process, one carries out God's will and embraces the higher righteousness through an unconditional love for all.[35]

Perfection as the Hallmark of the Christian Life

Both the letter of James and Matthew's Sermon on the Mount show how central and distinctive the concept of perfection is for both their texts. The ethos of the letter of James is one of perfection that informs the paraenesis of the letter. All the moral instructions illustrate how to live out that perfection in daily life. Perfection is attainable in the present, not something reserved only for a future state. The same is true for the Sermon on the Mount. The call to be perfect is the climax to the first part of the sermon (Matt 5:1-48) where the beatitudes are presented as those virtues that a child of God is to put into practice. The sermon gives expression to the real possibility of perfection, of right-

---

[34] Ibid., 173.

[35] Matthew uses the word "perfect" (τέλειος) on a second occasion in his Gospel, namely Jesus' encounter with the rich young man (Matt 19:16-22). A brief examination of this passage reveals again this same threefold understanding of perfection so characteristic of the letter of James and the Sermon on the Mount.

In comparing this passage (Matt 19:16-22) with its source in Mark 10:17-31, the most important change brought by Matthew was Jesus' response to the young man: "If you wish to be perfect [τέλειος] . . ." (Matt 19:21). The notion of "wholeness or completeness" undoubtedly lies behind the adjective "perfect" in this context. What prompted Jesus' remark was the young man's question: "What do I still lack?" (Matt 19:20). To this Jesus replied: "If you wish to be perfect . . ." (19:21). In this sense, "being perfect" is the counterpoint to "lacking" (Yarnold, "Τέλειος in St. Matthew's Gospel," 271). Thus, perfection in Matthew's context is reflective of the Old Testament understanding of perfection as completion or wholeness.

The idea of perfection (τέλειος) is also connected to the carrying out of God's will as is expressed in the commandments. However, this young man is asked to go further. This bears a similarity to the usage of perfection in Matt 5:48 where Jesus challenges the believer to go beyond the righteousness of the scribes and the Pharisees who see themselves obeying God's will by carrying out the commandments. Jesus shows that the young man must go beyond the literal observance of the commandments and do something more. The expression of God's will is still to be found in the law which continues to keep its validity (Matt 5:17-19). However, this law has to be fulfilled in a way that accomplishes more (see Schnackenburg, *Christian Perfection according to Matthew,* 181). For this young man, Jesus issues the challenge to go beyond the requirements of the law and to give up his wealth. In this way, he will demonstrate total dependence upon God. Perfection lies in this dependence upon and obedience to God.

The same aspects of perfection that were observed in Matt 5:48 are evident here with a somewhat different emphasis:

eousness, here and now in the present.[36] In essence, perfection is a call to discipleship, a call to show by one's actions that one is in a relationship with God that informs all one's dealings with others.

The letter of James is concerned with the life of the community and how that life of faith is lived out in action.[37] The letter concentrates on human action rather than on theological reflection. The exhortation "Be doers of the word, and not merely hearers who deceive themselves" (Jas 1:22) characterizes the direction of the letter's ethical advice. The Sermon on the Mount also gives a similar importance to the expression of faith in action: "Let your light shine before others, so that they may see your good works and give glory to your Father in heaven" (Matt 5:16). This gives further impetus for Matthew to stress the need to fulfill all the stipulations of the law (Matt 5:17-20).

---

(1) Perfection calls for wholeness and completeness. Jesus shows the young man how he can overcome what he lacks.

(2) This completeness or wholeness is obtained through a relationship with God. The young man is called to discipleship, and the fulfillment of the Torah is one way in which this discipleship is attained. Matthew's source, Mark 10:20, had implied that the rich person was advanced in age: "Teacher, I have kept all these since my youth [ἐκ νεότητός μου]." Matthew, however, omits this reference "since my youth" by commenting at the end of the narrative: "When the young man [ὁ νεανίσκος] heard this word . . ." (19:22). In focusing upon the young age of the rich man Matthew implies that he will come to maturity in discipleship by carrying out the injunctions of Jesus.

(c) Finally, wholeness and completeness are realized through a total carrying out of God's will in action. One must do more than keep the commandments; one needs to go beyond them. Just as Matt 5:20 called the disciples to go beyond the righteousness of the scribes and Pharisees, so too Jesus calls this young man to go beyond the mere observance of the commandments. The wholeness of the rich young man consists in giving total obedience to the word that Jesus addresses to him. Here the meaning of the call to be perfect reaches its universal application. As with this young man, everyone is called to be perfect. Everyone is called to give heed to the word that Jesus addresses to them and with which he challenges them. What that means concretely differs from person to person. While not everyone is called to give away all their possessions, as with the rich young man, everyone is called to attend to the word that Jesus addresses to them, a word which calls all to total allegiance and obedience. Once again this understanding of perfection remains close to the basic understanding as demonstrated in the letter of James and Matthew's Sermon on the Mount.

[36] DeWeerth, "Perfection, Righteousness and Justice in the Sermon on the Mount," 24.

[37] See Sophie Laws, "The Doctrinal Basis for the Ethics of James," *Studia Evangelica*, vol. 7, Papers Presented to the Fifth International Congress on Biblical Studies Held at Oxford, 1973 (Berlin: Akademie-Verlag, 1982) 299–305.

The opening verses of the letter of James (1:2-4) envisage a situation where the community's faith is being tested. A developmental progression runs from facing trials, through endurance, to attaining perfection and maturity. Endurance of sufferings and trials ultimately produces "the perfect person" who conforms to the original image God intended for humanity: "Let endurance have its full effect, so that you may be mature and complete, lacking in nothing" (1:4).

This call to perfection is very similar to the call expressed in Matt 5:48: "Be perfect, therefore, as your heavenly Father is perfect." Persecution is also a theme that runs throughout the sermon. The Beatitudes climax with two beatitudes on persecution (Matt 5:10-12). The theme is further remembered in the final antithesis: "But I say to you, 'Love your enemies and pray for those who persecute you . . .'" (Matt 5:44). The outcome of following this way of life is that "you may be children of your Father in heaven" (5:45). The believers' actions of love will bring them into a true familial relationship with God. By loving all people they realize their full potential as human beings. They have been brought to experience their true nature as God intended. In this perfection is found.

The Call to Be Perfect and to Imitate God

A further noteworthy similarity between the letter of James and Matthew's Sermon on the Mount in their understanding of perfection is the importance that the theme of the imitation of God plays in both writings. This is significant because this concept of the imitation of God does not play much of an important role in its Old Testament and Jewish contexts. In fact, the question as to whether the concept of the imitation of God is to be found at all in the Hebrew traditions has been the subject of much scholarly discussion.[38]

There are very few occasions where the imitation of God seems to underlie an Old Testament passage. The closest one comes to the concept of the imitation of God is in the call: "You shall be holy, for I the LORD your God am holy" (Lev 19:2). However, on closer examination one sees that the imitation of God is not what the verse has in mind. In Lev 19:2, one is called to holiness because God is holy. This verse expresses a relationship of *consequence*, not of *imitation*. The Hebrew conjunction used here (כִּי, "kî") expresses a result, not a comparison.[39] God is holy by nature. In leading the Israelites out of Egypt, God formed

---

[38]   Ibid., 302.
[39]   See Dupont, "L'Appel à imiter Dieu en Matthieu 5,48 et Luc 6,36," 140.

them into God's own nation at Sinai: "Now therefore, if you obey my voice and keep my covenant, you shall be my treasured possession out of all the peoples. Indeed, the whole earth is mine, but you shall be for me a priestly kingdom and a holy nation" (Exod 19:5-6). As a "holy nation," they are separated from the peoples of the earth and belong to God. This, then, has consequences for the Israelites. Their actions must reflect their nature. Because God has chosen them to be God's own people, they must lead their lives accordingly. This differs from Matthew's call in 5:48 to imitate God.[40] Basically, the understanding in Lev 19:2 is that one is to live in obedience to the Torah, to the will of God. This is not a matter of living in imitation of God, as is the case in Matthew's Gospel.[41]

A further example is Deut 10:17-19:

> For the LORD your God is God of gods and Lord of lords, the great God, mighty and awesome, who is not partial and takes no bribe, who executes justice for the orphan and the widow, and who loves the strangers, providing them food and clothing. You shall also love the stranger, for you were strangers in the land of Egypt.

This passage calls on the Israelites to extend love to strangers because God has freed them while they were slaves in Egypt. This passage, however, is not issuing a call to imitate God. It is rather a narrative that endeavors to actualize legal material.[42] Once again it is a call to obey the law and will of God rather than to imitate God directly.

Outside the Hebrew Scriptures, the writings of Philo show an awareness of the virtue of the imitation of God beginning to emerge. Philo sees that parents imitate God their creator in the procreation of children.[43] This development is probably due in large measure to the influence of Greek philosophical thought on this tradition. For example, Plato constantly appeals to the ideas of "imitating God" and of "following God" from the perspective of the relationship of the shadow and the ideal that is so basic to his whole thought.[44] Aristotle, on the

---

[40] Ibid.

[41] Hans Dieter Betz, *Nachfolge und Nachahmung Jesu Christi im Neuen Testament*, Beiträge zur historischen Theologie 37 (Tübingen: Mohr [Paul Siebeck], 1967) 89–90.

[42] Ibid., 91.

[43] *De Decalogo*, 107, 120; and *De Specialibus Legibus*, II, 225.

[44] See Henri Crouzel, "L'Imitation et la 'Suite' de Dieu et du Christ dans les Premières Siècles Chrétiens, ainsi que Leurs Sources Gréco-Romaines et Hébraïques," *Jahrbuch für Antike und Christentum*, Jahrgang 21 (Münster: Aschendorffsche Verlagsbuchhandlung, 1978) 7–8.

other hand, does not see that human virtue can bring people to become like or as gods. Instead, he argues that their actions can imitate
the virtues of the gods.[45]

The conclusion to be drawn from this brief study is that the concept
of the imitation of God is not distinctively Jewish. Absent from the Old
Testament, it only appears in some later Jewish sources. This conclusion
is supported by the detailed study of the topic by Hans Kosmala, who
concluded that the concept of the imitation of God was "foreign to the
Old Testament tradition."[46] Nevertheless, this theme plays a distinctive
part in both the letter of James and in the Sermon on the Mount. Consequently, it seems that the origin of this concept in James and the Sermon on the Mount is to be attributed, not directly to their Jewish
heritage, but rather to the influence of the thought patterns belonging to
the wider Hellenistic world.[47]

In James, as has been observed,[48] the imitation of God is not expressed directly, but it certainly operates in an indirect way. For James,
God is "the Father of lights" (1:17), the creator of the world. God is also
the re-creator whereby the believer becomes "a kind of first fruits of
his creatures" (1:18). Humanity has been created in "the likeness of
God" (3:9). The nature of humanity as "the likeness of God" provides
the basis for a notion of the imitation of God. Created in God's likeness, the human person must act like God. The very definition of religion in 1:27 ("to care for orphans and widows in their distress, and to
keep oneself unstained by the world") expresses one way to imitate
God. Care for "orphans and widows" is a key aspect of the Old Testament understanding of God's action. God is a God of the poor, those
marginalized by society. The biblical understanding of God presents
God as different from the world, and this forms the basis for keeping
oneself away from the world. Later, James defines God again in Old
Testament terms by saying that the "Lord is compassionate and merciful" (5:11). James's instructions throughout this letter draw attention
to actions that reflect the way God acts. The imitation of God provides
the horizon whereby one puts faith into action: avoidance of discrimination (2:1-13), concern for the poor (5:1-6), concern for the sick (5:13-
18)—these are all ways to imitate God's actions.

---

[45] Ibid., 9.

[46] Hans Kosmala, "Nachfolge und Nachahmung Gottes, II. Im Jüdischen
Denken," *Studies, Essays and Reviews,* vol. 2, New Testament (Leiden: Brill, 1978) 217.

[47] See Laws ("The Doctrinal Basis for the Ethics of James," 304), who makes a
similar conclusion. She refers to this concept of human actions imitating God as
"an idea that is so widespread in contemporary thought."

[48] See the section of chapter 5 entitled "The Imitation of God," p. 100.

The same spirit underlies the direct call in Matthew's Sermon on the Mount to imitate God (5:48). This concept of the imitation of God in Matthew's Gospel probably finds its origin within the evolving theology of his Gospel, especially in his concept of God as Father. God enters into a relationship with believers similar to that of a Father with children.[49] This image of God was first illustrated in the sermon in the Beatitudes (Matt 5:9) and is taken up again in the prayer that Jesus teaches his followers: the Our Father (6:9-13). The perfection to which the believers are called is a perfection the Father also demonstrates.

Matthew does not intend to propose a theological teaching. Rather, his accent is upon human behavior, and he appeals to the divine simply to stress this human behavior. The emphasis in Matthew's call to be perfect rests on human action. This is what Jesus requires of his disciples. Added to this is the idea that God's action is proposed as the way they are to act. What has happened, in effect, is that a quality of humanity has been applied to God. The same emphasis occurs elsewhere in the Sermon on the Mount and throughout Matthew's Gospel: an accent placed upon human action rather than theological reflection. The following section of the Sermon on the Mount (the Our Father, Matt 6:9-13) is followed by a saying that stresses one aspect of the Our Father, namely forgiveness: "For if you forgive others their trespasses, your heavenly Father will also forgive you; but if you do not forgive others, neither will your Father forgive your trespasses" (Matt 6:14-15).[50] In the Sermon on the Mount the focus is on the human action. God will respond with an action determined by human action.[51]

In the imitation of God, both the letter of James and the Sermon on the Mount remain focused on the actions of humans rather than on God's actions. Both Matthew and James believe that human conduct should give expression to God's will, or, as James expresses it, that human conduct should enable one to maintain friendship with God (4:4).

---

[49] See Crouzel, "L'Imitation et la 'Suite' de Dieu et du Christ," 24.

[50] Luke, by contrast, has the parable of the friend at midnight (Luke 11:5-8) in place of Matthew's commentary on forgiveness.

[51] The parable of the unforgiving servant (Matt 18:23-35) is another Matthean passage where God's action is seen to respond in the way in which humans act. Matthew presents this parable to show that the extent of forgiveness should be limitless. "So my heavenly Father will also do to every one of you, if you do not forgive your brother or sister from your heart" (Matt 18:35). Again, for Matthew the focus is upon human behavior, in particular the necessity to forgive others if one wishes to obtain God's forgiveness. His teaching starts with human behavior not with God's action (see Dupont, "L'Appel à imiter Dieu en Matthieu 5,48 et Luc 6,36," 153).

The advice in both writings is addressed to communities, not just to individuals. The communities are presented with demands that everyone can attain. They are called to total obedience in the fulfillment of God's will in order to maintain a right relationship with God. Perfection for both traditions consists in a total commitment to God that is realized through actions. For both Matthew and James, the paraenesis rests on the conviction that faith must be illustrated in action. Through action, one demonstrates the quality of one's relationship with God, a lifestyle that aims at perfection. Matthew states, "Not everyone who says to me, 'Lord, Lord,' will enter the kingdom of heaven, but only the one who does the will of my Father in heaven" (7:21), while Jas 2:18 says, "But someone will say, 'You have faith and I have works.' Show me your faith apart form your works, and I by my works will show you my faith."

Implications for Understanding the Emerging Traditions of Early Christianity

The consequence of this study does not argue for a knowledge of the Gospel of Matthew by the letter of James or vice versa. I do not think that such an argument can be made.[52] What I think this study shows is that the thought world of the letter of James is very similar to that of Matthew's Sermon on the Mount. Not only do both texts con-

---

A final example illustrating the importance that Matthew gives to the action of people in relation to the action of God can be seen in the parable of the lost sheep (Matt 18:10-14). Matthew has placed the parable in the discourse on the community (chapter 18) where it addresses the concern that the disciples must have in bringing back sinners. In contrast, the Gospel of Luke stresses the concern that God has for sinners (Luke 15:3-7).

In Matthew's eyes, human conduct should express God's will in the fullest possible way. As such, human action is an ethical consideration, not a theological one. While Luke wants to help the reader understand the conduct of God, Matthew wants to help his readers see the conduct of humanity (see Dupont, "L'Appel à imiter Dieu en Matthieu 5,48 et Luc 6,36," 157–8).

[52] Elsewhere I have examined the relationship between the letter of James and the traditions lying behind the Gospel of Matthew, more especially the Sayings Gospel Q (see *James and the Q Sayings of Jesus*, 144, n. 3). It is beyond the scope of the investigation to pursue this point here. The present purpose has been simply to illustrate that one aspect, namely the concept of perfection, is viewed in similar ways by both writings. What is of importance for my argument is that the Sermon on the Mount, as it now stands, bears similarities to the thought of the letter of James.

verge in their understanding of perfection, but they also show a number of other similar ideas. Both works stress the primacy of action as a reflection of one's faith. The imitation of God in one's actions is also of prime importance. While God's actions are proposed as an example, the focus is not with God, but with human actions. Neither text is attempting to give a theological understanding of God. The appeal to the divine simply emphasizes the call for humans to strive for perfection.

The letter of James must emerge from a religious context very similar to that of Matthew's Sermon on the Mount. It is not sufficient to say that their similarities are attributed to the common heritage they share with Judaism. It is true that much in both texts lies very close to the Jewish heritage, probably more so than most of the other New Testament writings. Nevertheless, what is so remarkable is the way both traditions have changed certain aspects of the Jewish tradition in similar ways. In particular, the notion of the imitation of God flourishes in each. As demonstrated, this was not a distinctively Old Testament or even Jewish concept, yet it is a crucial characteristic of both these texts. Further, the importance of fulfilling the entirety of the law (which undoubtedly is a characteristic Jewish understanding of the law and is also emphasized in both texts) has now been expanded by both the letter of James and Matthew's Sermon on the Mount to give attention to the importance of the law of love as the epitome of the law.

These connections point to the development of the traditions of early Christianity within a similar environment or milieu. They show that early Christians are still close to their Jewish roots, yet a development is proceeding in similar ways. The letter of James and Matthew's Sermon on the Mount are heirs to a remarkably similar heritage and similar development.[53] Ironically, the history of the transmission of the letter of James and of the Sermon on the Mount shows that they were received in surprisingly different ways. The Sermon on the Mount, as it now occurs in the Gospel of Matthew, has emerged almost as the "Magna Carta" of Christianity. It is one of the most well known parts, if not the most well known, of the Gospels and of the entire New Testament. This sermon gives expression to what Christians consider so

---

[53] Further study needs to be done to specify this connection. I have focused only on a number of aspects where connections are quite remarkable. But, to reach a firm conclusion with regard to the connections between the letter of James and the Sermon on the Mount would require a study in its own right. It would be necessary to examine the entirety of both texts and not just a few connections, as I have done. Nevertheless, I do believe that the striking connections I have isolated are indications of a similar development in the religious thought world of emerging Christianity.

characteristic of Jesus' teaching and in this way appeals to the imagination of Christians as the very heart of the Gospel message.

The letter of James, on the other hand, has been relegated to the
margins of the New Testament.[54] Accepted late into the Christian
canon,[55] it has always fallen under a cloud of suspicion because of the
way in which it has been compared to the writings of Paul. In fact,
James has most frequently been read from Paul's point of view. Because
James has been seen to challenge or even to oppose Paul's central
teaching on the relationship of faith and works, James's views have
been considered suspect.[56] However, it is now hoped that by showing
the connections of the letter of James to another tradition of early Christianity—a tradition very different from Paul but nonetheless valued as
the heart of the message of Jesus—James will be seen through new

[54] This has been the situation from the very beginning. However, especially
since the time of Martin Luther, the letter of James has fallen under a cloud of suspicion, receiving much distrust. Luther wrote in his Preface to the New Testament
(*Luther's Works: Word and Sacrament I*, vol. 35, ed. T. Backmann [Philadelphia:
Fortress Press, 1960] 362): "In a word St. John's Gospel and his first epistle, St.
Paul's epistles, especially Romans, Galatians, and Ephesians, and St. Peter's first
epistle are the books that show you Christ and teach you all that is necessary and
salvatory for you to know, even if you were never to see or hear any other book or
doctrine. Therefore St. James' epistle is really an epistle of straw, compared to these
others, for it has nothing of the nature of the gospel about it."

In a special preface to the letter of James, Luther wrote further (*Luther's Works:
Word and Sacrament I*, vol. 35, 397): "In a word, he wanted to guard against those
who relied on faith without works, but was unequal to the task. He tries to accomplish by harping on the law what the apostles accomplish by stimulating
people to love. Therefore I cannot include him among the chief books, though I
would not prevent anyone from including or extolling him as he pleases, for there
are otherwise many good sayings in him."

This negative assessment has undoubtedly influenced biblical scholarship greatly.
The approach of Luther was in stark contrast to that of John Calvin (*Commentaries
on the Catholic Epistles*, trans. and ed. J. Owen [Grand Rapids, Mich.: Eerdmans,
1959] 276–7), who appraised the letter of James very positively. Nevertheless, it was
largely Luther's attitude that was to have an enduring negative effect.

[55] It was only universally accepted as part of the Christian Canon by the fourth
century C.E. (Franz Mussner, *Der Jakobusbrief: Auslegung*, 4th ed. [Freiburg: Herder,
1981] 38–42).

[56] Luke Timothy Johnson (*The Letter of James: A New Translation with Introduction
and Commentary*, The Anchor Bible 37A [New York: Doubleday, 1995] 58–64) provides a very good "nuanced" analysis of the comparisons between James and Paul.
His conclusion is very balanced: "Despite the remarkable points of resemblance,
they appear not to be talking to each other by way of instruction or correction.
Rather, they seem to be addressing concerns specific to each author" (64).

eyes. Instead of being marginalized, James should be valued alongside Matthew's Sermon on the Mount as giving an insight into traditions of early Christianity that lie very close to the person of Jesus.

The final chapter will develop this importance of the letter of James by examining its relevance and value for today. In particular, this study will show the spirituality of perfection, as it emerges from the letter, urging today's reader to take seriously its ethical consequences and implications. Its message presents a challenge equal to that of Matthew's Sermon on the Mount.

CHAPTER SEVEN

On Reading James Today

Introduction

The letter of James is written to a community of Jewish-Christians living outside Palestine whom the author sees as heirs to Israel's heritage. The promises of the past have reached fulfillment in the present reconstitution of the twelve tribe kingdom. James calls his readers to authentic maturity as this twelve tribe kingdom. Such a call demands that the readers respond either positively or negatively to the instructions that outline their way of being in the world. As a protreptic discourse,[1] the letter of James presents an argument that uses exhortations to illustrate the community's lifestyle.

As part of the Christian canon, James's advice is significant, not just for first-century readers, but for readers of every age. James's argument presents the values that identify the believer as part of a new social order, namely "the twelve tribes in the Dispersion." The call to perfection that characterizes this writing is directed to the readers' present life. They are called to lead their lives in an integral way as members of the eschatological twelve tribes of the Dispersion. Luke Timothy Johnson has drawn attention to the need for the reader to discover the meaning of the text, as well as to engage the text within his or her own context.[2] This is an important insight and one that I wish

---

[1] See the discussion in the section of chapter 3 entitled, "The Paraenetic or Protreptic Nature of This Wisdom Advice," p. 45.

[2] Luke Timothy Johnson (*The Letter of James: A New Translation with Introduction and Commentary*, The Anchor Bible 37A [New York: Doubleday, 1995] 163) draws attention to this essential dimension of engagement with the text: "The reader is asked directly to test the *truth* and not only the *meaning* of the proposition. The question is not simply whether the statement makes sense given the author's worldview, but also whether it is true within the reader's worldview."

to pursue further. This study culminates in an examination of the importance of the letter's ethical stance for today. What does this study of the letter of James have to say to the present-day reader?

James issues a call for faith in action. This message has vital importance for today's world. This letter had a long history of struggle in gaining acceptance by the entire Christian tradition. The letter of James was among the last of the New Testament writings to gain universal acceptance as part of the Christian canon.[3] In the course of the sixteenth century, the letter was the subject of intense debate provoked by the influence of Martin Luther, who judged that James was reacting to Paul's teaching on justification by faith.[4] Luther approached James through the eyes of Paul.

Today the situation is different. The attitude toward the letter of James has shifted largely from a position of controversy to that of irrelevancy in the modern Christian world. Either consciously or unconsciously, Christians are operating with a "canon within a canon." The Gospels and the letters of Paul constitute the central canon of the New Testament. The letter of James is relegated to the margins of the New Testament because of James's perceived challenge to Paul's teaching. While James appears somewhat problematical for Lutheran and Protestant Christianity,[5] the Catholic Church also relegates it to the periphery in its liturgy. An examination of its liturgical use shows that James is read only on five Sundays in the course of the three-year Sunday cycle of readings.[6]

---

[3] See the detailed discussion on the canonical history of James in James H. Ropes, *A Critical and Exegetical Commentary on the Epistle of James* (Edinburgh: T. and T. Clark, [1916] 1978) 86–115. Origen (184–254) is the first writer to quote James explicitly by name. It seems that through Origen's influence and the ensuing acceptance of the letter of James within the Alexandrian church its wider importance began to grow. Ropes sums up the final acceptance of the letter of James in this way: "From the third century the epistle begins to be quoted, and to be included in the canon, first of all in the Greek church, then in the Latin, and finally in the Syrian church. Among the Greeks the process seems to have been complete before the time when Eusebius wrote his history (c. 324). In the West at the close of the fourth century, Jerome and Augustine mark, and did much to effect, the final acceptance of the book as sacred Scripture" (Ropes, *The Epistle of St. James*, 86–7). See also Johnson, *The Letter of James*, 126–40; and Sophie Laws, *A Commentary on the Epistle of James*, Black's New Testament Commentaries (London: Black, 1980) 20–6.

[4] See chapter 6, n. 54.

[5] See Andrew Chester, "James: Significance for Today," *The Theology of the Letters of James, Peter, and Jude,* ed. Andrew Chester and Ralph P. Martin (Cambridge: Cambridge University Press, 1994) 55.

[6] See Patrick J. Hartin, "'Come Now, You Rich, Weep and Wail . . .' (James 5:1-6)," *Journal of Theology for Southern Africa* 84 (1993) 57.

The message of James is important both for its own world as well as for our own. This message bears a particular relevancy by calling on believers to match their faith with action.

The Practice of Authentic Christian Existence

Perfection as a Way of Being in the World

James's urgent message appeals to believers to live out their faith in a particular way. Spirituality has been defined as a way of being in the world.[7] As such, James's spirituality shows a faith that informs one's way of being in the world. Faith leads to action. James does not present a well-rounded and systematic treatment of the content of the Christian faith in the way that Paul does. However, this does not suggest that James's message is any less important. The implications of James's faith call the believer to action at every age of the Christian Church.

As has been argued, James reflects the essence of the traditional threefold biblical understanding of perfection. The spirituality of perfection that emerges from this threefold understanding of perfection provides a particular importance and urgency for today.

Perfection as Wholeness

The fundamental meaning of perfection in James relates to the concept of wholeness and completeness: ". . . so that you may be mature and complete, lacking in nothing" (1:4). The essence of James's call to perfection is a challenge to its readers to harmonize faith and action in their lives. The person whose actions conform to his or her faith is a person of integrity. The image of the divided person, the double-minded person, is the counterpart to what James intends (1:8). This call remains as relevant today as it was in the time of James.

God alone accomplishes this wholeness and completeness. The believers are "the first fruits of God's creatures" (1:18), God's perfect gift (1:17). If anything should be lacking, God is the one who will provide for them when they ask (1:5). This gift enables believers to conform to the original constitution of God's people as the "twelve tribes in the Dispersion." The community is the reconstituted people of God that conforms to the image God desired for God's people from the beginning.

---

[7] See Ernest Kurtz and Katherine Ketcham, eds., *The Spirituality of Imperfection: Storytelling and the Journey to Wholeness* (New York: Bantam, 1992) 16.

The individual believer attains perfection as part of this reconstituted people of God.

As with any gift there comes responsibility. Being part of God's re-constituted people, they lead lives that remain true to this wholeness and integrity. Their lives reflect their faith. Today, as in every age, Christians are challenged to ensure that they do not just give lip service to their faith. Their way of being in the world must illustrate their faith. James uses the gift of speech to illustrate the perfect person: "Anyone who makes no mistakes in speaking is perfect" (3:2). Here the concept of integrity dominates. Those who always tell the truth are those who harmonize thought and speech. They conform to the way God has created them, by using speech to bless God and one another (3:9-10).

Perfection Demands a Wholehearted Dedication to God

The call to be friends of God (4:4) lies at the heart of James's teaching. Faith calls for total dependence upon God. The concept of perfection expresses this life of total dependence upon God. The image of the divided person captures the opposite situation of one who fails to show total allegiance to God. These are not time bound concepts, but ones that are central to the very message of Christianity. Faith as a relationship with God demands a wholehearted dedication to God where no half measures are conceivable. As Matthew says in another context: "No one can serve two masters; for a slave will either hate the one and love the other, or be devoted to the one and despise the other. You cannot serve God and wealth" (Matt 6:24).

James sees this opposition taking place between the world and God. In defining religion in 1:27, he says that "religion that is pure and undefiled before God, the Father, is this: . . . to keep oneself unstained by the world." The history of Christianity shows believers adopting different approaches to describe the relationship of the Christian to the world. This variety of approaches to the world is also evident in the Scriptures as well. For example, the Gospel of John sees the world as the theater of God's activity: "For God so loved the world that he gave his only Son, so that everyone who believes in him may not perish but may have eternal life" (John 3:16). Yet, in another context John views the world as equivalent to the forces opposed to Jesus: "I am not asking you to take them out of the world, but I ask you to protect them from the evil one. They do not belong to the world, just as I do not belong to the world" (John 17:15-16).[8]

---

[8] Vatican II (The Church in the Modern World [*Gaudium et spes*], *Vatican Council II: The Conciliar and Post Conciliar Documents*, ed. Austin Flannery [Collegeville:

James does not try to construct a fully developed theology. Instead, he argues a particular perspective. His concern here is to portray the world as a force that can lead one away from God. This is a valuable reminder for our present world. Amid the great technological advances in the past century, humanity needs to be reminded of the context of their efforts. While human beings have the ability to do many things, the further question always needs to be raised, "Should they be done?" The ability to perform an action does not necessarily mean that such an action should be done. The most obvious illustration of this is in the use of weapons. A nation does not possess a moral right to use certain weapons simply because that nation has the ability to make them. This is all the more urgent today where more countries are acquiring the ability to develop nuclear weapons. Because they possess the technology to develop weapons of mass destruction does not mean that they should actually produce them. For the more these nuclear arsenals are developed, the more the world is placed in jeopardy.

A positive approach to the world needs to be tempered with the reminder of the presence of evil in the world. The Christian is called upon to remain firm in allegiance to God by avoiding the enticements and attractions that emanate from the forces opposed to God. The community dimension of this call to perfection must remain in sight. Together, with other members of the reconstituted people of God, Christians live in friendship with God (Jas 4:4) and submit themselves to God (Jas 4:7).

Perfection Leads to Obedience of the Law

The Hebrew traditions show the fulfillment of the Torah as the ideal toward which every Israelite must strive. James is heir to the same traditions. The Torah is "the perfect law, the law of liberty" (1:25), because it gives expression to God's will. In carrying out God's will, one acquires the freedom to lead one's life in relationship with God and with the community. For James, the Torah continues to be vital for his community because it provides the way in which the

---

The Liturgical Press, 1980] 939–47) gives a very positive attitude to the world. The contributions of the Christian to the world are seen to contribute to the building up of the kingdom: "Whoever contributes to the development of the community of mankind on the level of family, culture, economic and social life, and national and international politics, according to the plan of God, is also contributing in no small way to the community of the Church insofar as it depends on things outside itself" (The Church in the Modern World, 44, 947).

community maintains its existence. As has been argued previously,[9] the Torah that James upholds is the moral law that gives expression to God's will for God's people. As such, the Torah provides those signposts giving the community direction on how to act. The Torah furnishes the members of the community with the means of social identification by providing them with moral signposts.

All the instructions in the letter of James give direction for maintaining the community's social identity. It constitutes them as a new society of the "twelve tribes in the Dispersion" and shows them how to act by providing a way of life that is distinctive from the wider society. James is not promoting a legalism with regard to law. Rather, the law functions as God's moral direction pointers for maintaining an identity in a world that is very different and often hostile. It does not call the community to separate from the world, but rather it shows them how they can maintain their identity while still functioning within the context of the wider society.

The community to whom James writes shares common bonds and a common way of life. The values of the community are the values of the individual separating them as individuals and as a community from the rest of the world. The love of neighbor becomes for James the epitome of the Torah illustrating the very heart of God's will for humanity. As such, the command to love one's neighbor encapsulates so perfectly the Torah's concern for the poor and powerless. James is in line with that tradition emanating from Jesus that subsumes the entire law under the law of love.

James's insight into the notion of law and how it functions within a Christian community is as important today as it was in the time of James. All laws and instructions express God's will for the community. They provide believers with guidelines that enable them to preserve their identity as God's people. In today's world where the Christian identity is becoming more and more nebulous, it is necessary to rediscover those values that distinguish the believing community from those of the wider society. The letter of James draws attention to the distinctiveness of the believing community and what it means to belong to such a community of faith. The laws and instructions are the means of socialization for believers within that faith community.

Since the concept of perfection captures what is meant by authentic Christian existence, the letter's moral instructions illustrate how to live out that perfection each day. It is a message that is always valid. These instructions are oriented toward helping the reader and the

---

[9] See the section of chapter 4 entitled "Perfection and the Law," p. 78.

community actualize here and now the reality of who they are and to preserve their social bonds. These exhortations are not teachings that view perfection as a future reward for good behavior. Instead, they encourage readers of every age to live in such a way that they will be found perfect at the end of time.[10]

Perfection as Integrity

As argued previously,[11] the notion of integrity expresses well the concept of perfection. Integrity demands consistency in word and action. This integrity is both personal and communitarian. The values that influence the lives of both the individual and the community are distinct from the world. In fact, believers should be a sign to the world of the consistency between their faith and their action. This harmony is the hallmark of James's message. James gives a very positive assessment of works (not "works of the law" in the sense that Paul attacks). James's focus on works centers on deeds of mercy that entail a constant concern for the needs and welfare of others, be it orphans and widows (1:27), the poor, or those discriminated against (2:1-7). Christian integrity demands a social conscience and response. James envisages that his readers (including present-day readers) demonstrate they are people of integrity in the following ways:

Sensitivity to the Pain of Others

The living out of faith in action must be a constant occurrence. The letter of James opens with a positive assessment of trials and oppression: "My brothers and sisters, whenever you face trials of any kind, consider it nothing but joy" (1:2). James envisages that the recompense for fidelity in the midst of oppression occurs in the present, in the lives of individuals and their communities. Through the endurance of trials they come close to wholeness, maturity, and perfection and experience solidarity with others.[12] The pain of the community becomes an individual's pain. A true community requires each member to embrace the trials of others and to journey together along the same road with them. A community that is whole, complete, and integral unites its members in the same struggles and sufferings. As Tamez notes: "The experience

[10] See Todd C. Penner, *The Epistle of James and Eschatology: Re-reading an Ancient Christian Letter,* JSNTS 121 (Sheffield: Sheffield Academic Press, 1996) 212.
[11] See the section of chapter 5 entitled "A Spirituality of Integrity," p. 101.
[12] See Elsa Tamez, *The Scandalous Message of James: Faith without Works Is Dead* (New York: Crossroad, 1992) 57.

of feeling perfect *(teleios)*, which in James means complete, total, integral, should remind those who suffer that they are human beings, not things."[13] A common humanity is evident in the pain that unites people and rightly brings a joy through this common experience. There is a desperate need in our present world to reawaken the human ties that bind the world together. The sufferings of others, particularly the poor in one's own society, demand a response of solidarity with their pain. One's humanity is experienced more existentially as one struggles to overcome whatever threatens to dehumanize society and the individual. James shows how dehumanizing forces are at work within his own society in the form of withholding unjustly the wages of the day laborers (5:4). Analogously, one can see similar dehumanizing tendencies at work in our present world. The exploitation of migrant workers, the sweat shops that demand hours of hard labor for meager returns, the pornographic exploitation of women and children; all these are but some of the evil forces within our society dehumanizing both the individual and the community. James's challenge is to be sensitive to these sufferings and to eradicate them from society.

People of Integrity Emulate the Integrity of God

In choosing to follow God, one chooses to be like God. God is always consistent in God's actions. This consistency implies that God will bestow every good gift on the believer.[14] "Every generous act of giving, with every perfect gift, is from above, coming down from the Father of lights, with whom there is no variation or shadow due to change" (Jas 1:17).

Belief in God consists in a belief that God is one: "You believe that God is one; you do well. Even the demons believe—and shudder. Do you want to be shown, you senseless person, that faith apart from works is barren?" (Jas 2:19-20). Commenting on the understanding that "God is one," Tamez argues that this phrase refers not merely to a monotheistic faith in God, as opposed to belief in the existence of other gods.[15] It also entails an understanding that "God acts consistently with the divine purpose, which for James is the cause of the

---

[13] Ibid., 58.

[14] As Laws (*A Commentary on the Epistle of James*, 73) argues forcefully: "The general point that James is making is clear: it is a further insistence upon the consistency of God as only and always the giver of good (an idea complementary to that of God as the single, i.e., ungrudging, giver of 1.5)."

[15] Tamez, *The Scandalous Message of James*, 61.

poor."[16] God is single-minded in bestowing good gifts on God's creatures. This single-mindedness undoubtedly brings with it a concern for action on behalf of the poor.

This understanding of God has serious repercussions for believers. Faith in God demands that this faith be demonstrated in action. If God has a single-minded dedication to the poor, so too believers must show their own concern through a single-mindedness that responds to the needs of the poor and those marginalized by society.

Integrity as Consistency between Faith and Action

"Religion that is pure and undefiled before God, the Father, is this: to care for orphans and widows in their distress, and to keep oneself unstained by the world" (Jas 1:27). Faith inspires a dedication to help the cause of those against whom society discriminates. The Christian faith calls for a reversal of attitudes toward the poor and the oppressed. The communities of believers must replace the unjust value systems of the world with a system that brings consistency to belief and practice.

James challenges communities of believers to demonstrate a consistency between their faith and action. James offers a graphic example to illustrate this:

> What good is it, my brothers and sisters, if you say you have faith but do not have works? Can faith save you? If a brother or sister is naked and lacks daily food, and one of you says to them, "Go in peace; keep warm and eat your fill," and yet you do not supply their bodily needs, what is the good of that? So faith by itself, if it has no works, is dead (2:14-17).

Faith brings with it a social consciousness and responsibility. A similar understanding is expressed in the final parable on the judgment of the nations in the Gospel of Matthew (25:31-46). Ultimately one's future depends upon the way one responds to the needs of those one encounters daily. One cannot pretend to be unaware of their urgent cries for help and pass them by. Faith calls forth a response.

An Integrity that Challenges Both the Individual and the Community

The letter of James presents no individualistic ethics. Its spirituality impacts both upon the individual and the community. Although it does address the individual, the letter generally has in mind the individual insofar as she or he forms part of a community. The community is guided by the same faith that inspires each individual member.

[16] Ibid.

Friendship with God, as opposed to friendship with the world, is the force inspiring every action. A spirituality of integrity brings about a specific attitude toward suffering or oppression within the community and promotes solidarity among all.

This concept of integrity defines well James's notion of perfection understood in the sense of wholeness. Integrity demonstrates that one is whole, that one strives for a consistency in faith and action, that one establishes a harmony in relationships with others and with God.[17] The conclusion to the letter of James radiates this agreement among the members of the community. The spirit of the final pericope (5:13-20) shines forth with concern for one another: the community prays for those who are sick (5:13), the elders pray over them (5:14), they confess their sins to one another (5:16), and, finally, the members of the community seek out those who stray from the path of truth (5:19) and bring them back (5:20).

Authentic Christian Existence Embraces a Concern for the Poor

Like the prophets before him, James gives expression to the voice of the poor and the marginalized. James resonates with conviction and hope as he speaks on their behalf. Such a voice can be uncomfortable for those readers who have no pressing material needs. Yet, the message of Jesus was never meant to be a message that was comfortable. His is a message that is challenging.

Both James and the Synoptic traditions emphasize the promise of the inheritance of a kingdom to the poor (Luke 6:20; Jas 2:5). One major difference between these two traditions is the way they express the message. Jesus' teaching about the rich and poor is most often couched in terms of parables (Luke 16:19-31), while James's attitude is very clear and direct.[18] Perhaps, as Ralph Martin observes, "James' community evidently had not fully identified with the poor, and the author hopes to steer them to a deeper identity with the oppressed."[19] "Listen! The wages of the laborers who mowed your fields, which you kept back by fraud, cry out, and the cries of the harvesters have reached the ears of the Lord of hosts" (Jas 5:4).

---

[17] As Tamez (*The Scandalous Message of James*, 69) defines it: "As we can see, integrity, in the sense of being consistent with oneself, with others, and with God, is a vital factor for praxis."

[18] See Ralph P. Martin, *James*, Word Biblical Commentary, vol. 48 (Waco, Tex.: Word Books, 1988) lxxxv.

[19] Ibid.

Neither Jesus' nor James's teaching considers poverty as desirable in its own right. Instead, they hold up the attitude of the poor person for emulation. Poverty takes on a spiritual dimension where the poor know their need of God. Since they are unable to help themselves, they need God's support and patrimony. Poverty in the time of Jesus and James was not only an economic plight. The economic situation stemmed from their inability to champion their own cause because they had no power or status.[20] In this context of powerlessness, the poor experience that they are "rich in faith" (Jas 2:5). They understand that God is on their side and that God will come to their assistance (Jas 5:4). Powerlessness is replaced with a power and status that comes from God, who will intervene on behalf of the poor in order to vindicate them (Jas 5:4-6).

James stands in that trajectory, reaching back from the prophets through Jesus and beyond, where God is recognized as the vindicator of the poor. James shows that the religion of Jesus and of the prophets is one that puts concern for the poor at the heart of its message. An honest respect for the poor person as a creature of God is ultimately what James champions.[21] This contrasts with the respect that the world gives to those with wealth and power. As an advocate for the poor, the letter of James condemns sharply every form of injustice experienced by the poor. James condemns unjust situations be they in his own or in our contexts. James is certain of one thing: God hears the cry of the poor (Jas 5:4) and ultimately the rich will be overthrown (Jas 5:5-6).

James does not incite the poor to take up arms in order to attain justice. God will accomplish this great reversal (Jas 1:9-10). Judgment rests in God's hands. Since God hears the cries of the poor, they have the right to demand justice from God. In particular, the poor have every right to demand just wages and humane working conditions. The demand is as valid today as it was in the first century. The poor have the consolation of knowing that God will champion their cause. The tirade against the rich does not intend to get the rich to change their ways. Instead, its concern is with the poor to whom James gives assurance that God will right their injustices. The poor place themselves in God's care.

A personal religion is meaningless without a social concern and involvement. Social commitment is what James demands. The challenge

[20] See Bruce J. Malina, "Wealth and Poverty in the New Testament and Its World," *Interpretation* 41 (1987) 354–67.

[21] See Wiard Popkes, *Adressaten, Situation und Form des Jakobusbriefes,* Stuttgarter Bibelstudien 125/126 (Stuttgart: Verlag Katholisches Bibelwerk Gmbtt, 1986) 197–9.

to adopt an option for the poor is as relevant today as it was in James's time. "That James takes up their cause as an apostle of Jesus Christ demonstrates his option for the poor. Like James, we, as modern representatives of Jesus Christ, are called to take that option and to take up the cause of the oppressed."[22] The message of James remains a vital challenge to present-day Christians and to society to assess their attitude to the poor.

Central to the whole discussion of James on the rich and the poor is the contrast between two very different attitudes of reality. The rich trust in themselves and their own efforts and achievements, while the poor turn outside themselves to place their trust in God. Those who adopt God's attitude to the world will be exalted, while those who exalt in the present world will experience a reversal (Jas 1:9-11). This illustrates further the thesis expressed in Jas 4:4 suggesting that one has to choose between friendship with the world and friendship with God. The world espouses the values of status, power, and wealth. God's values extend beyond the individual and the community to the needy, the poor, and those without status. As Jesus says in the parable on the judgment of the nations: "Come, O blessed of my Father, for I was poor, marginalized, and you welcomed me" (Matt 25:34).[23]

The value of the poor in God's eyes has a further important consequence. Every form of discrimination is to be avoided: "My brothers and sisters, do you with your acts of favoritism really believe in our glorious Lord Jesus Christ?" (Jas 2:1). While the example that follows involves discrimination against a poor person, this example embraces every form of discrimination as inconsistent with faith in a God who treats all people equally as creatures of God (1:18). James calls for a way of life, an authentic existence, that embraces the equality of all people. This challenge lies at the heart of the concerns of our present world where struggles for justice center around overcoming discrimination encountered in the areas of race, gender, and sexuality. In recent years, remarkable triumphs have occurred in overcoming racial discrimination, as witnessed, for example, in the transformation of South Africa through a non-racial democratic government. The efforts to bring an end to hostility between Protestants and Catholics in Northern Ireland is a further illustration of the desire to overcome religious prejudices. This is proof of the ability of the human spirit to replace

[22] Pedrito U. Maynard-Reid, *Poverty and Wealth in James* (Maryknoll, N.Y.: Orbis Books, 1987) 98.

[23] This is the way Pope John Paul II paraphrased the message of Matt 25:34-46 in his lenten message for 1998 (*L'Osservatore Romano*, weekly edition in English, 7 [1529] 18 February 1998, p. 1).

selfish concerns with an acceptance of the Christian vision of the equality and dignity of all people. The message of James remains a reminder to every generation of a truth as old as Christianity, but one that every generation has to rediscover for itself.

The option for the poor[24] and the avoidance of every form of discrimination illustrate the heart of James's message: faith must overflow into action. Following the example of God, Jesus, and James, we must make that option for the poor our own. James calls for a spirituality that takes seriously the equality of all, an equality that avoids every form of discrimination. Christians belong to a community of faith that embraces the same ways of acting with one another, with Jesus (through their faith in him), and with God (through their friendship with God [Jas 4:4]). Integrity demonstrates a consistency in faith and action, a consistency in relationships with others and with God. The wholeness of the individual and the community is rightly demonstrated through this faith in action. An option for the poor that embraces every human person regardless of their differences bears witness to what makes Christian existence authentic.

Challenge Addressed to Christian Communities Today

What Does It Mean to Be Perfect Today?

In today's society, the concept of perfection is radically different from that espoused by the letter of James. Today's world promotes a perfection that demands material success, achievements that occur at the expense of others, physical beauty that emphasizes externals and acknowledges no defects. Such perfection calls upon individuals to strive for economic wealth, to avoid every form of pain and suffering, to be successful always. Ultimately success depends upon how one is considered by others. Appearance is all that matters. This perfection is attained only through a struggle between individuals or groups where one overcomes another and is considered better than the other.

Tamez comments upon such standards for perfection: "If such is the case the great majority of the poor and exploited in Latin America are at a low level, a level of imperfection, because they never will have the opportunity to reach the image of perfection projected by our society."[25] One could add that not just the people of Latin America, but

---

[24] See Maynard-Reid, *Poverty and Wealth in James,* 98.
[25] Tamez, *The Scandalous Message of James,* 87.

the vast majority of the world's population would be excluded from this ideal of perfection.

James's concept of perfection is exactly the reverse. For James, authentic perfection demands consistency between what one believes and what one does. In the final analysis, one's faith proclaims a belief in a God who champions the cause of the poor and the oppressed. This faith challenges the believer both as an individual and as part of a community to respond in the same way as God does. If God shows a preferential option for the poor, so too must the Christian as an individual within a larger community. Since the vast majority of the world's population are poor, Christian communities must make a decided option to be involved with them. Churches today face the challenge to correct society's values by promoting a true understanding of the perfection to which the letter of James gives witness. Jesus' message did not endorse the status quo. The Jesus of the Gospels was highly critical of the religious establishment and its lack of concern for the poor and the seemingly less important members of society. James continues Jesus' spirit by demonstrating an equal concern for the poor.

James challenges readers to achieve a consistency between faith and action. This corrects a growing tendency today to separate the two. If faith is to be made alive, it must flower forth into actions that bear fruit. Ultimately these actions challenge the reader to transform the world by making it more human.[26] James addresses the reader not merely as an individual, but as a member of a community of faith. More can be achieved by working together as a group sharing the same vision and perspective than by working as individuals isolated from each other.

---

[26] Tamez (*The Scandalous Message of James*, 80–8) makes an interesting comparison between John Wesley and James in their understandings of perfection. She shows how central the idea of perfection is to both writers. She summarizes the thought of Wesley in this way: "In several places in his writings he condenses his thought on perfection by saying that the perfect Christians are those who have faith, love, joy, peace, and pray unceasingly, giving thanks for everything, bearing fruit in all their words and deeds. These are the Christians who are 'mature in Christ'" (85). The differences between Wesley and James lie more on the level of where they place their emphasis. Wesley tends to relate the concept of perfection to the level of the challenge of individual Christians in their relationship with God and Christ, while for James perfection occurs more in the interpersonal relationships within the community (86).

James Challenges Us to Re-Imagine the Development of Christianity

James reflects a closeness to the teaching of Jesus.[27] Concern for the poor and marginalized lies at the heart both of Jesus' teaching and of James's vision. "Has not God chosen the poor in the world to be rich in faith and to be heirs of the kingdom that he has promised to those who love him?" (Jas 2:5). This is remarkably close to the spirit of Jesus whose whole life demonstrated concern for the poor and the outcasts of society.

James bears witness to a development of the Jesus tradition that differed greatly from most of the other New Testament traditions. This is clearly seen in comparing James's thought on the issue of faith and works with that of Paul. The differences between the traditions of Paul and James caused of cloud of suspicion to fall upon the latter.[28] On the other hand, the study of the concept of perfection in the letter of James and Matthew's Sermon on the Mount[29] has demonstrated a remarkable similarity in their understanding of the Jesus tradition. Not only does their understanding of perfection show an agreement in perspective, but it also shows a convergence in the emphasis given to the primacy of action in reflecting one's faith. Further, both texts propose the imitation of God as important for human actions. This is an understanding that is characteristic of neither the Old Testament nor of Judaism in the first century C.E. Finally, the importance in fulfilling the entirety of the Torah (a characteristic Jewish understanding) is emphasized by both the letter of James and Matthew's Sermon on the Mount.

These connections argue for a common religious heritage for both the letter of James and Matthew's Sermon on the Mount. Just as the Sermon on the Mount reproduces the heart of Jesus' teaching, so does the letter of James continue Jesus' message. When Matthew's Sermon on the Mount was taken up into the larger context of the Gospel of Matthew, the starkness of its message dissipated as the wider context in which it was read transformed its meaning. On the other hand, the

---

[27] See Chester, "James: Significance for Today," 58.

[28] I have already drawn attention to the problem caused by reading James through the eyes of Paul (see chapter 4, n. 85, and chapter 6, n. 54). It has not been my intent to examine the relationship of James to Paul in depth. This would be a study in its own right. However, suffice it to say that I agree with the conclusion reached by Johnson, who sees each writer dealing with issues central to their own context and not engaging each other in any form of controversy (Johnson, *The Letter of James*, 64).

[29] See chapter 6.

brevity of the letter of James preserved the forcefulness of the message that concentrated on the poor and the marginalized. The letter of James, then, gives an insight into the development of the tradition of Jesus along a path different from that taken by the rest of the New Testament writings. This path reflects the radicality of Jesus' message and is extremely valuable in helping the reader to appreciate the richness and diversity of the early Christian movement.[30] In witnessing to a diversity within early Christianity, the letter of James opens up a perspective that resonates with the postmodern consciousness that embraces diversity. The distinctive message of James continues the concerns of Jesus in embracing the cause of the poor and in challenging the vested interests of the powerful within society. As such, the letter of James contains a message that continues to burn with urgency today.[31]

James Challenges Us to Reach Out Beyond the Boundaries of Christianity

The moral instructions of the letter of James provide social signposts to the members of James's community on how to preserve their identity. James's community is conscious that what drives and motivates them are the values that come from their faith. At the same time, the letter of James is a reminder that there are many things that it holds in common with other religious traditions. This letter provides the impetus to identify and acknowledge these common values that other religious traditions also hold sacred.

Of all the New Testament writings, James shows the greatest continuity with the Jewish inheritance. As a protreptic writing, James belongs to that literary world that knows no boundaries between Judaism and Christianity. Its form of expression transcends specific religious confines.

The letter provides believers with instruction on how to live out their faith in everyday life. The main concern lies with practice. James and Judaism adopt an identical attitude to the Torah as the expression of God's will for God's people. As such it is to be upheld in its entirety

---

[30] As Chester ("James: Significance for Today," 58) says: "This continuity with Jesus' teaching is relatively rare within the New Testament, and James stands as an important witness to one possible line of development for the Christian community, against the direction taken by the majority of early writers and communities."

[31] The urgency of the message of James for Third World countries and liberation theology's "preferential option for the poor" is beginning to be appreciated more and more. See, for example, Tamez, *The Scandalous Message of James,* and Maynard-Reid, *Poverty and Wealth in James.*

(Jas 2:10) and James remains concerned with its implementation. The Torah continues to be "the perfect law, the law of liberty" (1:25), the "royal law" (2:8). As the quintessential expression of God's will, the Torah maps out a way of being in the world for God's people and demands faithful obedience. Faith in action is what motivates every believer. As Chester notes: "James can, in this sense, be seen as making a case for Christianity as Judaism, to be primarily concerned not with belief, but practice, the people of God living in complete obedience to the divine command."[32]

With only two explicit references to Jesus in the course of the letter (1:1; 2:1), James's faith is centered more theologically than christologically.[33] This provides another link to the world of Judaism. The concept of God as creator and lawgiver holds much in common with a Jewish understanding of God. The identification of the community to whom it is addressed as "the twelve tribes in the Dispersion" (1:1), who are "the first fruits of God's creatures" (1:18), lies within the very heart of Judaism's self-identification. The letter of James holds more in common with Judaism than in separation from it. James offers a unique possibility to forge a dialogue between Judaism and Christianity. The dialogue should focus upon its overall ethical understanding that is grounded upon a theological vision. In this context, the letter of James shows how much of its ethical vision still resonates with that of Judaism. The awareness of this common heritage enables both Christian and Jewish communities to appreciate anew their common heritage.[34] This has importance for our present world where Christians endeavor to make amends to our Jewish sisters and brothers for the evils Christians of previous generations perpetrated against them in the name of the Christian religion.

In the wider religious world beyond Judaism and Christianity, James also stands poised to offer a contribution. For James, God is the creator who has made humanity in God's likeness (3:9). The ethical consequences of this reality demand that all human beings be treated with the dignity and respect they deserve. James again provides the unique possibility for enunciating an understanding of how a human being should act in the world without specifically drawing upon the

[32] Chester, "James: Significance for Today," 57–8.

[33] See Johnson, *The Letter of James*, 164.

[34] As Johnson (*The Letter of James*, 164) says: "Rather than an embarrassment to a Christianity that defines itself as much as possible in terms of its *difference* from Judaism, James is a gift (particularly in a post-Holocaust generation) to the Christian community to examine how the 'faith of Jesus Christ' can positively be affirmed as much in continuity with 'the perfect law of freedom' as in discontinuity."

distinctiveness of its Christian understanding of God. The concern for the poor, the avoidance of discrimination in every form, the appeal to take control of one's tongue, the critique of conflicts and disputes that stem from desires at war within the human heart, all these are ethical issues that relate to the human condition irrespective of their religious or humanistic origin. James shows an awareness of and promotes a concern for issues of a social nature that reach across the religious divide. He offers possibilities for dialogue with other traditions on areas of common concern. In a postmodern world that celebrates multiculturalism and religious diversity, the letter of James remains a valuable document for fostering dialogue. It gives impetus to social action that resonates with all people of good will irrespective of their religious background.

Once again, I can cite another example from my own South African background where divergent religious traditions united in moral outrage. In the South African struggle against the evils of apartheid, common ethical values transcended the narrow confines of religious denominationalism. The evils of segregation and the atrocities perpetrated by the state to keep people separate unleashed an opposition that transcended religious bounds as nothing else could. Jews, Muslims, Communists, Atheists, Catholics, Christians of every denomination together with members of African Traditional Religions all banded together in a common human response to oppose and resist the evils of apartheid. In its opposition to discrimination, the letter of James reflects this common human sentiment so admirably (Jas 2:1).

An Urgent Challenge to Embrace James's Vision

James's Vision Is to Be Read in the Context of the Other Biblical Witnesses to the Christian Faith

While the importance of James and his vision has been emphasized throughout this study, this message must be read within the context of other voices emerging from the Christian Scriptures. James's vision cannot stand alone. James is a reminder to the reader of a basic dimension of Jesus' message that stands out from other reflections and presentations of the Christian faith. This message does not claim to be an all inclusive or comprehensive presentation of the Christian faith. Just as the letters of Paul need a wider context in order to appreciate their meaning and significance, so too does the letter of James. This letter draws upon the wider context of the canon of Scripture and cannot be read in isolation from the rest of the Scriptures. In preserving its canonical position, James offers an urgent witness to the importance of one dimension of

Jesus' teaching. This is no isolated message, but one that reaches back into the heart of the biblical teaching where the voices of the Hebrew prophets call their people to exercise an option for the poor. This message is exemplified as well in the wisdom writings that are concerned with providing guidelines for leading one's life according to the faith one professes. Finally, this message is exemplified in the rich, cultic language of perfection. The call to wholeness and integrity expresses the very essence of a believer who strives to remain true to the creative power of God, re-creating this community of believers as the "first-fruits." This is what Robert Wall terms "the canonical approach to biblical interpretation."[35] The vision of James is one among many other visions witnessing to the Christian reflection on God and humanity's relationship to God and to one another. James needs to be heard together with the other biblical voices so that the richness and the diversity of the Christian message may emerge. The importance of James's theological message is not to be exaggerated. Neither is it to be silenced. Together with the rest of the canonical writings, James emerges as one among many other lights illuminating the reality of the Christian faith.[36]

James's Spirituality Acts as a Corrective to
Present-Day Approaches to Spirituality

Western spirituality tends to place great emphasis upon a spirituality of the individual in isolation from a larger community. This has more to do, perhaps, with Western society's focus upon the individual. While James's spirituality of perfection embraces the individual, he shows that this spirituality can be worked out only in relationship to the community. The spirituality of perfection is a spirituality of authentic Christian existence. It calls upon Christian believers to activate their faith through an awareness of the bonds that unite them with other Christian believers in their common option for the poor and those marginalized by society. James provides a serious reminder of the community dimension of the Christian faith and way of life. The spirituality of James is a real counter to the forces at work both within society and within the Christian faith that wish to reduce Christianity to a private, individualistic religion.

[35] Robert W. Wall, *Community of the Wise: The Letter of James*, The New Testament in Context (Valley Forge, Pa.: Trinity Press International, 1997) 23–7.

[36] As Wall so well expresses it: "The special significance of this book's particular witness to God, then, is best understood in relationship to the witnesses of other biblical books and collections, precisely because each understands God in different although complementary ways and forms, if finally by 'mutual criticism,' a more objective and discriminating faith" (*Community of the Wise*, 24).

The spirituality of James remains an urgent witness to the heart of the Christian message. In its option for the poor, in its condemnation of all forms of discrimination, in its call for friendship with God, the letter of James provides its readers with a distinctive way of being in the world. This distinctiveness is more evident when viewed against the background of the materialistic values of today's society. Read in today's context, there is an urgency in the letter of James for Christians to take this message seriously and to put it into practice. James calls into account the integrity of Christians both as individuals and as a community. If Christians are to make an impact on today's society, their faith must match their actions. As Chester says: "However this may be, the fact is that Christianity has no reason to be taken seriously if it fails to live out its faith at real cost to itself (financially, socially, and emotionally), and therefore represent a real challenge to the complacency and deep helplessness of modern Western society."[37]

James's attitude to the world provides an important guide. The letter warns its readers against the world and its allurements. What is distinctive about James's approach is that the letter does not advocate that its community separate themselves from the world physically through some form of ascetic lifestyle, as was evidenced in the monastic development of the early centuries in North Africa. For James, Christians continue to live "in the world," but the values that direct their lives and their communities are ones that are meant to transform and overcome the world.[38]

The Spirituality of James Provokes an Identity Crisis among Believers[39]

If we are honest, we realize that many Christian communities and churches are far from the ideal that James sets forth. The values of society have permeated the Christian communities instead of Christian

---

[37] Chester, "James: Significance for Today," 59.

[38] Elsewhere I have investigated an interesting comparison between the letter of James and the Gospel of Thomas with regard to their understanding of the world and their attitude to the poor. Both the letter of James and the Gospel of Thomas speak of the world in similar terms as a hostile force that is to be opposed: "In both the relationship to the world ultimately determines the relationship to the kingdom or to God. What is most noteworthy is the attitude of *mistrust of the world* that dominates both traditions. For the Gospel of Thomas the rejection of the world involves a radical ethos that embraces an itinerant life ('Be passersby' [GTh 42]), which includes a rejection of wealth (GTh 63) and a total renunciation of the world . . ." (Patrick J. Hartin "The Poor in the Epistle of James and the Gospel of Thomas," *Hervormde Teologiese Studies* 53:1 and 2 [1997] 158).

[39] See Tamez, *The Scandalous Message of James*, 78–9.

values permeating society. Values of competition, prestige, and wealth tend to dominate churches instead of the values of integrity, equality, and concern for the poor where faith and actions coincide. This is the real challenge that James offers today. In fact, it is more than a challenge. It should provoke an identity crisis. James gives expression to the voice of the poor and challenges his readers to evaluate their own stance with regard to the poor. James calls Christian believers to see themselves as part of a larger whole, namely, the Christian community, as well as the human community. The Christian is called to respond through faith and joy to the challenges emanating from both communities: "My brothers and sisters, whenever you face trials of any kind, consider it nothing but joy, because you know that the testing of your faith produces endurance; and let endurance have its full effect, so that you may be mature and complete, lacking in nothing" (Jas 1:2-4). Both the individual and the community accept these challenges because they lead to an integration of faith and life, an integration that lies at the heart of the spirituality of perfection or integrity that is the horizon of the letter of James.

Bibliography

Adamson, James B. *James: The Man and His Message*. Grand Rapids, Mich.: Eerdmans, 1989.

———. *The Epistle of James*. New International Commentary on the New Testament. Grand Rapids, Mich.: Eerdmans, 1976.

Aland, Barbara, Kurt Aland, Johannes Karavidopoulos, Carol M. Martini, and Bruce M. Metzger. *Nestle-Aland: Novum Testamentum Graece*. 27th ed. Stuttgart: Deutsche Bibelgesellschaft, 1994.

Alonso Schökel, Luis. "Literary Genres, Biblical." *New Catholic Encyclopedia*. Vol. 8. Ed. William J. McDonald, 803–9. New York: McGraw-Hill, 1967.

Amphoux, C. B. "A propos de Jacques 1,17." *Revue d'histoire et de philosophie religieuses* 50 (1970) 127–36.

Anderson, H., trans. "4 Maccabees." *The Old Testament Pseudepigrapha*. Vol. 2. Ed. James A. Charlesworth, 531–64. London: Darton, Longman and Todd, 1985.

Arnt, William F., and F. Wilbur Gingrich, eds. *A Greek-English Lexicon of the New Testament and Other Early Christian Literature: A Translation and Adaptation of Walter Bauer's Griechisch-Deutsches Wörterbuch zu den Schriften des Neuen Testaments und der übrigen urchristlichen Literature*. 4th rev. ed. Chicago: University of Chicago Press, 1957.

Baasland, Ernst. "Der Jakobusbrief als Neutestamentliche Weisheitsschrift." *Studia Theologica* 36 (1982) 119–39.

Babbitt, Frank Cole, trans. *Plutarch's Moralia*. Vol. 1. Cambridge, Mass.: Harvard University Press, 1960.

Bacher, W. *Die exegetische Terminologie der jüdischen Traditionsliteratur. I. Die bibelexegetische Terminologie der Tannaiten*. Darmstadt: Wissenschaftliche Buchgesellschaft, 1899.

Bailey, Cyril. *Epicurus: The Extant Remains with Short Critical Apparatus, Translation and Notes*. Oxford: Clarendon Press, 1926.

Basore, John W., trans. *Seneca Moral Essays*. Vol. 1. The Loeb Classical Library. Cambridge, Mass.: Harvard University Press, 1958.

Bauer, Walter. *Rechtgläubigkeit und Ketzerei im ältesten Christentum*. BHT 10. Tübingen: Mohr-Siebeck, 1934. English translation: *Orthodoxy and Heresy in Earliest Christianity*, trans. R. A. Kraft and G. Krodel. Philadelphia: Fortress Press, 1971.

Bauernfeind, Otto. "ἁπλοῦς." *Theological Dictionary of the New Testament*. Vol. 1. Ed. Gerhard Kittel, trans. Geoffrey W. Bromiley, 386. Grand Rapids, Mich.: Eerdmans, 1969.

Baur, Ferdinand C. *Paul, the Apostle of Jesus Christ, His Life and Work, His Epistles and His Doctrine: A Contribution to the Critical History of Primitive Christianity*. 2d ed. London: Williams and Norgate, 1876.

Berger, Peter, and Thomas Luckmann. *The Social Construction of Reality: A Treatise in the Sociology of Knowledge*. Garden City, N.Y.: Doubleday, 1966.

Betz, Hans Dieter. *Nachfolge und Nachahmung Jesu Christi im Neuen Testament*. Beiträge zur historischen Theologie 37. Tübingen: Mohr-Siebeck, 1967.

————. *The Sermon on the Mount*. Minneapolis: Fortress Press, 1995.

Borchert, Gerald L. "Matthew 5:48: Perfection and the Sermon." *Review and Expositor* 89 (1992) 265–9.

Borg, Marcus, ed. *Jesus at 2000*. Boulder, Colo.: Westview Press, 1997.

Browne, R. W., trans. *The Nicomachean Ethics of Aristotle*. London: Henry G. Bohn, 1950.

Burchard, Christoph. "Zu Jakobus 2,14-26." *Zeitschrift für die neutestamentliche Wissenschaft und die Kunde der älteren Kirche* 71 (1980) 27–45.

Calvin, John. *Commentaries on the Catholic Epistles*. Trans. and ed. J. Owen. Grand Rapids, Mich.: Eerdmans, 1959.

Cantinat, Jean. *Les Epîtres de Saint Jacques et de Saint Jude*. Sources biblique. Paris: Libraire Lecoffre, 1973.

Cargal, Timothy B. *Restoring the Diaspora: Discursive Structure and Purpose in the Epistle of James*. SBL Dissertation Series 144. Atlanta: Scholars Press, 1993.

Carlston, Charles. "The Vocabulary of Perfection in Philo and Hebrews." *Unity and Diversity in New Testament Theology: Essays in Honor of George E. Ladd*, ed. Robert A. Guelich, 133–60. Grand Rapids, Mich.: Eerdmans, 1978.

Chaine, Joseph. *L'Epitre de Saint Jacques*. Paris: J. Gabalda et Fils, 1927.

Charles, Robert H., ed. *The Apocrypha and Pseudepigrapha of the Old Testament in English with Introduction and Critical and Explanatory Notes to the Several Books*. Oxford: Clarendon Press, 1913.

Charlesworth, James A., ed. *The Old Testament Pseudepigrapha*. Vol. 1, *Apocalyptic Literature and Testaments*. Garden City, N.Y.: Doubleday, 1983.

————, ed. *The Old Testament Pseudepigrapha*. Vol. 2, *Expansions of the "Old Testament" and Legends, Wisdom and Philosophical Literature, Prayers, Psalms, and Odes, Fragments of Lost Judeo-Hellenistic Works*. London: Darton, Longman and Todd, 1985.

Charue, A. M. "Quelques Avis aux Riches et aux Pauvres dans l'Epître de St. Jacques." *Collationes Namurences* 30 (1936) 177–87.

Chester, Andrew, and Ralph P. Martin. *The Theology of the Letters of James, Peter, and Jude*. Cambridge: Cambridge University Press, 1994.

Collins, John J. "Introduction: Towards the Morphology of a Genre." *Semeia* 14 (1979) 1–20.

————. *The Apocalyptic Imagination*. New York: Crossroad, 1992.

Conn, Joann Wolski. "Spirituality." *The New Dictionary of Theology.* Ed. Joseph A. Komonchak, Mary Collins, and Dermot A. Lane, 972–86. Wilmington, Del.: Michael Glazier, 1987.

Copleston, Frederick. *A History of Philosophy.* Vol. I, *Greece and Rome.* An Image Book. New York: Doubleday, 1985.

Copley, Frank. O., trans. *Cicero: On Old Age and On Friendship.* Ann Arbor: University of Michigan Press, 1967.

Crossan, John D. *The Historical Jesus: The Life of a Mediterranean Jewish Peasant.* San Francisco: HarperSan Francisco, 1991.

Crouzel, Henri. "L'Imitation et la 'Suite' de Dieu et du Christ dans les Premières Siècles Chrétiens, ainsi que Leurs Sources Gréco-Romaines et Hébraïques." *Jahrbuch für Antike und Christentum.* Jahrgang 21, 7–41. Münster: Aschendorffsche Verlagsbuchhandlung, 1978.

Dautzenberg, Gerhard. "Ist das Schwurverbot Mt 5,33-37; Jak 5,12 ein Beispiel für die Torakritik Jesu?" *Biblische Zeitschrift, Neue Folge* 25 (1981) 47–66.

Davids, Peter H. "James and Jesus." *Gospel Perspectives: The Jesus Tradition Outside the Gospels.* Vol. 5. Ed. David Wenham, 63–84. Sheffield: JSOT, 1985.

———. *The Epistle of James: A Commentary on the Greek Text.* The New International Greek Testament Commentary. Grand Rapids, Mich.: Paternoster Press, 1982.

———. "The Meaning of ἀπείραστος in James i.13." *New Testament Studies* 24 (1978) 386–92.

Davies, W. D. *The Setting of the Sermon on the Mount.* Atlanta: Scholars Press, 1989.

———, and Dale C. Allison. *A Critical and Exegetical Commentary on the Gospel according to Saint Matthew.* The International Critical Commentary. Vols. 1–3. Edinburgh: T. and T. Clark, 1988–97.

De Graaf, J. *Elementair Begrip van de Ethiek.* 2d ed. Amsterdam: De Erven Bohn Bv, 1974.

Delling, Gerhard. "τέλος, τελέω, τέλειος, τελειόω." *Theological Dictionary of the New Testament.* Vol. 8, ed. Gerhard Friedrich, trans. Geoffrey W. Bromiley, 49–87. Grand Rapids, Mich.: Eerdmans, 1972.

De Mello, Anthony. *One Minute Wisdom.* New York: Doubleday, 1986.

De Vogel, Cornelia J. *Greek Philosophy: A Collection of Texts, with Notes and Explanations.* Vol. 3, *The Hellenistic-Roman Period.* 2d ed. Leiden: Brill, 1964.

DeWeerth, Jennifer. "Perfection, Righteousness and Justice in the Sermon on the Mount." *Criterion* 35 (1996) 23–5.

Dibelius, Martin. *Der Brief des Jakobus.* 11th ed. Göttingen: Vandenhoeck und Ruprecht, 1964. English translation: *James: A Commentary on the Epistle of James.* Trans. Michael A. Williams. Philadelphia: Fortress Press, 1975.

Doohan, Leonard. *Luke: The Perennial Spirituality.* Santa Fe, N.M.: Bear & Company, 1985.

———. *Matthew: Spirituality for the 80's and 90's.* Santa Fe, N.M.: Bear & Company, 1985.

Dreyer, Elizabeth. "Christian Spirituality." *The Harper Collins Encyclopedia of Catholicism.* Ed. Richard P. McBrien, 1216–20. New York: HarperCollins, 1995.

Driver, Samuel R., and George B. Gray. *A Critical and Exegetical Commentary on the Book of Job.* International Critical Commentary. New York: Charles Scribner's Sons, 1921.

Du Plessis, Paul J. *ΤΕΛΕΙΟΣ: The Idea of Perfection in the New Testament.* Kampen: J. H. Kok, 1959.

Dupont, Jacques. "L'Appel à imiter Dieu en Matthieu 5,48 et Luc 6,36." *Rivista Biblica* 14 (1966) 137–58.

Edwards, Richard A., and Robert A. Wild, trans. *The Sentences of Sextus.* Chico, Calif.: Scholars Press, 1981.

Elliott-Binns, L. E. "James I.18: Creation or Redemption?" *New Testament Studies* 3 (1956/57) 148–61.

Eslick, Leonard. "Plato as Dipolar Theist." *Process Studies* 12 (1982) 243–51.

Fabris, Rinaldo. *Legge della Libertà in Giacomo.* Supplementi alla Rivista Biblica, 8. Brescia: Paideia Editrice, 1977.

Felder, Cain. "Partiality and God's Law: An Exegesis of James 2:1-13." *The Journal of Religious Thought* 39 (1982/83) 51–69.

Fiore, Benjamin. *The Function of Personal Example in the Socratic and Pastoral Epistles.* AB 105. Rome: Biblical Institute Press, 1986.

Fitzmyer, Joseph A. *The Gospel according to Luke (I–XI).* Vol. 1. The Anchor Bible 28. New York: Doubleday, 1981.

Flannery, Austin, ed. The Church in the Modern World *(Gaudium et spes).* Vatican Council II: The Conciliar and Post Conciliar Documents. Collegeville: The Liturgical Press, 1980.

Fowler, Harold N., trans. *Plato in Twelve Volumes.* Vol. 1, *Euthyphro, Apology, Crito, Phaedo, Phaedrus.* The Loeb Classical Library. Cambridge, Mass.: Harvard University Press, 1977.

Francis, Fred O. "The Form and Function of the Opening and Closing Paragraphs of James and 1 John." *Zeitschrift für die neutestamentliche Wissenschaft und die Kunde der älteren Kirche* 61 (1970) 110–26.

Frankemölle, Hubert. "Das semantische Netz des Jakobusbriefes: Zur Einheit eines umstrittenen Briefes." *Biblische Zeitschrift, Neue Folge* 34 (1990) 161–97.

————. "Zum Thema des Jakobusbriefes im Kontext der Rezeption von Sir 2,1-18 und 15,11-20." *Biblische Notizen* 48 (1989) 21–49.

Fuller, Reginald H. "The Decalogue in the New Testament." *Interpretation* 43 (1989) 243–55.

Gammie, John G. "Paraenetic Literature: Toward the Morphology of a Secondary Genre." *Semeia* 50 (1990) 42–77.

Geyser, Albert S. "The Letter of James and the Social Condition of His Addressees." *Neotestamentica* 9 (1975) 25–33.

Goodenough, Erwin R. *An Introduction to Philo Judaeus.* 2d ed. Oxford: Basil Blackwell, 1962.

Goodspeed, Edgar J. *An Introduction to the New Testament.* Chicago: University of Chicago Press, 1937.

Gottwald, Norman, ed. *The Bible and Liberation: Political and Social Hermeneutics.* Maryknoll, N.Y.: Orbis Books, 1983.

Halson, B. R. "The Epistle of James: 'Christian Wisdom?'" *Studia Evangelica.* Vol. 4. Papers presented to the Third International Congress on New Testament Studies held at Christ Church, Oxford, 1965. Part I: The New Testament Scriptures. Ed. F. L. Cross, 308–14. Berlin: Akademie-Verlag, 1968.

Hanks, Thomas D. *God So Loved the Third World: The Biblical Vocabulary of Oppression.* Trans. James C. Dekker. Maryknoll, N.Y.: Orbis Books, 1983.

Harrington, Daniel. *The Gospel of Matthew.* Sacra Pagina Series, 1. Collegeville: The Liturgical Press, 1991.

Hartin, Patrick J. "Call to Be Perfect through Suffering (James 1,2-4). The Concept of Perfection in the Epistle of James and the Sermon on the Mount." *Biblica* 4:77 (1996) 477–92.

———. "'Come Now, You Rich, Weep and Wail . . .' (James 5:1-6)." *Journal of Theology for Southern Africa* 84 (1993) 57–63.

———. *James and the Q Sayings of Jesus.* JSNTS 47. Sheffield: Sheffield Academic Press, 1991.

———. "James and the Sermon on the Mount/Plain." *Society of Biblical Literature 1989 Seminar Papers.* Ed. D. J. Lull, 440–57. Atlanta: Scholars Press, 1989.

———. "James: A New Testament Wisdom Writing and Its Relationship to Q." D.Th. Dissertation. University of South Africa: Pretoria, 1988.

———. "The Poor in the Epistle of James and the Gospel of Thomas." *Hervormde Teologiese Studies* 53:1–2 (1997) 146–62.

———. "'Who Is Wise and Understanding among You?' (James 3:13). An Analysis of Wisdom, Eschatology and Apocalypticism in the Epistle of James." *Society of Biblical Literature Seminar Papers,* 483–503. Atlanta: Scholars Press, 1996.

Hauck, Friedrich. "μακάριος." *Theological Dictionary of the New Testament.* Vol. 4, ed. Gerhard Kittel, trans. Geoffrey W. Bromiley, 362–70. Grand Rapids, Mich.: Eerdmans, 1969.

Held, Heinz Joachim. "Glauben ohne 'Ansehen der Person': Zu Jakobus 2,1-13 zugleich ein biblischer Beitrag zum Thema Diskriminierung." *Zukunft aus dem Wort.* Ed. Günther Metzger, 209–25. Stuttgart: Calwer Verlag, 1978.

Hengel, Martin. *Acts and the History of Earliest Christianity.* Trans. J. Bowden. Philadelphia: Fortress Press, 1979.

———. "Jakobusbrief als antipaulinische Polemik." *Tradition and Interpretation in the New Testament.* Ed. G. F. Hawthorne and O. Betz, 248–78. Grand Rapids, Mich.: Eerdmans, 1987.

Hiebert, D. Edmond. "The Unifying Theme of the Epistle of James." *Bibliotheca Sacra* 135 (1978) 221–31.

Hoppe, Rudolf. *Der theologische Hintergrund des Jakobusbriefes.* Würzburg: Echter Verlag, 1977.

Horst, Johannes. "μακροθυμία, μακροθυμέω." *Theological Dictionary of the New Testament.* Vol. 4, ed. Gerhard Kittel, trans. Geoffrey W. Bromiley, 374–87. Grand Rapids, Mich.: Eerdmans, 1969.

Hort, F.J.A. *The Epistle of St. James.* London: Macmillan, 1909.

Jackson-McCabe, Matt A. "A Letter to the Twelve Tribes in the Diaspora: Wisdom and 'Apocalyptic' Eschatology in the Letter of James." *Society of Biblical Literature Seminar Papers,* 504–17. Atlanta: Scholars Press, 1996.

Johanson, B. C. "The Definition of 'Pure Religion' in James 1:27 Reconsidered." *Expository Times* 84 (1973) 118–9.

Johnson, Luke Timothy. "Friendship with the World/Friendship with God: A Study of Discipleship in James." *Discipleship in the New Testament.* Ed. Fernando F. Segovia, 166–83. Philadelphia: Fortress Press, 1985.

————. "James 3:13–4:10 and the Topos περὶ φθόνου." *Novum Testamentum* 25 (1983) 327–47.

————. *The Letter of James: A New Translation with Introduction and Commentary.* The Anchor Bible 37A. New York: Doubleday, 1995.

————. *The Real Jesus: The Misguided Quest for the Historical Jesus and the Truth of the Traditional Gospels.* San Francisco: HarperSanFrancisco, 1996.

————. "The Social World of James: Literary Analysis and Historical Reconstruction." *The Social World of the First Christians: Essays in Honor of Wayne A. Meeks.* Ed. L. Michael White and O. Larry Yarbrough, 178–97. Minneapolis: Fortress Press, 1989.

————. "The Use of Leviticus 19 in the Letter of James." *Journal of Biblical Literature* 101:3 (1982) 391–401.

Kilpatrick, G. D. "Übertreter des Gesetzes, Jak. 2,11." *Theologische Zeitschrift* 23 (1967) 433.

Kingsbury, Jack Dean. *Jesus Christ in Matthew, Mark and Luke.* Philadelphia: Fortress Press, 1981.

Kirk, J. A. "The Meaning of Wisdom in James: Examination of a Hypothesis." *New Testament Studies* 16 (1969/70) 24–38.

Kittel, Gerhard. "Der geschichtliche Ort des Jakobusbriefes." *Zeitschrift für die neutestamentliche Wissenschaft und die Kunde der älteren Kirche* 41 (1942) 71–105.

Klein, Martin. *"Ein vollkommenes Werk": Vollkommenheit, Gesetz und Gericht als theologische Themen des Jakobusbriefes.* Stuttgart: Verlag W. Kohlhammer, 1995.

Koester, Helmut. "Epilogue: Current Issues in New Testament Scholarship." *The Future of Early Christianity: Essays in Honor of Helmut Koester.* Ed. Birger A. Pearson, 467–76. Minneapolis: Fortress Press, 1991.

Kosmala, Hans. "Nachfolge und Nachahmung Gottes, I. Im griechischen Denken; II. Im jüdischen Denken." *Studies, Essays and Reviews.* Vol. 2, New Testament, 138–231. Leiden: Brill, 1978.

Kurtz, Ernest, and Katherine Ketcham, eds. *The Spirituality of Imperfection: Storytelling and the Journey to Wholeness.* New York: Bantam, 1992.

Lake, Kirsopp, trans. *The Apostolic Fathers.* Vol. 1, *I Clement, II Clement, Ignatius, Polycarp, The Didache, Barnabas.* Vol. 2, *The Shepherd of Hermas, The Martyrdom of Polycarp, The Epistle to Diognetus.* The Loeb Classical Library. Cambridge, Mass.: Harvard University Press, 1965–70.

La Rondelle, H. K. *Perfection and Perfectionism. A Dogmatic-Ethical Study of Biblical Perfection and Phenomenal Perfectionism.* Berrien Springs, Mich.: Andrews University Press, 1971.

Layton, Bentley. *The Gnostic Scriptures.* A New Translation with Annotations and Introductions by Bentley Layton. Garden City, N.Y.: Doubleday, 1987.

Laws, Sophie. *A Commentary on the Epistle of James.* Black's New Testament Commentaries. London: Black, 1980.

———. "The Doctrinal Basis for the Ethics of James." *Studia Evangelica.* Vol. 7. Papers Presented to the Fifth International Congress on Biblical Studies Held at Oxford, 1973, 299–305. Berlin: Akademie-Verlag, 1982.

———. "Does Scripture Speak in Vain? A Reconsideration of James iv.5." *New Testament Studies* 20 (1973/74) 210–15.

Lenski, R.C.H. *The Interpretation of the Epistle to the Hebrews and of the Epistle of James.* Columbus, Ohio: Lutheran Book Concern, 1938.

Liddell and Scott. *An Intermediate Greek-English Lexicon.* 7th ed. Oxford: Clarendon Press, 1968.

Limberis, Vasiliki. "The Provenance of the Caliphate Church: James 2.17-26 and Galatians Reconsidered." *Early Christian Interpretations of the Scriptures of Israel: Investigations and Proposals.* Ed. Craig A. Evans and James A. Sanders, 397–420. JSNTS 148. Sheffield: Sheffield University Press, 1997.

Lodge, John G. "James and Paul at Cross-Purposes? James 2,22." *Biblica* 62 (1981) 195–213.

Longman, Thomas, "Form Criticism, Recent Developments in Genre Theory, and the Evangelical." *Westminster Theological Journal* 47 (1985) 46–67.

Lorenzen, Thorwald. "Faith without Works Does Not Count before God! James 2:14-26." *Expository Times* 89 (1978) 231–5.

Louw, Johannes P., and Eugene A. Nida. *Greek-English Lexicon of the New Testament Based on Semantic Domains.* Vol. 1. New York: United Bible Societies, 1988.

Lovell, Ora D. "The Present Possession of Perfection in First John." *Wesleyan Theological Society* 8 (1973) 38–44.

Luther, Martin. *Luther's Works: Word and Sacrament I.* Vol. 35, ed. T. Backmann. Philadelphia: Fortress Press, 1960.

Luz, Ulrich. *Matthew 1–7: A Commentary.* Trans. Wilhelm C. Linss. Minneapolis: Augsburg, 1989.

———. "'Weisheit' und Leiden: Zum Problem Paulus und Jakobus." *Theologische Literaturzeitung* 92 (1967) 253–8.

Malina, Bruce J. *Christian Origins and Cultural Anthropology: Practical Models for Biblical Interpretation.* Atlanta: John Knox Press, 1986.

———. "The Social Sciences and Biblical Interpretation." *Interpretation* 37 (1982) 229–42.

———. "Wealth and Poverty in the New Testament and Its World." *Interpretation* 41 (1987) 354–67.

Marmorstein, Arthur. "The Imitation of God (Imitatio Dei) in the Haggadah." *Studies in Jewish Theology: A Marmorstein Memorial Volume.* Ed. J. Rabbinowitz and M. S. Lew, 106–42. London: Oxford University Press, 1950.

Martin, Ralph P. *James.* Word Biblical Commentary. Vol. 48. Waco, Tex.: Word Books, 1988.

Martinez, Florentino García, ed. *The Dead Sea Scrolls Translated: The Qumran Texts in English*. Trans. Wilfred G. E. Watson. Leiden: Brill, 1994.

Massebieau, L. "L'Epitre de Jacques est-elle l'Oeuvre d'un Chrétien?" *Revue de l'Historie des Religions* 32 (1895) 249–83.

Mayer, Gunther. *Index Philoneus*. Berlin/New York: De Gruyter, 1974.

Maynard-Reid, Pedrito U. *The Bible and Liberation*. Maryknoll, N.Y.: Orbis Books, 1983.

———. *Poverty and Wealth in James*. Maryknoll, N.Y.: Orbis Books, 1987.

Mayor, Joseph B. *The Epistle of St. James: The Greek Text with Introduction, Notes, Comments and Further Studies in the Epistle of St. James*. Grand Rapids, Mich.: Zondervan, 1954.

Mazzaferri, F. D. *The Genre of the Book of Revelation from a Source-Critical Perspective*. Beihefte zur Zeitschrift für die neutestamentliche Wissenschaft, 54. Berlin: De Gruyter, 1989.

Meier, John P. *A Marginal Jew: Rethinking the Historical Jesus*. Vols. 1 and 2. New York: Doubleday, 1991 and 1994.

Merk, Otto. "Nachahmung Christi: Zu ethischen Perspektiven in der paulinischen Theologie." *Neues Testament und Ethik*. Für Rudolf Schnackenburg. Ed. Helmut Merklein, 172–206. Freiburg: Herder, 1989.

Meyer, Arnold. *Das Rätsel des Jakobusbriefes*. Beihefte zur Zeitschrift für die neutestamentliche Wissenschaft und die Kunde der älteren Kirche, 10. Giessen: Töpelmann, 1930.

Michel, Otto. *Der Brief an die Hebräer*. Göttingen: Vandenhoeck und Ruprecht, 1936.

Miller, Patrick D. "The Place of the Decalogue in the Old Testament and Its Law." *Interpretation* 43 (1989) 229–42.

Miller, Walter, trans. *Xenophon's Cyropaedia*. Vol. 1. The Loeb Classical Library. New York: The Macmillan Co., 1954.

Moo, Douglas J. *The Letter of James: An Introduction and Commentary*. Grand Rapids, Mich.: Eerdmans, 1985.

Moreland, Milton C., and James M. Robinson. "The International Q Project: Work Sessions, 6–8 August, 18–19 November, 1993." *Journal of Biblical Literature* 113 (1994) 497.

Mosala, Itumeleng J. *Biblical Hermeneutics and Black Theology in South Africa*. Grand Rapids, Mich.: Eerdmans, 1989.

———, and Buti Tlhagale. *The Unquestionable Right to Be Free: Black Theology from South Africa*. Maryknoll, N.Y.: Orbis Books, 1986.

Murray, A. T. *Homer: The Iliad*. New York: G. P. Putnam's Sons, 1928.

Mussner, Franz. "Das Toraleben im jüdischen Verständnis." *Das Gesetz im Neuen Testament*. Questiones Disputatae 108. Ed. Karl Kertelge. Freiburg: Herder, 1986.

———. *Der Jakobusbrief: Auslegung*. 4th ed. Fribourg: Herder, 1981.

———. "Die ethische Motivation im Jakobusbrief." *Neues Testament und Ethik*. For Rudolf Schnackenburg. Ed. Helmut Merklein, 416–23. Freiburg: Herder, 1989.

———. "Die Idee der Apokatastasis in der Apostelgeschichte." *Lex Tua Veritas*. Festschrift für Hubert Junker zur Vollendung des siebzigsten Lebensjahres

am 8. August 1961. Ed. Heinrich Gross and Franz Mussner, 293–306. Trier: Paulinus-Verlag, 1961.

New Revised Standard Version of the Bible: Catholic Edition. Nashville: Thomas Nelson, Catholic Bible Press, 1989.

Nickelsburg, George W. E. *Jewish Literature between the Bible and the Mishnah.* Philadelphia: Fortress Press, 1981.

———. "Wisdom and Apocalypticism in Early Judaism: Some Points for Discussion." *Society of Biblical Literature Seminar Papers.* Ed. Eugene H. Lovering, 715–32. Atlanta: Scholars Press, 1994.

Overman, J. Andrew. *Matthew's Gospel and Formative Judaism: The Social World of the Matthean Community.* Minneapolis: Fortress Press, 1990.

Paul, Garrett E. "Jesus' Ethic of Perfection." *Christian Century* 113 (1996) 270–4.

Pearson, Birger A. "James, 1–2 Peter, Jude." *The New Testament and Its Modern Interpreters.* Ed. Eldon Jay Epp and George W. MacRae, 371–406. Society of Biblical Literature, The Bible and Its Modern Interpreters. Atlanta: Scholars Press, 1989.

Peck, George. "James 5:1-6." *Interpretation: A Journal of Bible and Theology* 42 (1988) 291–6.

Penner, Todd C. *The Epistle of James and Eschatology: Re-reading an Ancient Christian Letter.* JSNTS 121. Sheffield: Sheffield Academic Press, 1996.

Perdue, Leo G. "The Death of the Sage and Moral Exhortation: From Ancient Near Eastern Instructions to Graeco-Roman Paraenesis." *Semeia* 50 (1990) 81–109.

———. "Liminality as the Social Setting of Wisdom Instructions." *Zeitschrift für die alttestamentliche Wissenschaft* 93 (1981) 114–26.

———. "Paraenesis and the Epistle of James." *Zeitschrift für die neutestamentliche Wissenschaft und die Kunde der älteren Kirche* 72 (1981) 241–56.

———. "The Social Character of Paraenesis and Paraenetic Literature." *Semeia* 50 (1990) 5–39.

———. "The Wisdom Sayings of Jesus." *Forum* 2 (1986) 1–34.

———. *Wisdom and Creation: The Theology of Wisdom Literature.* Nashville: Abingdon Press, 1994.

Pines, S. "Notes on the Twelve Tribes in Qumran, Early Christianity and Jewish Tradition." *Messiah and Christos: Studies in the Jewish Origins of Christianity.* Presented to David Flusser on the Occasion of His Seventy-Fifth Birthday. Ed. Ithamar Gruenwald, Shaul Shaked, and Gedaliahu G. Stroumsa, 151–4. Tübingen: Mohr-Siebeck, 1992.

Pope John Paul II. Encylical letter. The Splendor of Truth *(Veritatis Splendor).* Addressed by the Supreme Pontiff Pope John Paul II to All the Bishops of the Catholic Church Regarding Certain Fundamental Questions of the Church's Moral Teaching. Boston: St. Paul Books and Media, 1993.

———. "I Was Poor and You Welcomed Me." Holy Father's Lenten Message for 1998. *L'Osservatore Romano,* weekly edition in English, 7 (1529) 18 February 1998, p. 1.

Popkes, Wiard. *Adressaten, Situation und Form des Jakobusbriefes.* Stuttgarter Bibelstudien 125/126. Stuttgart: Verlag Katholisches Bibelwerk GmbH, 1986.

————. "The Composition of James and Intertextuality: An Exercise in Methodology." *Studia Theologica* 51 (1997) 91–112.

Preisker, Herbert. *Das Ethos des Urchristentums.* Gütersloh: Bertelsmann, 1949.

Prümm, Karl. "Das neutestamentliche Sprach-und Begriffsproblem der Vollkommenheit." *Biblica* 44 (1959) 76–92.

Rahlfs, Alfred. *Septuaginta.* Stuttgart: Deutsche Bibelgesellschaft, 1979.

Random House Webster's College Dictionary. New York: Random House, 1995.

Ridderbos, H. *Paulus Ontwerp van Zijn Theologie.* Kampen: J. H. Kok, 1973.

Rigaux, Beda. "Révélation des Mystères et Perfection à Qumran et dans le Nouveau Testament." *New Testament Studies* 4 (1957–58) 237–62.

Roberts, D. J. "The Definition of 'Pure Religion' in James 1:27." *Expository Times* 83 (1971/72) 215–6.

Ropes, James H. *A Critical and Exegetical Commentary on the Epistle of St. James.* Edinburgh: T. and T. Clark, 1978.

Ross, Alexander. *The Epistles of James and John.* New International Commentary on the New Testament. Grand Rapids, Mich.: Eerdmans, 1954.

Sabourin, Leopold. "Why Is God Called 'Perfect' in Mt 5:48?" *Biblische Zeitschrift, Neue Folge* 24 (1980) 266–8.

Saldarini, Anthony J. *Matthew's Christian-Jewish Community.* Chicago: University of Chicago Press, 1994.

Sasse, Hermann, "κόσμος." *Theological Dictionary of the New Testament.* Vol. 3, ed. Gerhard Kittel, trans. Geoffrey W. Bromiley, 868–98. Grand Rapids, Mich.: Eerdmans, 1972.

Schlier, Heinrich, "θλίβω, θλῖψις." *Theological Dictionary of the New Testament.* Vol. 3, ed. Gerhard Kittel, trans. Geoffrey W. Bromiley, 139–48. Grand Rapids, Mich.: Eerdmans, 1972.

Schmidt, Karl Ludwig. "διασπορά." *Theological Dictionary of the New Testament.* Vol. 2, ed. Gerhard Kittel, trans. Geoffrey W. Bromiley, 98–104. Grand Rapids, Mich.: Eerdmans, 1971.

Schmitt, John J. "You Adulteresses! The Image in James 4:4." *Novum Testamentum* 28 (1986) 327–37.

Schnabel, Eckhard J. *Law and Wisdom from Ben Sira to Paul.* Wissenschaftliche Untersuchungen zum Neuen Testament. 2 Reihe 16. Tübingen: Mohr-Siebeck, 1985.

Schnackenburg, Rudolf. "Christian Perfection according to Matthew." *Christian Existence in the New Testament.* Vol. 1, 158–89. Notre Dame, Ind.: University of Notre Dame Press, 1968.

————. "The Sermon on the Mount and Modern Man." *Christian Existence in the New Testament.* Vol. 1, 128–57. Notre Dame, Ind.: University of Notre Dame Press, 1968.

Schoeps, Hans Joachim. "Von der Imitatio Dei zur Nachfolge Christi." *Aus früchristlicher Zeit. Religionsgeschichtliche Untersuchungen.* 286–301. Tübingen: Mohr-Siebeck, 1950.

Seitz, Oscar J. F. "Afterthoughts on the Term 'Dipsychos.'" *New Testament Studies* 4 (1957/58) 327–34.

————. "Antecedents and Signification of the Term ΔΙΨΥΧΟΣ." *Journal of Biblical Literature* 66 (1947) 211–9.

————. "James and the Law." *Studia Evangelica*. Vol. 2. Papers Presented to the International Congress on "The Four Gospels in 1957," 472–86. Berlin: Akademie Verlag, 1964.

Shorey, Paul, trans. *Plato in Twelve Volumes*. Vol. 6, *The Republic*. The Loeb Classical Library. Cambridge, Mass.: Harvard University Press, 1980.

Shutt, R.J.H. "Letter of Aristeas." *The Old Testament Pseudepigrapha*. Vol. 2, ed. James H. Charlesworth, 7–34. London: Darton, Longman and Todd, 1985.

Sidebottom, E. M. *James, Jude, 2 Peter*. New Century Bible. Grand Rapids, Mich.: Eerdmans, 1967.

Slingerland, Dixon. "The Nature of *Nomos* (Law) within the Testaments of the Twelve Patriarchs." *Journal of Biblical Literature* 105:1 (1986) 39–48.

Spitta, F. "Der Brief des Jakobus." *Zur Geschichte und Literatur des Urchristentums*. Vol. 2, 1–239. Göttingen: Vandenhoeck und Ruprecht, 1896.

Spittler, R. P. "The Testament of Job." *The Old Testament Pseudepigrapha*. Vol. 1, *Apocalyptic Literature and Testaments*. Ed. James H. Charlesworth, 829–68. Garden City, N.Y.: Doubleday, 1983.

Stagg, Frank. "Exegetical Themes in James 1 and 2." *Review and Expositor* 4:66 (1969) 391–402.

Stanton, Graham. *Gospel Truth? New Light on Jesus and the Gospels*. Valley Forge, Pa.: Trinity Press International, 1995.

Stauffer, Ethelbert. "Das 'Gesetz der Freiheit' in der Ordensregel von Jericho." *Theologische Literaturzeitung* 77 (1952) 527–32.

Stowers, Stanley K. *Letter Writing in Greco-Roman Antiquity*. Library of Early Christianity. Philadelphia: Westminster Press, 1986.

Tamez, Elsa. *The Scandalous Message of James: Faith without Works Is Dead*. New York: Crossroad, 1992.

Theissen, Gerd. "Die soziologische Auswertung religiöser Überlieferungen: Ihre methodologischen Probleme am Beispiel des Urchristentums." *Kairos* 17 (1975) 284–99.

————. "Theoretische Probleme religionssoziologischer Forschung und die Analyse des Urchristentums." *Neue Zeitschrift für systematische Theologie und Religionsphilosophie* 16 (1974) 35–56.

The Shorter Oxford English Dictionary on Historical Principles. Prepared by William Little, H. W. Fowler, and Jessie Coulson. Revised and edited by C. T. Onions. 3rd ed., completely reset with etymologies revised by G.W.S. Friedrichsen and with revised addenda. Vol. 1. Oxford: Clarendon Press, 1986.

Thurston, Bonnie Bowman. "Matthew 5:43-48: You, therefore, must be perfect." *Interpretation* 41 (1987) 170–3.

Thyen, Hartwig. *Der Stil der jüdisch-hellenistischen Homilie*. Forschungen zur Religion und Literature des Alten und Neuen Testaments, Neu Folge 47. Göttingen: Vandenhoeck und Ruprecht, 1955.

Thysman, R. "L'Ethique de L'Imitation du Christ dans le Nouveau Testament Situation, Notations et Variations du Thème." *Ephemerides Theologicae Lovanienses* 42 (1966) 138–75.

Tredennick, Hugh, trans. *Aristotle in Twenty-Three Volumes.* Vol. 17, *The Meta-physics, Books I–IX.* The Loeb Classical Library. Cambridge, Mass.: Harvard University Press, 1989.

Tsuji, Manabu. *Glaube zwischen Vollkommenheit und Verweltlichung.* Eine Untersuchung zur literarischen Gestalt und zur inhaltlichen Kohärenz des Jakobusbriefes. Tübingen: Mohr-Siebeck, 1997.

Van der Ploeg, J.P.M. *The Excavations at Qumran: A Survey of the Judaean Brotherhood and Its Ideas.* Trans. Kevin Smyth. London/New York: Longmans, Green and Co., 1958.

Via, Dan O. "The Right Strawy Epistle Reconsidered: A Study in Biblical Ethics and Hermeneutics." *Journal of Religion* 49 (1969) 253–67.

Vokes, F. E. "The Ten Commandments in the New Testament and in First-Century Judaism." *Studia Evangelica.* Vol. 5. Papers Presented to the International Congress on "The Four Gospels in 1957," 146–54. Berlin: Akademie Verlag, 1968.

Von Lips, Hermann. *Weisheitliche Traditionen im Neuen Testament.* Wissenschaftliche Monographien zum Alten und Neuen Testament 64. München: Neukirchener Verlag, 1990.

Vouga, François. *L'Epître de Saint Jacques.* Commentaire du Nouveau Testament. Genève: Labor et Fides, 1984.

Waanders, F.M.J. *The History of ΤΕΛΟΣ and ΤΕΛΕΩ in Ancient Greek.* Amsterdam: Grüner, 1983.

Wall, Robert W. *Community of the Wise: The Letter of James.* The New Testament in Context. Valley Forge, Pa.: Trinity Press International, 1997.

————. "James as Apocalyptic Paraenesis." *Restoration Quarterly* 32 (1990) 11–22.

Walters, Orville S. "John Wesley's Footnotes to Christian Perfection." *Methodist History* 12 (1973) 19–36.

Ward, Roy Bowen. "Partiality in the Assembly: James 2:2-4." *Harvard Theological Review* 62 (1969) 87–97.

————. "The Works of Abraham: James 2:14-26." *Harvard Theological Review* 61 (1968) 283–90.

Way, Arthur S., trans. *Euripides.* Vol. 2. The Loeb Classical Library. Cambridge, Mass.: Harvard University Press, 1939.

Wesley, John. "A Plain Account of Christian Perfection." *John and Charles Wesley: Selected Writings and Hymns.* Ed. Frank Whaling. New York: Paulist Press, 1981.

Wickgren, Allen. "Patterns of Perfection in the Epistle to the Hebrews." *New Testament Studies* 6 (1959/60) 159–67.

Wolverton, Wallace I. "The Double-Minded Man in the Light of Essene Psychology." *Anglican Theological Review* 38 (1956) 166–75.

Wuellner, Wilhelm H. "Der Jakobusbrief im Licht der Rhetorik und Textpragmatic." *Linguistica Biblica* 43 (1978) 5–66.

Yarbro Collins, Adela. "Introduction: Early Christian Apocalypticism." *Semeia* 36 (1986) 1–11.

Yarnold, E. "Τέλειος in St. Matthew's Gospel." *Studia Evangelica.* Papers Presented to the International Congress on "The Four Gospels" in 1957. 102:4, 269–73. Berlin: Akademie-Verlag, 1968.

Yonge, Charles D., trans. *The Works of Philo.* Peabody, Mass.: Hendrickson, 1993.

Index of Scripture References

Index of Subjects